"This is the book on Revelation we need now. Bringing contemporary issues and thinking into conversation with the first-century world of John, Greg Carey offers scholars, students, pastors, and anyone interested in Christian tradition a thoughtful and readable guide to a book that has been used and abused for millennia. Carey's reading of Revelation is equally critical and compassionate, taking the text's call to resistance seriously while not letting it off the hook for the misogynistic and violent messages it voices. This is a really great book!"

—LYNN HUBER
Elon University

"Lucid. Judicious. And even vulnerable. Greg Carey delivers a masterful reappraisal of social, political, and religious issues raised by the author of Revelation. *Rereading Revelation* is personal, ethical, and enriched by years of careful erudition and sustained critical reflection. Readers will invariably experience a wide-ranging and deeply human conversation undertaken with sensitivity, openness, and grace. The result is a collection of theological essays that foster life, community, sustainability, dignity, and equity. A rare achievement."

—JUAN HERNÁNDEZ JR.
Bethel University

"Revelation remains a dangerous and frequently misinterpreted text. Too often a chasm lies between the interpretations offered by biblical scholars and popular readings that apply Revelation to the contemporary world. In this remarkable and engaging book, Greg Carey resists such a chasm. Drawing upon his insights as a biblical scholar and theologian, Carey interprets Revelation as 'counterimperial literature' that can offer modern readers a vision of hope and a way of imagining resistance. The result is a brilliant and instructive reading of Revelation that is attentive to authority, violence, gender, emotion, economics, and politics."

—ROBYN WHITAKER
Pilgrim Theological College

T0407133

Rereading Revelation

Theology, Ethics, and Resistance

Greg Carey

William B. Eerdmans Publishing Company
Grand Rapids, Michigan

Wm. B. Eerdmans Publishing Co.
2006 44th Street SE, Grand Rapids, MI 49508
www.eerdmans.com

31 30 29 28 27 26 25   1 2 3 4 5 6 7

ISBN 978-0-8028-7812-0

Library of Congress Cataloging-in-Publication Data

A catalog record for this book is available from the Library of Congress.

*I dedicate this book to the legacy of Lancaster Theological Seminary
on the occasion of its two hundredth anniversary.
This seminary has embraced an ecumenical witness, attended closely
to the personal formation of each individual student,
and pursued justice and equity.*

Contents

All scriptural abbreviations follow *The SBL Handbook of Style*, 2nd ed. (Atlanta: SBL Press, 2014).

Ancient Sources

Agr.	Tacitus, *Agricola*
Ant.	Josephus, *Antiquities*
Ascen. Isa.	Ascension of Isaiah
2 Bar	2 Baruch
De or.	Cicero, *De oratore*
Did.	Didache
1 En.	1 Enoch
Ep.	Pliny the Younger, *Epistulae*
Ign. *Phld.*	Ignatius, *To the Philadelphians*
Inst.	Quintilian, *Institutio oratoria*
4 Macc	4 Maccabees
Mart. Pol.	Martyrdom of Polycarp
Prog.	Aelius Theon, *Progymnasmata*
Rhet.	Aristotle, *Rhetorica*
Rhet. Her.	Rhetorica ad Herennium
Sat.	Juvenal, *Satirae*
Sib. Or.	Sibylline Oracles
T. Jos.	Testament of Joseph

Secondary Sources

AY	Anchor Yale Bible
BBR	*Bulletin for Biblical Research*

BibInt	*Biblical Interpretation*
BibInt	Biblical Interpretation Series
BNTC	Black's New Testament Commentaries
BTCB	Brazos Theological Commentary on the Bible
BZNW	Beihefte zur Zeitschrift für die neutestamentliche Wissenschaft
CBQ	*Catholic Biblical Quarterly*
CBQMS	Catholic Biblical Quarterly Monograph Series
CBR	*Currents in Biblical Research*
ESEC	Emory Studies in Early Christianity
ExAud	*Ex Auditu*
HBT	*Horizons in Biblical Theology*
HDR	Harvard Dissertations in Religion
HTR	*Harvard Theological Review*
ICC	International Critical Commentary
IDB	*The Interpreter's Dictionary of the Bible*. Edited by George A. Buttrick. 4 vols. New York: Abingdon, 1962
JANES	*Journal of the Ancient Near Eastern Society*
JBL	*Journal of Biblical Literature*
JRS	*Journal of Roman Studies*
JSNTSup	Journal for the Study of the New Testament Supplement Series
JSP	*Journal for the Study of the Pseudepigrapha*
JSPSup	Journal for the Study of the Pseudepigrapha Supplement Series
LCL	Loeb Classical Library
LNTS	Library of New Testament Studies
NIDB	*New Interpreter's Dictionary of the Bible*. Edited by Katharine Doob Sakenfeld. 5 vols. Nashville: Abingdon, 2006–2009
NIGTC	New International Greek Testament Commentary
NovT	*Novum Testamentum*
NovTSup	Supplements to Novum Testamentum
NTL	New Testament Library
NTS	*New Testament Studies*
PMLA	*Proceedings of the Modern Language Association*
PRSt	*Perspectives in Religious Studies*
RBS	Resources for Biblical Study
RevExp	*Review and Expositor*
SemeiaSt	Semeia Studies
SHBC	Smyth & Helwys Bible Commentary
SNTSMS	Society for New Testament Studies Monograph Series
StABH	Studies in American Biblical Hermeneutics

STR	Studies in Theology and Religion
SymS	Symposium Series
VT	*Vetus Testamentum*
WGRW	Writings from the Greco-Roman World
WUNT	Wissenschaftliche Untersuchungen zum Neuen Testament

Opening Words

THIS BOOK OFFERS A FRESH AND BROAD theological interpretation of Revelation organized according to topics ranging from the dogmatic to the ethical and the political. Without question, these interpretations speak to a particular time and place. Without reciting my demographic characteristics, I hope these questions I discuss will resonate with many contemporary Western readers. This book does not attempt to construct a systematic theology of Revelation or to fit the book into the church's traditional dogmatic categories. Nor does it claim to present "the theology of Revelation," as if I have identified the book's core convictions, primary concerns, or deep theological structure. Instead, I intend to find contemporary Christian meaning in Revelation, meaning that involves bringing traditional and contemporary questions to the book and exploring how modern readers may engage it in life-giving ways. I hope my reflections will interest non-Christian readers as well.

There are many different types of books on Revelation out there. Commentaries introduce readers to the book and then work through it passage by passage, verse by verse, or phrase by phrase. Some commentaries address technically trained audiences, while others speak to preachers, teachers, and students. Monographs present focused investigations related to specific topics concerning Revelation, including its textual history, literary features, historical and cultural context, aspects of its theological or ethical significance, or its history of influence. There are books that offer general treatments of Revelation, some of them somewhat similar to this book in their approach. Other books serve as popular guides to Revelation intended for individual benefit or group discussion. As far as I can tell, this book is a little bit different than all the abovementioned publications. Very few studies of Revelation seek to address the book topically and from a theological perspective, as I do here.

In seeking theological meaning, my approach to Revelation in this book is without bias. Biblical exegetes and theologians often pose as advocates for particular interpretive postures in their reading of Scripture. Some proclaim a hermeneutics of trust. These interpreters generally seek a positive word—the living word of God—through the study of Scripture. They expect good news. Others foreground a hermeneutics of suspicion. Aware that biblical texts were composed to promote specific agendas often freighted with misogyny, domination, and enslavement, these interpreters expect to engage in critique or counterreading. I do not pretend to be neutral or objective in my interpretation, but I wish to avoid preparing in advance for submission or resistance to biblical texts. I aim to read Revelation in ways that foster life, community, sustainability, dignity, and equity. By no means do I offer an explicit methodology for this process.

Public interpretation is messy by default. It requires not only careful study of the text, its cultural context, and its reception history but also engagement with interpreters and communities who may see things differently than one another. If we're honest, we can admit that textual interpretation depends a great deal upon the communities that form us. Those communities shape our questions and our preoccupations. A primary way to expand and critique those starting places requires engaging other readers—not just readers of Revelation but also readers of all texts. Interpretation is always provisional, never final. One day, I'll wince at some of the proposals contained in this book. I don't really cherish the thought, but maybe I should.

I now regard Revelation as a dangerous and necessary part of the New Testament canon. I will not try to explain away aspects of Revelation that lead many readers to reject it outright. Revelation relishes the hope that its enemies will suffer. To the degree that it resists Roman imperialism, it nevertheless presents Jesus as ruler of a new empire and his followers as rulers in their own right. Although Revelation does not promote violence on the part of its reader/hearers, many have read its violent imagery as legitimating violence. They may misread Revelation in these ways, but several passages celebrate when the Lamb's enemies suffer. Revelation is irredeemably misogynistic; it cannot imagine female identity in categories other than sexual ones and envisions only female characters as undergoing sexualized punishment. I would add that Revelation addresses its audience with an absolutist and authoritarian voice. I do not try to make these things okay.

Readers reject Revelation for other reasons that I do not share. Many regard it as hopelessly esoteric and impossible to understand. Revelation is that at many points, but we can get the general drift by reading it within the poetic and rhetorical conventions of ancient apocalyptic literature. Lots of readers also regard Revelation as an empty form of pie in the sky escapism completely untethered from the demands of real life. Here I disagree fiercely: Revelation is very much concerned with faithful witness to Jesus in its own time and place. Moreover, its hope is grounded in Israel's Scriptures and in the resurrection of Jesus. I believe a close examination of hope is relevant and worthwhile. Similar to the pie in the sky objection is the argument that Revelation imagines the destruction of our world, a dangerous notion in a world that faces dire ecological and technological threats. I think a case can be made that Revelation imagines a new age, even one that renews our world. Many also reject Revelation because of its exclusivity: one follows the Lamb or faces unbearable suffering. This objection strikes home, but I believe it is possible to read Revelation more optimistically. Finally, some readers push Revelation aside because John is an extremist who brooks no compromise. Again, this concern is well founded, but it requires further reflection. Many of our heroes were extremists in their day.

In this book, I address all the issues presented in the previous two paragraphs. Some receive more attention than others. In this book, I want to name why Revelation is essential reading for Christians despite its flaws, the challenging questions that come with it, and the difficulty of understanding it. Revelation confronts contemporary readers with pressing questions more directly than does any other New Testament document. Many of these questions feel particularly relevant.

Revelation's primary challenge involves loyalty. John composed Revelation to call worshipers of Jesus to resist imperial culture, specifically worship devoted to the emperors and the imperial gods. The primary category is not some abstract Protestant "faith" but "faithfulness" as a matter of relationship, allegiance, and conduct. John identifies Jesus as "the faithful witness" (1:5), applies the same label to a martyr named Antipas (2:13), and then promises victory over the Beast through the "testimony" of Lamb followers who risk their lives. This language foregrounds absolute loyalty when loyalty can be costly.

I write in a context of high social and political polarization. In particular, I am thinking of the burgeoning Christian nationalism movement and its demands that one narrow construal of Christian values take dominion over society. Christian nationalism also requires followers to demonstrate an uncritical patriotism intertwined with commitment to Christian identity. Those who resist those values, even on Christian grounds, are nevertheless attacked as being "anti-Christian" or even demonic. As a result, many people experience alienation from loved ones who reject them because of their refusal to blend loyalty to Christ with loyalty to the state. This is something that I have experienced myself. In turn, hot button issues have become loyalty tests for religious leaders especially as well as for ordinary citizens. Religious leaders are now challenged if they speak to social issues they once were free to address, such as racism and immigration. They also receive challenges if they choose not to speak into public controversy on other issues. Serious as they are, our contemporary concerns are mild in comparison to those others face today and have faced throughout history. Revelation cannot and ought not prescribe when conditions constitute tests of loyalty to the gospel. It speaks from its own time and place, but it does raise that question in a particularly acute way.

Revelation's demand for loyalty requires political and theological discernment. If we limit Revelation to the topic of "idolatry," we play into the vapid pietism in which many of us were raised. I intend no criticism of piety here but only of the context-less religiosity decried by Dietrich Bonhoeffer, who wrote, "Here and there people flee from the public altercation into the sanctuary of private virtuousness. But anyone who does this must shut his mouth and his eyes to the injustice around him. Only at the cost of self-deception can he keep himself pure from the contamination arising from responsible action."[1] When Revelation judges Rome, idolatry certainly represents a key issue. Revelation engages Rome through two primary symbols: the Beast and the Prostitute. The Prostitute rides the Beast, who receives worship and promotes blasphemy (13:5–6, 15; 17:3). Revelation critiques Rome not as an imperial center that rules from a distance but as a cultural force that implicates the seven assemblies and corrupts their cities.[2] Local elites in Roman Asia promoted cults to Roman emperors and deities (13:15), while ordinary people—Revelation calls them "the Inhabitants of the Earth"—participated in those festivals and shrines and in Roman commerce. Moreover, Revelation condemns more than idolatry in the Roman system. Rome rules with violence (13:4). It makes war upon those who insist upon worshiping Jesus alone (13:7; 17:6). And it arranges diplomacy and commerce in ways that extract wealth from other peoples, a critique that includes the slave trade (18:9–20). Some readers even believe Revelation indicts Rome's exploitation of natural resources.[3] This multidimensional condemnation of Rome invites contemporary readers to examine analogous systems in our own cultures. More than any other New Testament document, Revelation presses contemporary Christians to ask how our social and commercial entanglements may compromise our loyalty to Jesus Christ.

1. Bonhoeffer 1971, 258.
2. A. Yarbro Collins 2021, 200–204.
3. Most pointedly, Kiel 2017.

Let us return to the objection that Revelation is just too hard to understand. Admittedly, Revelation presents countless interpretive details that defy resolution. I do not envy those who produce commentaries on this book, as I have little idea what I would say regarding many matters. For example, I do not know why the Lamb has seven horns and seven eyes (5:6). We might argue that seven depicts perfection, while horns and eyes connote power and knowledge, respectively. Thus, the Lamb is all-powerful and all-knowing. Those views make sense, but they do not exhaust the symbolism. For example, the seven eyes "are" seven spirits God has sent to patrol the earth (see 1:4; 4:5; 5:6). We also recognize in this imagery allusions to Daniel and Jeremiah.[4] But why, then, is the Beast allotted ten horns and seven heads (13:1)? While I can say some things about this phenomenon with some confidence, I would not dare "explain" it. Nor does this book attempt that kind of reading.

Although biblical scholars continue to debate the meaning of some of the more opaque symbolism presented in Revelation, this does not mean that the book as a whole has defied the analysis of interpreters. Despite the challenges of interpreting Revelation, most scholarly readings fall within a fairly well-defined range of opinion. To sketch a basic outline of these opinions:

1. While there is still debate over whether Revelation was written in the immediate context of the First Jewish Revolt or decades later, the vast majority of readers agree that Revelation responds in part to Roman imperialism with a particular emphasis upon imperial cults. As I argued above, Revelation reads Rome as idolatrous but also as violent, arrogant, and oppressive. Like other ancient Jewish apocalypses, Revelation is an example of counter-imperial resistance literature.

2. Revelation addresses seven early Christian assemblies. These assemblies resided among significant cities in Roman Asia, the region we would now locate in western Turkey. Revelation's author identifies himself as John and pits himself in opposition to other Christian prophet-teachers who were active among those assemblies. His Christian opponents apparently propounded an ethic that allowed for accommodation to the larger society, which thoroughly participated in Roman commerce and religiosity, including the imperial cults. John allows no compromise with these things. He calls for absolute withdrawal from Roman imperial culture, including its cults and its commerce.

4. See Beale 1999, 350–56 for the kind of exhaustive research I have in mind here.

3. John and his reader/hearers were experiencing pressure regarding their
    exclusive witness. Revelation contains several references to persecution and
    martyrdom (e.g., 1:9; 2:10, 13; 6:9–11; 12:11; 13:7, 16–17; 17:6; 18:24; 19:2). It
    gives the impression that followers of Jesus were facing ongoing persecu-
    tion, both locally and from Roman authorities. However, historians debate
    the extent and nature of persecution in Roman Asia during the first century.
    Our New Testament sources commonly reflect concern with persecution,
    but it is extremely difficult to make the case for widespread or systematic
    persecution from sources beyond the New Testament. My own view is that
    the seven assemblies may already have experienced a measure of social
    pressure along with occasional violence for their exclusive devotion to Jesus.
    But Rome had no official persecution policy in John's day.

4. Revelation also indicates hostility to persons outside the assemblies. We
    deal primarily with two phrases: the "synagogue of Satan" (2:9; 3:9) and
    the "Inhabitants of the Earth." (Throughout the book, I use capitalization
    to indicate specific characters in Revelation.) References to the Inhabitants
    almost surely indicate the general population outside of the assemblies—
    persons who went about daily life, observed imperial festivals and wor-
    shiped at imperial shrines, and participated in the flow of culture. Revela-
    tion describes such ordinary people as worshipers of the Beast. The phrase
    "synagogue of Satan" is more hotly debated. Does it refer to actual Jewish
    communities beyond the seven assemblies? Does it point to gentile Jesus
    followers "who say that they are Jews but are not," a phrase linked to both
    references to a synagogue of Satan? Or, given that Revelation is a Jewish
    book that reflects devotion to Jesus, is John pointing to fellow Jews whose
    faithfulness he finds lacking? I tend to think John uses "synagogue of Satan"
    to point to other Jews (as John himself is Jewish) who do not follow Jesus;
    thus, the phrase indicates conflict between the *ekklēsia* and the synagogue.
    However we might identify the "synagogue of Satan," Revelation imagines
    the outside world as hostile to those who follow the Lamb and worthy of
    divine judgment.

This broad range of general agreement (not quite a consensus) is familiar
to every scholar and to many persons who have been introduced to biblical
scholarship on Revelation. Of course, most people who have opinions about
Revelation have never been introduced to academic biblical scholarship. Many
Christians instead look to Revelation for predictions of world events, and
many other people dismiss those Christians as kooks. Within the general
agreement outlined above, scholars still have room for disagreement. Some

involve matters of detail, while other points of disagreement involve our assessment of Revelation's theological, ethical, and political significance. This project focuses on that latter set of issues.

In an effort to reach a broad audience while presenting a well-researched argument, I have avoided extensive engagement with secondary literature in the main text. Here I use footnotes to point readers to my primary conversation partners whose work merits attention. Where opinions differ widely, I occasionally report simply that "some" or "many" readers hold an opinion without providing specific examples. Where I cite my own work, which is too often, I am referring to fuller arguments supporting the opinions I advance here.

Several chapters and some sections of this book have evolved from work I have published earlier. I have updated them all, sometimes expressing changes of opinion. Chapters 8 and 9 in particular represent updated and lightly revised versions of articles I have published in *Perspectives in Religious Studies*. Chapter 8 first appeared as "Revelation's Violence Problem: Mapping Essential Questions," *PRSt* 42 (2015): 295–306; chapter 9 as "What Counts as 'Resistance' in Revelation?," *PRSt* 45 (2018): 199–212. I give thanks to Baylor University Press and to Senior Editor Mikeal C. Parsons for permission to publish these light revisions of those articles and to Mark McEntire, Amanda C. Miller, and Mitchell G. Reddish for their editorial work on those publications. Chapter 5 originated as "Moving an Audience: One Aspect of Pathos in the Book of Revelation," in *Words Well Spoken: George Kennedy's Rhetoric of the New Testament*, ed. C. Clifton Black and Duane F. Watson (Waco: Baylor University Press, 2008), 163–78. I have redeveloped that chapter substantially.

Unless indicated otherwise, all biblical quotations are taken from the New Revised Standard Version updated edition (NRSVue).

The editorial staff at Eerdmans has welcomed this project, coached me through its conceptualization, and shown patience due to delays caused by changes in my home institution and by the COVID-19 pandemic. I would like to single out Trevor Thompson, Executive Editor, and James Ernest, Editor-in-Chief, respectively, for their wisdom and guidance. Laurel Draper directed the project with grace and insight, Blake Jurgens improved the manuscript on points of substance and style, and anonymous eagle-eyed proofreaders have saved me countless embarrassments. Jeff Dundas, Jason Pearson, and Clare Galloway conducted beautiful work with design and marketing and welcomed me as a partner in that project.

I extend my gratitude to Jaime Clark-Soles, who told me I should write this book, and to a host of other colleagues for various kinds of help in resourcing and conceptualizing this project: Eric Barreto, Brigidda Bell, Scott Coley,

David deSilva, Sarah Emanuel, David Frankfurter, Beverly Gaventa, Rhiannon Graybill, Meghan Henning, Lynn Huber, Lindsey Jodrey, Chris Keith, Vanessa Lovelace, Laura Nasrallah, Julia O'Brien, Justin Jeffcoat Schedtler, David Smith, and Robyn Whitaker. As I write these words, I am concluding my twenty-fifth year on the faculty of Lancaster Theological Seminary. Countless students, colleagues, staff members, and alumni have shaped my character and my theological understanding, and I am profoundly grateful to them. Much of this book came together during a spring 2024 sabbatical leave granted by the Seminary and supported by our partner institutions, Moravian University and Moravian Theological Seminary. That support is an enormous privilege, and I am grateful to our Board of Trustees for supporting this work. As Lancaster enters its two hundredth year, I dedicate this book to the Seminary that has nurtured me, welcomed my family, and blessed my life.

Reading Revelation as Apocalypse, Prophecy, and Letter

R EVELATION'S FIRST WORD, *APOKALYPSIS*, gives the book its name: the Apocalypse or Revelation. The word's fundamental meaning involves an uncovering or unveiling, perhaps a disclosure. As many have observed, the Greek word *apokalypsis* sometimes describes the moment when a bride removes her veil, revealing her face to her new husband. *Apokalypsis* also applies to mystical disclosures, experiences of sight and sound in which visionaries transgress the normal boundaries of human perception to encounter heavenly beings and heavenly worlds. On multiple occasions, the apostle Paul refers to his own apocalypses. One of them involves an ascent into the "third heaven," where he holds a brief conversation with "the Lord" Jesus (2 Cor 12:1–10; see also Gal 1:12, 15; 2:2).

This information is common knowledge for many, but deep theological engagement with Revelation requires more reflection concerning what it means to read it as a literary apocalypse. People who have studied the New Testament in academic settings will know what an apocalypse is and why the term applies to Revelation. In Revelation, John enters a state he describes as being "in the spirit." He encounters the risen Jesus, ascends into God's heavenly throne room, and observes a cosmic drama play out that culminates with the New Jerusalem coming down to earth. There God dwells with mortals, presumably forever. Many will have heard that, as an apocalypse, Revelation does not predict the remote future and certainly not current events, contrary to what contemporary Bible prophecy preachers would tell us. We will discuss all this here, but ultimately we are after something else. *How may contemporary Christian readers find meaning through an encounter with an ancient apocalypse with its formidable symbols, its alien mythological framework, and its frequently offensive narrative dynamics?*

Here I will propose some responses to that question. The path to that proposal requires a circuitous route, one that starts with the acknowledgment that Revelation is not "only" an apocalypse. Apocalypse is a literary category, a genre developed by modern scholars. It is not even the primary way in which Revelation presents itself; prophecy and letter are more prominent. But Revelation is a literary apocalypse, and that raises at least three concerns for theological interpretation. First, an apocalypse entails an extraordinarily high claim to authority. In chapter 2 we will discuss how Revelation builds its authority claims, and we will reflect there on the role of authority claims in Christian discourse. This is important for many reasons, not least that we are living through a resurgence of authoritarian politics in the United States and around the world. Second, apocalypses claim to "reveal" a reality more profound than the one we generally perceive. That reality may involve a blessed future or a heavenly realm, but it is more real than the one we accept and is more worthy of our allegiance. And third, apocalypses tend to promote a markedly sectarian outlook: our group may be small, but we alone know the truth. I will argue that these three features of apocalypses all hold a measure of promise. They also come with a big, bright "handle with care" tag.

APOCALYPSE, PROPHECY, LETTER

Before we delve more deeply into what it means to approach Revelation as an apocalypse, we should reflect just a bit on the book's self-presentation. Warning: this will be a lengthy detour, but it is foundational to the process of reading Revelation theologically.

Revelation's author introduces himself as John, and that's how we shall refer to him. He provides almost no other identifying information, and we shall honor that as well. But he plays an active role in the story not only as a visionary and reporter but also as a participant.

John presents his vision as an apocalypse, a prophecy, and a distributed letter.[1] Although it introduces itself as an *apokalypsis* (1:1), Revelation never uses that term again. Right after referring to itself as an apocalypse, it presents itself as prophecy (1:3) and as a sort of open letter (1:4-5).

> Blessed is the one who reads aloud the words of the prophecy, and blessed are those who hear and who keep what is written in it, for the time is near.
>
> John to the seven churches that are in Asia: Grace to you and peace from him who is and who was and who is to come and from the seven spirits who are before his throne. (1:3-4)

1. Linton 1991.

John sets forth his message as a prophecy, carrying divine authority to his audiences. Immediately after appealing to prophecy, John forwards letters to each of the seven assemblies dictated by the risen Jesus. He returns to both themes at the end of the book. "The words of the prophecy of this book" remain open precisely because they function as a "testimony" to the churches addressed at the book's beginning (22:10, 16).

All three modes of communication—apocalypse, prophecy, and letter—are relevant for understanding Revelation. We should be careful not to assume we know how John's ancient reader/hearers would have processed these signals, though we may venture educated guesses. Nor should we reduce Revelation to just one of these analytical categories. Nevertheless, Revelation most frequently identifies itself as a prophecy, albeit one that resembles other Jewish literary apocalypses. Most likely, John's reader/hearers received Revelation as a prophecy delivered in an apocalyptic mode and addressed specifically to them and to their circumstances.

Revelation as Apocalypse

Scholars have long identified a certain set of ancient writings as "apocalypses." Prominent ancient Jewish and Christian examples would include the five books constituting 1 Enoch, Daniel, 2 Baruch, 3 Baruch, 4 Ezra, the Apocalypse of Abraham, Revelation, the Shepherd of Hermas, the Ascension of Isaiah, and the Apocalypse of Peter. Experts still debate the genre's exact boundaries, with some questioning whether we should define apocalypse as a genre at all. After all, no one in the ancient world ever referred to "apocalypse" as a literary genre. This use of apocalypse as a modern analytical category in part reflects scholars' attempts to identify analogies for Revelation's self-identification as "the apocalypse" (1:1). But Revelation shares with the other literary apocalypses mentioned above a common framework: it tells the story of a visionary who experiences a mystical disclosure of otherworldly realities, like heaven and hell or history's ultimate outcome, and the visionary receives instruction or explanation from a heavenly being, such as an angel. We need not work through all the details and debates here. It is enough to say that the first reader/hearers of Revelation likely recognized its affinity with other ancient literature sharing similar characteristics.[2]

I have come to identify four categories that help me understand apocalyptic literature: poetry, scribal activity, constructive theology, and rhetoric. As

---

2. On the apocalypses, see J. Collins 2016; Carey 2005.

poetry, Revelation trades in richly textured images, symbols, and allusions, often playing these in combination and contrast with one another. It may be a mistake to pin discrete meanings to each symbol. As Jamie Davies notes, symbols and images can perform multiple functions all at once, sometimes creating tension among possible meanings.[3] Revelation may communicate some things directly, but it generally relies upon these word pictures.

Many readers find themselves stumped by Revelation's many striking symbols: unidentified heavenly beings, numbers freighted with significance, massive natural disasters, and monsters. Quite a few literary apocalypses, not least Daniel, trade in symbols like these. I certainly cannot claim to understand them all at any compelling level of detail. It is helpful to regard these symbols, along with other features of Revelation, as a kind of *poetry*.

Let us consider two examples. First, Revelation presents the risen Jesus primarily as the Lamb. The Lamb's chief antagonist is the Beast, a violent monster. If we pay close attention, we will notice that the Lamb and the Beast reflect against one another. They share crucial features: they exercise power; they receive worship; they have received mortal wounds; their followers bear marks of allegiance on their bodies; and they have "sponsors" (the Beast receives its power from the Dragon, while the Lamb receives an important scroll from the One seated upon the throne). The Beast conquers the Lamb's followers, but the Lamb and its followers ultimately conquer the Beast. By juxtaposing the Lamb and the Beast in such direct ways, Revelation presents a stark conflict, thereby forcing readers to align with one or the other. Revelation rarely explains its outlook in discursive language; instead, it conveys the message through images.

Our second example comes with ethical and theological problems that we will discuss later. Toward the end of Revelation, we encounter two women—the Prostitute and the Bride. Revelation represents female symbols primarily according to sexually defined roles; it also depicts a prophet named Jezebel as promoting sexual misconduct (*porneia*, 2:21) and presents the Woman Clothed with the Sun as vulnerable through pregnancy and childbirth (12:1–9). Both the Prostitute and the Bride are identified as (or represent) cities: the Prostitute is called Babylon, a cipher for Rome (17:5, 9), and the Bride is referred to as "the holy city, the New Jerusalem" (21:2). Revelation also calls attention to their dress: the Prostitute is dressed elaborately (17:1–6), while Roman brides were dressed modestly.[4] The Prostitute is filthy, but the Bride is clean (19:8). Perhaps most important, the Prostitute rides the Beast (17:3), a suggestive image that

---

3. J. Davies 2023, 15–16.
4. Huber 2007, 130–33, 148–60.

works at multiple levels, while the Bride marries the Lamb. No wonder, then, that Revelation exhorts its readers and hearers to "Come out" from Babylon (18:4), while the New Jerusalem constitutes the site where God dwells with mortals (21:3).[5] Once again, Revelation juxtaposes symbols in order to dramatize a direct conflict in values: Readers should abandon Babylon so that they can inhabit the New Jerusalem.

Perhaps this is the moment to reflect upon Revelation's recourse to demeaning language, in this case its presentation of Babylon as a prostitute. Recognizing that the language is hurtful, violent, and derogatory, I nevertheless identify Babylon as a *prostitute* rather than with a contemporary term like *sex worker*. I am not entirely confident in this choice, but I am aware that prominent feminist interpreters continue to adopt it.[6] Part of the logic dictating my choice here is the issue of status: the Greek noun *pornē* likely identifies an enslaved woman who labors in a brothel as opposed to a *hetaira* or courtesan. Oddly, Revelation's description of the *pornē*, with her fine clothing and jewelry, in some ways resembles what we would expect of a higher level courtesan. But there is also the question of meaning, that is, what Revelation connotes by identifying Babylon as a *pornē*. Here, the issue is not so much the common usage of a particular Greek word in first-century Roman Asia but rather the term's scriptural resonances. The Hebrew prophets—most notably Hosea but also Isaiah, Jeremiah, and Ezekiel—used prostitution and adultery as metaphors for Israel's participation in pagan worship. Such language could not be harsher and often accompanies images of sexual violence, like those deployed by Revelation. Revelation's Prostitute particularly draws upon imagery from Ezek 16.[7] In summary then, while I use "Prostitute" throughout this book to communicate that level of meaning, by no means am I condoning John's point of view. Rather, my intention here is to communicate the hostility John addresses against Rome.[8]

These two examples demonstrate how Revelation uses poetic means to motivate believers' behavior in Roman Asia and to shape their theological imaginations. Revelation presents itself as a vision report: a narrative of John's visionary encounter with the risen Jesus. It may be that on the whole or in part. But Revelation also participates in the literary tradition set forth by literary apocalypses such as Daniel and 1 Enoch.

---

5. In addition to Huber, other literature addresses the juxtaposition of these cities. See Pippin 1992; Humphrey 1995; Rossing 1999; Carey 2009; and S. Smith 2014.

6. See the more fulsome discussion in Huber with O'Day 2023, 242–44; cf. Whitaker 2023, 84.

7. For a concise discussion, consult Yeatts 2003, 322–23.

8. Moore and Glancy 2014, 104–5; Huber 2013, 61–67.

If the ancient apocalypses are poetic, they also have a peculiar *scribal* quality in the sense that they sustain intense conversations with other texts. This is especially important for Revelation, which alludes to passages from the Hebrew Scriptures (Old Testament) more frequently than any other New Testament document. It can be instructive to read Revelation with a good study Bible in hand, one that indicates parallel passages from other parts of Scripture. The most popular critical Greek texts of the New Testament—the *Novum Testamentum Graecae* and the *Greek New Testament*—offer the most authoritative tabulations, although every such accounting is debatable. Although it never quotes the Scriptures directly, Revelation alludes to biblical passages between 250 and 1,000 times, depending on who does the counting. Revelation draws most heavily from Isaiah, Daniel, Ezekiel, and Jeremiah. These scriptural allusions can be dense; in one case, we encounter at least eight such allusions in only seven verses (1:12–18). And the patterns can be striking. For example, Revelation draws from sections of Ezekiel in the same order in which they appear in Ezekiel.[9] Revelation also invokes key scriptural scenes, such as Daniel's description of the Ancient of Days and "one like a Son of Man" (7:8–14) or Isaiah's appearance in the divine throne room (6:1–13). Just as remarkable, Revelation demonstrates familiarity with five Hebrew and Greek versions of the text of Zechariah.[10]

Scholars have generally underplayed Revelation's possible allusion to other New Testament texts, but we may certainly note moments when the book resonates with other early Christian documents.[11] For example, the distinctive "grace and peace" formula in Revelation's epistolary introduction (1:4–5) suggests that John may be familiar with Paul's letters (e.g., Phil 1:2). Revelation also draws twice upon the tradition that Jesus would return "like a thief" (Rev 3:3; 16:15), a motif that appears in the New Testament Gospels (Matt 24:43; cf. Luke 12:39), in Paul's letters (1 Thess 5:2, 4), and in 2 Pet 3:10. While some of these allusions may be referring to specific ancient texts, others may derive from popular motifs within early Christian discourse.

These data are at once impressive and disorienting. While we can only speculate concerning the resources and methods by which John accessed scriptural texts, clearly John was deeply engaged with Scripture and thickly resourced. Revelation stands apart for its density of scriptural allusions and for the ways John uses them, but John engages the Scriptures in ways ancient readers would have recognized. Ancient authors, Jewish and Christian alike, frequently appealed to

9. Moyise 2012a, 111–12.
10. G. Allen 2017.
11. See J. Davies 2023, 22.

prominent texts in order to draw upon their authority. That being said, modern scholars debate whether Revelation uses scriptural allusions and images in ways that are faithful to their canonical meanings. That debate often participates in conversations about the Bible's general accuracy, a concern that does not interest me much, as that framework has limited use for helping us understand Revelation's argument. A more promising approach would attend to how John uses Scripture to construct meaning, regardless of how much interpretive freedom John exercises. This approach requires us to assess how Revelation shapes meaning and promotes communication through its engagement with Scripture.[12]

The case of the Lamb in Rev 5 indicates a third interpretive category we may apply to apocalyptic writings: *constructive theology*. Revelation 5 also reflects our previous two categories. Its poetic nature involves introducing two symbols that carry very different connotations: the Lion and the Lamb. And Revelation's scribal dimension appropriates the resonances of lion and lamb imagery throughout Israel's Scriptures. In Genesis, Jacob blesses Judah as a "lion's whelp," who perpetually holds the scepter of royal authority (Gen 49:9–10). If the Lion of Rev 5 has "conquered" (5:5), the Lamb "ransoms" the saints with its own blood (5:9). In this way, the Lamb recalls the Passover lamb, whose blood makes possible Israel's redemption from slavery.

John has entered God's throne room in heaven, where God holds a sealed scroll. We do not yet know this, but opening the scroll will unleash all the events that lead to God's ultimate victory over those who oppose God and oppress God's people. In other words, the scroll contains the fate of the world.[13] John weeps greatly because no one in heaven, or anywhere else for that matter, is qualified to open the scroll. A heavenly voice commands John to stop crying: "the Lion of the tribe of Judah, the Root of David, has conquered, so that he can open the scroll and its seven seals." This is messianic language drawn from the Hebrew Scriptures: Isaiah refers to the root of Jesse, who will bring glory to Judah (Isa 11:10), while Jacob blesses his son Judah as a lion (Gen 49:9).

Now we are ready for a lion. But the Lion does not appear either here or later in Revelation. Instead, John beholds a strange lamb, standing with seven horns and seven eyes and bearing the marks of its own slaughter. The Lamb takes the scroll, and heaven breaks out in song (5:13). Many interpreters hold that Revelation is combining the two images of the Lion and the Lamb, but I would argue that the Lamb displaces the Lion entirely.[14] John deploys poetry to communicate

12. Especially helpful is deSilva 2009, 147–74.
13. See Whitaker 2015, 147–48.
14. J. Davies (2023, esp. 95, 239) notes that Revelation often presents images that con-

a powerful theological message, one articulated very differently by Paul: God's power works through vulnerability, not domination (see 1 Cor 1:22–25). It is worth noting that the Beast, the Lamb's enemy, has "a mouth like a lion's mouth" (13:2). John is performing a profound act of theological interpretation—the Messiah Jesus does not govern with leonine force but rather with vulnerable sacrifice.

Apocalyptic discourse is far more flexible than many readers realize. Its capacity to speak poetically, draw upon literary resources in a scribal fashion, and frame novel theological ideas all position it to accomplish *rhetorical* aims. This fourth dimension of apocalyptic literature involves its capacity to persuade audiences to adopt particular points of view and to behave accordingly, that is, to shape belief, attitude, and behavior. Revelation sets forth a direct conflict between following Jesus and participating in Roman imperial religion and exploitation. It also seeks to alienate members of the seven assemblies from competing *Christian* points of view identified as Balaam, the Nicolaitans, and Jezebel. All three of these terms probably function as fictitious nicknames. Although it is conceivable that the Nicolaitans circulated around a prophet named Nikolaus, the names Balaam and Jezebel derive from clear scriptural precedents.

Once again, we observe a combination of poetic and scribal activity. Balaam is best remembered as a non-Israelite prophet who was commissioned to curse the Israelites but blessed them instead (Num 22–24). But later the Israelites slaughter Balaam, who is condemned for having led Israel into idolatry (31:8, 16; see also Josh 13:22; Mic 6:5). Jezebel is a great scriptural villain, a Phoenician who marries King Ahab of Israel, promotes idolatry, and persecutes the prophets of Yahweh. Both Balaam and Jezebel meet violent deaths. John deploys Scripture to apply these fictitious names to his enemies. His rhetorical aim is to alienate persons in his audience from these enemies and their message by presenting their teaching as idolatrous and by associating them with the judgments enacted against Balaam and Jezebel. All this occurs through the voice of the risen Jesus, who addresses these rival prophets in the letters to the churches.

Revelation as Prophecy

Ancient prophecy shares with literary apocalypses the claim to represent divinely given disclosure. This claim implies an exceptionally high level of authority. Revelation asserts John's prophetic authority by blessing those who

---

flict with one another, arguing that this feature reflects poetry's capacity to hold concepts in tension and to allow all symbols to interpret one another without forcing an exclusive choice among them.

heed its authoritative prophetic message and cursing those who do not. John emphasizes this message by placing it at the beginning and end of the book (1:3; 22:7, 10, 18–19).

Prophecy, like magic, is a contested category. Just as people distinguish legitimate miracles from illicit magic, so too true prophets are often set in contrast to false ones. The early Christian work known as the Didache provides several tests for doing just that: among other things, true prophets will not demand food or money, and their lifestyles will be compatible with their speech (Did. 11.7–12). Deuteronomy discerns true from false prophets based on the accuracy of their predictions (Deut 18:21–22; see also Ezek 13:9–10). A false prophet might also entice people to worship deities other than Yahweh (Deut 13:1–5; 18:20).[15] Paul seems to claim that prophets govern themselves as a group and expects them to recognize his own authority (1 Cor 14:32, 37). Even then, he reminds the Corinthian assemblies that "real" prophets will not curse Jesus. Claims to prophecy clearly involve contests over authority.[16]

Revelation mentions competing prophets both as a group within the assemblies and as a symbolic individual located outside them. The letter to the assembly in Thyatira targets a certain Jezebel, "who calls herself a prophet" and practices deception (2:20). As we have seen, the name alludes to the biblical Jezebel, who is characterized in the Hebrew Scriptures as promoting Baal worship in Israel (1 Kgs 16:31; 21:25). For many years biblical commentators described Jezebel as a "false prophet," and sometimes they still do, thereby adopting John's point of view. But historical sensitivity requires us to recognize instead a competition for prophetic authority among the assemblies. Jezebel is as much a Jesus-following prophet as John is, but the two disagree regarding issues John regards as essential.[17] Most scholars read Jezebel as aligned with Balaam and the Nicolaitans. John accuses Jezebel of teaching Jesus's followers to practice *porneia* and eat idol-food (Rev 2:20), the same charge he weighs against Balaam, whom he links with the Nicolaitans (2:14–15). It is possible that these prophets are not aligned with each other. John may simply be attacking all competing voices with one blanket accusation. It seems more likely, however, that he is attacking competing prophets who, in his view, promote compromise with idolatry.

---

15. Koester 2014, 658.

16. On Paul, see Nasrallah 2003, 61–94. On Revelation and apocalyptic discourse, see Carey 1999. With gratitude to Julia O'Brien for guiding me through this subject matter in a personal conversation.

17. See discussion in deSilva 2009, 58–63.

Revelation also mentions a "false prophet" (16:13), who aligns with the Dragon (Satan; 12:9) and the Beast. Evidently, this image applies to the Other Beast from Rev 13:11–18, who promotes worship of the Beast (19:20). We cannot identify this symbol with certainty. Most interpreters regard this Other Beast or false prophet not as an individual but as a collective reality—elites in Roman Asia who promote worship of the emperor and other imperial cults. Steven J. Friesen assesses "the use of *neokoros* as a technical title for a city with a provincial temple of the emperors" as an "explosive" innovation that transformed public discourse in Roman Asia.[18] Remarkably, John characterizes the promotion of these cults as a competing prophecy. This move constitutes a "distinctive synthesis" of early Jewish and Christian traditions concerning false prophets.[19] Unfortunately, we can only speculate as to why John adopts this language.

Theological interpretation of Revelation requires us to acknowledge John's perspective but not necessarily adopt it. It is not difficult to imagine a perspective like that of the so-called Jezebel. To abstain entirely from participation in the many cults of an Asian city could threaten believers' social security, including their livelihoods and the familial and social networks that sustained them.[20] If such abstention also attracted repression (which, perhaps, is a better term to use than "persecution"), then the threat would have been further amplified. The apostle Paul found it plausible to declare that "no idol in the world really exists" as a justification for eating "idol-food," precisely the charge John levies against his opponents (1 Cor 8:4; see Rev 2:14, 20). We cannot know whether or not Paul identified with this application—there are good reasons to think not—but he takes it seriously as something a Christian could claim.[21] "Jezebel" and others like her probably argued that participating in the cults did not damage one's loyalty to Jesus, a position John regards as idolatrous and characterizes as sexual misconduct, following the example of prophets like Hosea. Our theological assessment can thus recognize the range of opinions reflected in Revelation without necessarily choosing sides.

We as readers are responsible for how we make sense of prophetic claims. The historical default among commentators has involved "seeing things John's way," to use David deSilva's words.[22] Interpretation, then, would amount to explicating and amplifying John's authority claims. Luke Timothy Johnson ex-

18. Friesen 2001, 150.
19. Koester 2014, 659.
20. Bowden 2021.
21. Works 2014, 79–80.
22. DeSilva 2009.

emplifies how scholars tend to accept rather than analyze prophets' assertions of divine inspiration: "[Prophets claim] that the origin of their message is God. Their prophecy does not arise from their own volition or from a process of logical reasoning. It is not a political formulation devised by a committee of priests and prophets with official cultic status. . . . The word of the prophet is God's word in human speech."[23]

Another approach is to take seriously what John has to say by recognizing that Revelation is a rhetorical document that aims to shape people's attitudes and behaviors, examining how John's claims regarding true and false prophecy function as part of his argument, and asking what contemporary readers might learn by engaging these questions. While this is not a submissive response to Revelation, it is also not a hostile one either.

While modern scholars have attempted to distinguish between apocalypse and prophecy as literary genres, John perceives no such boundary. Maybe we should pay attention to John on this point not necessarily as a reason to dismantle useful categories but in order to understand what John aims to do. Although researchers have devoted more energy to assessing Revelation as "apocalyptic literature" rather than as prophecy, John refers to his book as a prophecy several times and as an apocalypse only once. As prophecy, Revelation claims to present a divinely authorized perspective. It does so using the conventions interpreters assign to apocalyptic discourse.

Revelation as Letter

As soon as John presents his message as "this prophecy," he also frames it as a letter. He sounds very much like Paul for a moment, employing the "grace and peace" formula familiar from Paul's letters (Rev 1:4). Unlike Paul's letters, John embeds within Revelation seven little letters dictated by the risen Jesus to the Christian assemblies in seven Asian cities (Rev 2–3). Scholars debate how to classify these seven letters, which sound very much like prophetic proclamations in their use of the phrase "Thus says." In any case, they are presented as seven shorter letters embedded within one grand letter. These seven letters occur very near the book's beginning, essentially after John has greeted his audience and described his encounter with a resplendent Jesus.

Embedded letters are a common device in ancient literature, including histories, plays, and novels.[24] Some occur in other ancient apocalypses, which

23. L. T. Johnson 2018, 123–24.
24. Rosenmeyer 2001; D. Smith 2020, 53–57.

frequently include divine commands to write. First Enoch includes a lengthy epistle (1 En. 92–105) addressed by "Enoch the scribe" (92:1) to "all my sons who will dwell on the earth, and to the last generations who will observe truth and peace."[25] This letter likely functioned as a conclusion to 1 Enoch as it existed in the second century BCE.[26] Second Baruch, likely composed not long after Revelation, concludes with an epistle to the exiles of Israel (2 Bar 77–87). In the Hebrew Scriptures, the prophet Jeremiah sends a letter to the exiles in Babylon (Jer 29:1–23) that may be relevant for Revelation. While no other apocalypse presents itself entirely as a letter like Revelation does, the book nevertheless utilizes embedded letters much like other literary apocalypses and prophetic works.

Embedded letters, including those in Revelation, layer voices. Such letters enable the author to allow another voice, whether actual or fictional, to speak for a while.[27] Revelation's letters present themselves as coming from the ultimate authority, the risen Jesus. From another perspective, the letters allow John the opportunity to present his point of view by appropriating the voice of Jesus. John represents Jesus speaking to the churches through his own activity of recording the letters. This question of authority presents a theological question: is Jesus speaking through John, or is John speaking for Jesus?

The seven letters follow a common, albeit flexible, formula. They begin with an address to the angel (or messenger) of the assembly in question followed by the direction to "write" and a "Thus says" declaration that attributes the letter to Jesus. (Many English translations do not translate "Thus says," *tade legei*, literally.) In each case, Jesus is described in terms of an attribute found in Revelation itself (usually derived from his appearance in 1:13–20). What follows next is the address to the assembly, whether praise, admonition, or a blend of the two. Each letter concludes with an address to those who have ears to hear (again, often translated otherwise) and an eschatological promise for "those who conquer." These two final elements occur in reverse order in the last four letters.

The "Thus says" formula evokes oracles delivered by Israel's prophets and signals that each letter also functions as an oracular prophecy. The formula occurs in other ancient prophetic discourse, including two other early Christian examples (Acts 21:11; Ign. *Phld.* 7.3).[28] It is not rare for ancient letters to convey

25. Translation of 1 Enoch from Nickelsburg and VanderKam 2004.
26. Nickelsburg and VanderKam 2004, 12.
27. Rosenmeyer 2001, 69.
28. Aune 1990, 188.

oracular messages or, rather, for oracular messages to present themselves as letters. Once again, apocalyptic, prophetic, and epistolary conventions blur together.[29] John presents these messages within his revelatory encounter with Jesus, in which Jesus addresses prophetic oracles to the seven assemblies.

Historians often turn to these seven letters to reconstruct the circumstances of the seven assemblies and to discern John's motivation for writing. This is usually done in part because the letters invite our trust as readers. But we should also remember that these letters reflect John's framing of the situation as an attempt to persuade a complex audience. We should also bear in mind that social networks rarely conform to our expectations. While biblical scholars tend to treat participants in early Christian assemblies as sharing a common identity, more typically individuals in a social network bear diverse relationships to that network and to others. Not every person prioritizes a given network to the same degree.[30] Read carefully, the letters to the churches suggest such complexity. Each letter assesses the status of the assembly in question. Some receive praise, some receive admonition, and some receive a mixture of the two. To the degree that the letters represent John's impression of the assemblies, they include persons who belong to multiple social networks and prioritize them differently.

It looks as if John is addressing a conflicting teaching that resides at least among the assemblies of Ephesus, Pergamum, and Thyatira. The letters mention self-appointed apostles (2:2) and one self-appointed prophet (2:20). As noted earlier, John also identifies three opponents: the individuals he calls Balaam and Jezebel and a group he labels the Nicolaitans. He accuses the two individuals of encouraging believers to eat idol-food and to participate in sexual misconduct. He does not level an accusation against the Nicolaitans directly, but in one instance he condemns Balaam and then condemns "some who hold to the teaching of the Nicolaitans" (2:14–15). As mentioned above, historians typically identify the Nicolaitans, Balaam, and Jezebel with a single position—toleration for participation in pagan meals, rituals, and festivals—that John condemns as idolatrous. I share that view, but we must also remember that we are hearing only John's representation of the conflict. He has imposed biblical monikers upon the individuals he identifies as Balaam and Jezebel, two scriptural personae remembered for leading Israel into idolatry. (We can speculate concerning the name "Nicolaitans.") We have no way of knowing whether John holds the upper hand in any of these assemblies.

---

29. In a previous work, I interpret this phenomenon through John Briggs's image of the *reflectaphor* (Carey 1999, 96–108; Briggs 1987).

30. D. Smith 2020, 21–23.

Historians draw three other data points among the seven letters. First, the letters suggest tensions related to wealth and status.[31] John addresses the assembly in Smyrna as persecuted and poor yet also rich according to Jesus's perspective (2:9). Conversely, the assembly in Thyatira believes itself to be rich, but Jesus regards it as poor and miserable (3:17). So too the assembly in Philadelphia possesses "but little power" (3:8) and has endured persecution. Revelation elsewhere condemns exploitative wealth and power, which is a primary critique John wages against Rome (18:9–19), and it specifically mentions rulers and the rich among those who face God's judgment (6:15), although typically in a context that includes all the Inhabitants of the Earth (13:16). Contemporary scholars intensely debate the proportion of poverty, wealth, and more basic prosperity in the Roman Empire, specifically how many people might have lived with excess income as opposed to those living near or below subsistence level.[32] I am not competent to assess that debate, but it is salient that the capacity to enjoy meat, as opposed to fish paste and the like, and to participate in group banquets, where meat was served and deities were honored, relates to prosperity. Those who enjoyed a measure of status and prosperity would feel greater inclination to eat meat, especially in public settings, than those who were poor. Such persons had more to lose by alienating themselves from the meals shared by associations and guilds.[33] Revelation's letters condemn assemblies that regard themselves as rich or powerful, and it blesses those on the opposite end of the spectrum.

Once again we are making much from small clues in a tendentious document. For example, it is highly unlikely that all the participants in the assembly at Thyatira saw themselves as rich. Perhaps they were relatively prosperous in comparison to other assemblies, but on no account was prosperity the norm in ancient cities. And we must factor in that we are dealing with John's characterization of these assemblies in a contentious context.

A second data point involves allusions to persecution, some of which are more explicit than others. On three occasions the letters mention *hypomonē* (2:2, 19; 3:10), which I understand to mean "resistance" in the context of Revelation. *Hypomonē* appears ten times in the context of torture and martyrdom in 4 Maccabees (e.g., 1:11; 11:12). Revelation deploys *hypomonē* in the context of persecution and victory (*nikē*, see 12:11; 13:10; 14:12).[34] Revelation also men-

---

31. Duff 2001 constitutes the classic study along the lines presented here.
32. Friesen 2004; Scheidel and Friesen 2009; Longenecker 2010; Oakes 2020.
33. See Harland 2003, 262.
34. Carey 2018, 204–6; Schüssler Fiorenza 1991, 51.

tions slander from a group labeled "the synagogue of Satan" (2:9; 3:9–10)—an issue we shall address shortly—along with threats of imprisonment (2:10) and outright martyrdom (2:13). These notes resonate with others that point to repression elsewhere in the book.

Traditionally, Christian readers have understood these data points as evidence that Revelation was composed in response to imperial persecution of Christians. Research over the past several decades, however, has greatly complicated that picture. Beyond early Christian literature, we have no direct indications of widespread or systematic persecution of Jesus followers during this period. If a persecution policy existed, that would certainly have been news to Pliny the Younger, governor of the adjacent province of Bithynia from 110 to 113 CE, who claims to have no awareness of any such policy concerning Christians (*Ep.* 10.96–97). Historians more generally now debate the prevalence of persecution throughout the first four centuries of the Common Era.[35] The image of the emperor Domitian as a persecutor of Christians, often regarded as the context for Revelation, has also received serious reassessment.[36]

It seems most plausible to me that John wrote at a period in which the Asian Jesus followers were subject to a measure of repression with known instances of martyrdom. Although it is possible that John concocted the fear of persecution out of his own anxiety, as a rhetorical technique, or out of his own engagement with literature like Daniel, Revelation assumes an audience that recognizes itself as being under duress and is familiar with at least one outbreak of violence.[37] It seems further likely that this general tension may have motivated other leaders in the assemblies to recommend that people avoid behavior that would call negative attention to themselves, namely, abstention from festive meals and imperial festivals. To associate Revelation with persecution, we need not conjure Roman troops banging on doors and searching caves. Many groups that imagine themselves as being persecuted face much lower levels of tension with their larger society than their claimed experiences of oppression suggest. That various Christian leaders might assess these threats differently and recommend conflicting responses to them should scarcely surprise us.

More vexing and particularly troublesome given the legacy of Christian anti-Semitism are Revelation's two references to the "synagogue of Satan"

---

35. Moss 2013; Kinzig 2021.

36. L. Thompson 1990, 15–18.

37. On Daniel as a possible source for Revelation's persecution imagery, see Moloney 2020, 33–36.

(2:9–10; 3:9–10). The first alludes to slander or perhaps blasphemy and evokes the fear of prison, while the second occurs in a broader context that suggests persecution. Contemporary scholarly debate regarding this phrase concerns whether this group (assuming it existed) represents "non-Christian" Jews or followers of Jesus who appropriated a Jewish identity for themselves. External evidence exists to support both interpretations. On the one hand, the mid- to late second-century Martyrdom of Polycarp claims Jews in Smyrna (one of Revelation's seven cities) cheered and gathered wood for the bishop's execution (Mart. Pol. 13.1).[38] On the other hand, early in the second century Ignatius warns against uncircumcised persons who propound Judaism, which likely is a reference to gentiles who practiced Jewish customs before embracing Jesus faith and continued to do so afterward (*Phld.* 6.1).[39] Alternatively, John may have in view gentiles who were not Jewish enough in their Jesus discipleship to meet John's own standards.[40] We cannot be certain, but in my view it is likely that actual Jewish persons outside the assemblies experienced conflict with Jesus followers in the assemblies, perhaps even identifying them as not being Jews in public settings. We should handle the matter with caution because the notion of early Jewish persecution toward Jesus followers has often been accompanied by anti-Semitic sentiments. Additionally, in the late first century the boundaries between "Jewish" and "Christian" identities were scarcely fixed. Therefore, we should not assume that members of these assemblies drew exclusive boundaries between church and synagogue. Revelation never identifies itself as a "Christian" book and should instead be read as a Jewish literary work composed by a Jesus believer. The tensions indicated in Rev 2:9 and 3:9 make the most sense when they are interpreted as conflicts among neighbors for identity and security in a stressful period, noting that such conflicts can turn intensely ugly.

We might still ask how the conflicts suggested by the seven letters stand among John's motivations for writing Revelation. For example, did John write these letters primarily in response to conflict within the assemblies, or did he do so in response to the challenges posed by following Jesus within Roman imperial culture, especially after Jerusalem's destruction by Roman forces? Although it is not necessary to prefer one set of concerns above the other, we should recognize that the letters themselves fit awkwardly within the rest of the book, so much so that many interpreters regard them as a later addition to the

---

38. Reddish 2001, 56.
39. Wilson 1995, 163–65.
40. Frankfurter 2001, 403.

larger work.[41] If we excised the letters from the rest of Revelation, we would never know John was addressing competing prophets within the assemblies. Nor would we recognize eating idol-food as a pressing concern for Revelation without the seven letters. Although I am not much interested in source-critical solutions for these issues (only because we cannot verify them), these factors do demand attention. However, I propose that we instead frame the issues this way: the seven letters reflect disagreements among the prophets, conflicts determined by the larger dilemmas faced by following Jesus in the face of Roman worship, militarism, and commercial exploitation.

So what is Revelation, and how do we read it? We need not choose among apocalypse, prophecy, and letter as if they are mutually exclusive options. Reading Revelation alongside other ancient literary apocalypses helps us appreciate that Revelation is using symbolic and even poetic language to shape how members of the seven assemblies interpreted and responded to their own circumstances. Revelation proposes to *unveil* the fundamental truth about their culture. John knows no distinction between apocalypse and prophecy—that formal literary distinction is one constructed by modern scholars. Instead, John presents the entire work as a divine word he must write and distribute. Moreover, the letter framework is not a literary flourish but an essential part of Revelation's message. John appears to address the actual seven assemblies, and perhaps others as well, as a personal intervention on John's part to rebuke the teaching of competing prophets.

Unveiling

Reading Revelation as an apocalyptic prophecy requires that we take seriously what apocalypses purport to do. As we understand them, apocalypses claim to reveal a reality that is not readily apparent. That reality may involve the realms of heaven and its inhabitants and potentially include hell. Or it may involve the destiny of humankind and the cosmos. Conventionally, scholars have classified apocalypses as otherworldly or historical, spatial or temporal, according to these interests.[42] Some apocalypses address both spatial/otherworldly and temporal/historical concerns. Revelation is one of those: John ascends into the heavenly throne room, from which he observes the unfolding of history, the final climax between the forces of good and evil, and the descent of the New Jerusalem.

41. Classically, Aune 1998, 1:cxviii–cxxxiv.
42. Classically expressed in J. Collins 1979, 9.

We cannot know how John expected his reader/hearers to receive his message. Commentators have generally assumed that John expected them to receive his book as the record of an authentic revelatory experience. I tend to agree. The apostle Paul seems to expect the same of the Corinthians when he claims to have visited the third heaven (2 Cor 12:1–10). Yet, it is also possible that John and many of his reader/hearers were familiar with the literary conventions we today identify with apocalyptic writing. We should keep that possibility in mind. In either case, John presents to these seven assemblies an unveiling of a great and sacred reality that demands their obedience.

Apocalypses confront their audiences with a profound claim: the world they think they inhabit, the one that seems absolutely real and is not subject to question, is not the ultimate reality. Revelation presents an alternative reality, one that transcends the mundane perceptions and values that occupy our minds most of the time. Moreover, this alternative reality *judges and interprets* the world we think we inhabit. Not only does it relativize that world, but it also critiques it.

Revelation attempts this by recharacterizing Rome, its authority, and its system of empire through its use of symbols. The book's most compelling negative symbols are the Beast and the Prostitute, even though the Dragon (i.e., Satan) resides above the Beast and the Prostitute in the hierarchy of evil, as the Dragon bestows its authority upon the Beast (13:2, 4). But the Beast and the Prostitute receive far more attention than the Dragon; it is with the Beast and the Prostitute that John and the seven Asian assemblies must contend. Through this direct yet powerful use of symbolic rhetoric, Revelation unveils the true nature of Rome and the Roman system. At the most obvious level, Revelation interprets Rome as a disgusting monster, known as the Beast, and the Roman system of diplomacy and commerce as Babylon the Prostitute. At the same time, Revelation acknowledges Rome's apparent grandeur. Its power is awe-inspiring: "Who is like the beast, and who can fight against it?" (13:4). Rome holds authority "over every tribe and people and language and nation" (13:7), just as the Lamb gathers followers from "every tribe and language and people and nation" (5:9; see also 7:8; 14:6). Rome also receives worship from the Inhabitants of the Earth (13:4, 8). Seated upon many waters, the Prostitute also exercises power over "peoples and multitudes and nations and languages" (17:15). Despite her licentious title and less than becoming introduction (17:1–2), the Prostitute is decked out in purple and scarlet, and she is adorned with gold, jewels, and pearls. If she is a prostitute, she is a "Prostitute-Empress."[43] The description of the Prostitute's clothing employs the language

---

43. Huber 2013, 67.

of excess; her outfit uses not one but two opulent colors prized by emperors and the elite, and she wears jewelry stacked upon jewelry.[44] Perhaps her clients are kings and excessively wealthy merchants, as we shall learn later in the book (18:9, 11, 17).[45] For this reason, she drinks from a golden cup (17:4). Both the Beast and the Prostitute evoke amazement (13:3; 17:6).[46] Rome meant to intimidate through its military power, wealth, and architecture. John acknowledges the wonder inspired by the imperial system but aims to undermine it.

Revelation's "revealing" intertwines this amazement with disgust. The Beast may inspire awe, but it is, first of all, a hideous monster given to arrogance, blasphemy, and murder. So too the prostitute Babylon may be opulent, but she rides that same hideous monster, her life is defined by wantonness, and her cup is filled with human blood. Revelation's audience hears the demise of both figures in the most debasing terms. The Beast's minions strip the Prostitute naked, eat her flesh, and burn her (17:16), while the Beast is thrown alive into the lake of fire (19:20).

Jamie Davies links the Beast of Revelation with other imperial monsters in Daniel and 4 Ezra. (The Animal Apocalypse in 1 En. 85–90 also uses allegorical animals to tell the story of Israel and its oppressors.) Both Revelation and 4 Ezra draw upon Daniel's beastly imagery, although Revelation does so more directly. As Davies writes, "This is how apocalyptic beast visions work: they concern the conflict between oppressive political powers and the kingdom of God. These depictions of political realities, as with all apocalyptic imagery, function not as a coded system of symbols that can be neatly unpacked into prose, but as transformative imagery that changes how we imagine our world and its systems. They are a powerful form of anti-imperial political theology exposing deceptive imperial propaganda."[47]

This rhetorical pattern is well suited to resistance literature, the kind of literature that parodies the powerful by turning their own arrogance against them. The earliest literary apocalypses have their roots in Jewish scribal circles, who resisted the imperial program of Antiochus IV Epiphanes (r. 175–164 BCE), which Anathea Portier-Young characterizes as "Seleucid state terror," that threatened the integrity of Judean culture. Daniel and significant parts of 1 Enoch emerged during that period of conflict.[48] At the same time, literary

---

44. Huber 2013, 64.
45. Royalty 1998, 192, cited in Huber 2013, 64.
46. See Whitaker 2015, 203–7.
47. J. Davies 2019, 116.
48. Portier-Young 2011.

apocalypses are scribal products at some remove from grassroots resistance. People who could compose such writings possessed cultural resources that were relatively scarce within their societies.[49] Moreover, as we see from Daniel, the Book of Dreams (1 En. 83–90), and the Apocalypse of Weeks (1 En. 93:1–10; 91:11–17), apocalypses reflect conflict as originating both from within Judean society as well as from outside oppressors. All these insights apply to Revelation as well. John's vision "reveals" the violence, corruption, and blasphemy of Roman imperial culture, but that does not mean John represents the view of either an ordinary citizen or the majority of his reader/hearers.

Revelation's *unveiling* strategies can evoke ambi*veil*ent responses, to borrow a term from Shanell T. Smith.[50] That is, readers find themselves at once inspired and entangled by the book. Many interpreters of Revelation note that resistance literature often replicates the imaginative structures of the empires it resists. In doing so, they argue that Revelation does just that by critiquing Rome without escaping the orbit of imperial imagination.[51] If Roman sculpture depicts conquered peoples as women exposed to rape, Revelation follows that lead. This and similar examples compromise Revelation's status as "good news," an issue we will address in later chapters. At the same time, Revelation counters Roman imperial iconography with a subversive iconography of its own. Dwellers of the seven Asian cities would have had intimate cultural familiarity with Roman grandiosity through its architecture and sculptures. Even today, many visitors to the ruins of a grand Roman city such as Ephesus experience a sense of awe. In addition to its devotion to Artemis, which extended beyond its famous temple to countless other shrines throughout the city, Ephesus also dedicated massive public edifices to Roman emperors and their families. These included an aqueduct, a grand gate, and a theater that could seat well over twenty thousand spectators.[52] Depending on how late we date Revelation, we might also add to this list the Ephesian Temple of the Sebastoi. Dedicated in 89 or 90 CE to Vespasian, Titus, and Domitian, its remains include portions of a massive statue of one of the Flavian emperors, including a forearm as long as an adult human. How many other gigantic imperial statues did this temple once contain? We can only begin to imagine the scale of these edifices and their impression upon people who walked the city's narrow streets. The Temple of the Sebastoi rested on a terrace constructed on the slope of Mount

---

49. See Horsley 2007.
50. S. Smith 2014.
51. With Revelation, see Royalty 1998; Carey 1999; Emanuel 2020, 52.
52. Koester 2014, 256–59.

Koressos. The temple proper resided within a portico not much smaller than an American football field, the temple itself measuring 7.5 × 13 meters.[53] Rome did not impose these structures upon the citizens of Asia; instead, local elites competed with one another to share these messages through these construction projects. Nevertheless, anyone who visited an ancient Asian city would have been surrounded by imposing monuments to Rome's grandeur. "Who is like the beast, and who can fight against it?" indeed (13:4).[54]

Revelation's *unveiling* activity mocks Roman rulers, commerce, and piety by means of parody and satire.[55] "By satirizing Rome and imperial Roman leaders," writes Sarah Emanuel, "Revelation constructs a cosmic counternarrative in which an empire and its followers come undone" while those who resist (see 12:11) "reign supreme."[56] Parody and satire played a significant role in Greek and Roman cultural critique, as they have done and continue to do in resistance literature throughout history. The Russian literary theorist Mikhail Bakhtin maintained that ancient satire features "scandal scenes, eccentric behavior, . . . violations of the generally accepted and customary course of events and the established norms of behavior and etiquette."[57] Its primary target is hubris (Greek: *hybris*) or presumptive behavior. Thus, the Roman satirist Juvenal mocks the emperor Domitian, writing that while he awakens the old laws, he impregnates his niece and forces her to undergo an abortion that results in her death (*Sat.* 2.29–33).[58] According to Juvenal, Domitian arrogantly self-identifies as a restorer of traditional morality, when in fact he is incestuous and murderous.

Revelation specifically targets Roman *hybris*. The Dragon endows the Beast with its own power, throne, and authority (Rev 13:2). The Beast is, well, a monster who speaks "haughty and blasphemous words," echoing the arrogant words spoken by the little horn that sprouts from Daniel's fourth beast (Dan 7:8, 11, 20; 8:11). And the Prostitute has "glorified herself and lived luxuriously," perceiving herself to be a queen who will never come to grief (Rev 18:7). All three meet violent and debasing ends.

Specifically, Rome claims invincibility, attracts illicit worship, and practices commercial exploitation. This is what Revelation unveils. Revelation acknowledges the Beast's ferocity; the monster, after all, makes war against the Lamb

---

53. Friesen 2001, 50–51.
54. Lopez 2016.
55. Laws 1998; Carey 1999, 150–54; Meier 2002, 164–97.
56. Emanuel 2020, 126.
57. Bakhtin 1984, 117.
58. Bakhtin 1984, 114.

and its followers, while the Prostitute drinks their blood. The Inhabitants of the Earth regard the Beast as invincible: "Who is like the beast, and who can fight against it?" (13:4). Less commonly emphasized, Revelation indicts the Prostitute not only for the blood of the prophets and saints but also for the blood of "all who have been slaughtered on earth" (18:24). A second beast from the land sponsors worship of the Beast (13:11–17). Local Asian elites sponsored worship of Rome, its gods, and its emperors. According to Revelation, the Other Beast imposed economic sanctions against persons who refused to participate. Historians cannot verify this practice; in any case, John regards such worship as idolatrous. And Revelation portrays the Prostitute as adorned with gold, jewels, and pearls, dressed in purple and scarlet, and drinking from a golden cup (17:4). Kings, merchants, and sailors lament her demise, indicating the system of imperial commerce that enriched Rome. Merchants in particular lament the loss of luxurious cargo items:

> cargo of gold, silver, jewels and pearls, fine linen, purple, silk and scarlet, all kinds of scented wood, all articles of ivory, all articles of costly wood, bronze, iron, and marble, cinnamon, spice, incense, myrrh, frankincense, wine, olive oil, choice flour and wheat, cattle and sheep, horses and chariots, slaves—and human lives. (18:12–13)

Although Revelation directly emphasizes Rome's violence against the Lamb and his followers, it also recognizes the suffering Rome inflicts on humanity in general. Through these portraits, John acknowledges Rome's apparent invincibility, systemic idolatry, and commercial exploitation, portraying Rome instead as monstrous, murderous, filthy, and doomed to destruction.

Reading Apocalypse

Modern scholars identify Revelation as a literary apocalypse. As such, it reinterprets the reality most people perceive by pulling away a veil that obscures the truth. Apocalypses do this by constructing complex webs of symbols and creating narrative relationships among them. It is impossible to achieve absolute certainty regarding the full meaning of these symbols, but most interpreters have arrived at a general consensus: Revelation presents a cosmic conflict in which the risen Jesus and his heavenly and earthly allies fight against Rome and its allies. This conflict is absolute; from John's perspective, there can be no compromise with Rome or the trappings of its culture. Those who follow Jesus must reject prophetic teachers who accommodate to the point of compromise. In the end, Jesus and his followers will conquer and inherit a blessed new world.

John's unveiling involves an implicit acknowledgment of diverse perspectives, and likely direct conflict, among the assemblies. Read with historical sensitivity, John's allusions to competing prophets like Balaam, the Nicolaitans, and Jezebel reflect clashing opinions concerning how to navigate their common culture rather than a condemnation of "false prophets." These competing prophets have followers. John's unveiling activity also presumes that some among the assemblies may be quite impressed by Roman glory, whether monumental, commercial, military, or cultic. Rhetorically speaking, John is pulling his wagon uphill.

We have noted that John does not quite escape an imagination shaped by empire and domination. This reality goes along with reading Revelation as an apocalypse. Not all ancient Jewish and Christian apocalypses emphasized empire and domination, but many do, and all of them rely on the vision of God as Israel's true king, judge, and deliverer. (So did Jesus.) Revelation's promise of conquest or victory epitomizes the book's entanglement with domination and conflict, as do its depictions of war and judgment. Even Revelation's depictions of women as either brides, mothers, or prostitutes comport with Rome's self-representation in monuments and coins, where defeated nations appear as half-naked women subjugated by their captors.[59] If Rome claimed universal dominion, however hyperbolic, so does Revelation.

Approaching Revelation as an apocalypse is critical for understanding the book. However, we should also remember that Revelation is not *only* an apocalypse; it also presents itself as a letter and as prophecy. In other words, John wrote Revelation to influence real assemblies of Jesus followers. According to John, they face a crisis. Various kinds of persecution have emerged, posing dangers that include martyrdom. Moreover, divisions concerning how to relate to the trappings of Roman culture, which John regards as idolatrous, expose them to Jesus's judgment. We do not know how many of those involved in these Jesus assemblies regarded things the way John does—modern readers have conflicting reactions too—but this is John's assessment, and Revelation is his message.

In my view, Revelation poses distinctive challenges for Christian readers, challenges not pressed with the same acuity elsewhere in the New Testament. First, how exclusive is loyalty to Jesus, and what potential allegiances threaten this loyalty? Second, Revelation is the only New Testament document to condemn Roman power in an overt way. How should followers of Jesus weigh

---

59. Lopez 2008.

their relationships to the state? Third, John claims an extraordinarily high level of authority for his vision. Many religious leaders do so, but most Christians reject authoritarianism. At the same time, do we not occasionally face moral crises for which there can be no compromise? Fourth, Revelation presses us with the question of hope. For what do we hope, and what grounds our hope? Fifth, how do we relate to this world? Lots of Christians long to leave this world and go to heaven. At least in the United States, many Christians are fine dispensing with this world in hope of a better one. Revelation depicts the destruction of this world and its replacement with another, one that features one city, no sea, and a river.[60] Folks who are likely to read this book will not desire this world's destruction, and neither do I. Yet, what language shall we borrow to envision dramatic change and cosmic renewal?

Revelation will not answer these questions for us, but it presses them in ways we should not ignore. Moreover, careful attention to Revelation provides readers with pointed case studies that open the possibility for sophisticated and faithful conversations.

---

60. Kiel (2017, 80–84) calls particular attention to the displacement of the sea in Revelation, reading the sea as the location from which empires come to plunder.

Authority and Authoritarianism in Revelation

IN CHAPTER 1 WE OBSERVED THAT Revelation claims an extraordinarily high level of authority. In some sense, all apocalypses do, as they purport to reveal truths inaccessible to ordinary human understanding.[1] Revelation demands absolute obedience, blessing those who hear and obey its teaching (1:3) while condemning anyone who fails to keep their "robes" clean (3:4–5) and forbidding even minor alterations to its text (22:18–19): whoever adds to the text is cursed with the plagues narrated throughout the book, and whoever subtracts from it is excluded from the tree of life and the holy city.

Revelation's elevated authority claims create a problem for many modern readers. Some readers accept these claims on a variety of theological and literary grounds. Others, and I stand among them, cannot avoid seeing Revelation as *authoritarian* in a fundamental way. That is, Revelation insists that its message carries absolute authority and will brook no dissent. Revelation's authority claims, along with the literary and rhetorical strategies that support them, merit close attention and raise critical questions for theologically engaged readers.

Ancient rhetoricians applied the term *ēthos* to denote how a speaker's character (or perceived character) contributes to the work of persuasion. An audience that trusts, likes, or admires a speaker is far more likely to accept that person's point of view. Greek and Roman theorists so valued *ēthos* that it stood alongside *logos* (logical force) and *pathos* (the appeal to affect and emotion) as one of three fundamental "proofs" or elements of persuasion. Aristotle classically ranked *ēthos* as the most effective among these three elements (*Rhet.* 1356a), involving hearers' confidence that the speaker is a person of good sense, virtue, and goodwill (1378a). Aristotle held that *ēthos* does not come from one's social status but rather involves the authority that comes from trust (1356a). The Latin rhetorical tradition more strongly acknowledged a speaker's

---

1. O'Leary 1994.

identity and reputation before the rhetorical moment (e.g., Rhet. Her. 1.6–11; Cicero, *De or.* 2.35).[2]

This chapter shows that John demonstrates acute sensitivity toward building trust with his audience. This is not to say that he had formal rhetorical training, only that Revelation offers hints that John is competing with other Christian teachers among the seven assemblies and goes out of his way to build a rapport with his reader/hearers. Sometimes he reaches out as a peer, as if to communicate that "We're all in this together." But other times he appeals to his unique status as the recipient of a divine revelation. The result is a push-pull between two kinds of appeal, one egalitarian and the other authoritarian.

The question of authoritarianism is particularly acute as I write. Over the past several years, observers have documented a resurgence of authoritarianism around the globe. Whereas authoritarianism was once assumed to flourish in less prosperous societies, its recent rise in Europe and the United States has led to a reassessment.[3] Yascha Mounk attributes this rise of authoritarianism and corresponding decline of liberal democracy to several factors: social media and its deleterious effects upon communication and social cohesion; economic and social stagnation that prevents many people from imagining economic progress for themselves; and identity crises brought on by global population shifts. "Today's populists," he writes, "claim that they seek to deepen the democratic elements of our current system." Contemporary populist authoritarianism generally relies upon democratic institutions and rhetoric to establish itself, only later to render legitimate democratic processes inoperative. Mounk identifies the trend as a threat to liberal democracy. Liberal democracy requires not simply rule through electoral institutions that presumably reflect the popular will (democracy) but also democratic rule where individual rights and the rule of law flourish (liberal).[4] As Wendy Brown observes, in a neoliberal context that takes no account of a common good or collective endeavor, even the discourse of individual freedom hollows out the meaning of democracy.[5] In the United States, we observe this phenomenon among advocates for religious freedom who promote anti-LGBTQ+ policies and cancel diversity, equity, and inclusion initiatives.

Research demonstrates a thick intersection between political and religious authoritarianism. Here in the United States, this fusion primarily expresses

2. Wisse 1989, 2145–46; Enos and Schnakenberg 1994; Carey 1999, 52–56; Zhuang 2023, 3.
3. Frantz 2018, 43; see also Applebaum 2020.
4. Mounk 2018, 52; see also Gushee 2023, 16–20.
5. Brown 2018, 19.

itself in Christian nationalism—the belief that God has set apart the United States for a particular privilege and vocation and that one sectarian Christian outlook should determine national policy and culture. Additionally, once an authoritarian defines just what their "Christian worldview" is, it leaves little room for other interpretations of Christianity, much less other religious and secular value systems. For example, the social and political outlooks of White Christian nationalists diverge sharply from those of Black Christians, who by and large share their theology and religious experience.[6] Put another way, Christian nationalism is largely a White phenomenon that often accompanies racist sentiments.[7] Thus, authority and authoritarianism stand as pressing interpretive and theological issues in our cultural moment.

I would suggest that Revelation holds particular value for Christian readers as we grapple with the challenges of authority and authoritarianism. I do not propose to use Revelation as a positive or negative example but rather as a case study that raises important questions and (ahem) reveals theological dilemmas. If that is the case, we should work through how Revelation builds its own authority claims and then develop our assessments.

READING AUTHORITY IN REVELATION

I devoted my 1996 doctoral dissertation, which was later revised and published as my first book, to a deep exploration of Revelation and authority, little knowing then how acute the issue would become over the coming decades.[8] During that time, I was concerned with the kind of religious authoritarianism associated with Christian fundamentalism, particularly the Bible prophecy movement. Bible prophecy adherents believe we are living in the last days, that Jesus's return is imminent, and that current events are fulfilling biblical prophecies. At the time, few Americans were concerned that authoritarian politics would threaten democracy in the United States and Europe, but that is the context in which I now write. Here, I will rehearse some of the key arguments from that earlier project, which have been refined and augmented over an additional two decades of study and in response to the critiques of other interpreters.

In the previous chapter, we noted that apocalypses claim inherently high levels of authority by depicting their visionary authors as directly encountering

6. Jones 2020, 158.
7. Gorski and Perry 2022.
8. Carey 1999.

perspectives that are unavailable to ordinary mortals. We also reviewed how Revelation blesses those who obey its message and curses those who would alter it (1:3; 22:6, 18–19). But Revelation uses several other devices to buttress its claims to authority. The seven letters promise eschatological blessing to those who conquer by following the risen Jesus's commands and warn those who do not conform of Christ's judgment. The letter to Thyatira threatens the so-called Jezebel with being thrown on a bed to die, with the death of her children, and with "great distress" to her followers unless they change their ways (2:22–23). It is open to question whether Jezebel's bed suggests sickness, as most commentators believe, or relates to the message concerning *porneia*.[9] Her "children" are likely, but not necessarily, her followers. The Greek word translated "distress" (*thlipsis*) is often taken to be a reference to persecution or suffering. In this context, the distress could indicate direct divine punishment. It could also suggest persecution of the kind John anticipates for believers (1:9; 2:9), such that their conduct will save them from neither danger nor a final end-time crisis (7:14). John may even be interpreting present persecution as the beginning of that great crisis. In any case, John asserts that his reader/ hearers' fate depends upon their response to his message and voices this admonition with particular venom toward the so-called Jezebel and her allies.

John insists upon the supernatural origin of his prophecy. Over forty times, he reports what "I saw," and twenty-seven times he recounts what "I heard." The book begins with a command for John to write what he sees (1:1, 19) and reiterates the command to write a dozen more times, eight of them appearing in the letters to the churches. John purports that he has recorded everything he has seen (1:2). On one occasion when John begins to write what he hears, he is prevented from doing so: "Seal up what the seven thunders have said, and do not write it down" (10:4). Writing is a major motif in ancient literary apocalypses, and this one moment recalls other instances where writing blurs with secrecy in apocalyptic literature (2 Cor 12:4; 4 Ezra 14:23–48).[10] It also reinforces the authority of what John does share; John knows even more than he is allowed to disclose. John's access to truth greatly exceeds that of his readers and hearers.

A network of heavenly voices reinforces John's message. All literary apocalypses include heavenly voices, most prominently those of nonhuman beings, such as angels, who guide and instruct the visionary. Revelation exceeds most apocalypses in the degree to which it draws upon this kind of ventriloquy, in

9. Graybill in Huber with O'Day 2023, 52–53; Emanuel 2020, 109–10.
10. Ruiz 1994.

which the speech of heavenly characters serves its author's overall message. In Revelation, John receives such assistance from the risen Jesus, multiple angels, and other heavenly beings. As a case in point, the seven miniature epistles embedded early in Revelation present themselves as communicating the speech of Jesus himself. From a literary perspective, the risen Jesus in these letters speaks not only to John but *for John* by setting forth John's point of view to the seven assemblies. (The seven letters also present themselves as "what the Spirit is saying to the churches.") Also among this extraordinary network of voices are heavenly choruses, whose numbers defy counting, which announce and celebrate the events transpiring in the book (5:11; 7:9; 19:1, 6). The voices supporting John's vision also include other saints, especially those who have endured martyrdom (6:9–11; 15:2), mighty inanimate forces such as thunders (10:3), and the Holy Spirit (14:13; 22:17).[11] In short, through this network of voices John aligns his perspective with those of Jesus and other heavenly beings, not to mention with martyrs and inanimate forces.

The heavenly voices play a key role in justifying John's message against possible objections. Many contemporary readers resist Revelation's depiction of gruesome punishment meted out upon the Inhabitants of the Earth. Some ancient readers probably felt the same revulsion. On multiple occasions, these heavenly voices break out in song precisely when John's vision provokes these concerns.[12] When the Lamb opens the first four seals, war, famine, and pestilence break forth. Just then, the martyrs in heaven cry out for vengeance, reminding reader/hearers that the Inhabitants of the Earth deserve punishment (6:9–11). After a great earthquake devastates the holy city, more heavenly voices celebrate the victory of God and of the Messiah (11:15–18). Just before seven angels pour out the bowls of the final seven plagues, those who have conquered the Beast break out in the song of Moses:

> Great and amazing are your deeds,
>> Lord God the Almighty!
> Just and true are your ways,
>> King of the nations!
> Lord, who will not fear
>> and glorify your name?

11. The conquering saints of Rev 15:2 may or may not specifically have martyrs in view. I think they do. See Moloney 2020, 231–32; Reddish 2001, 291.

12. Hansen 2014 argues that the saints in heaven contribute to the judgment through their petitions and praise.

> For you alone are holy.
>   All nations will come
>   and worship before you,
>   for your judgments have been revealed. (15:3b–4)

This song justifies the divine wrath that precedes it and the harsh judgments to come (15:1).

After the second bowl kills every living thing in the sea and the third bowl turns the earth's fresh water into blood, an angel sings:

> You are just, O Holy One, who are and were,
>   for you have judged these things;
>   because they shed the blood of saints and prophets,
>   you have given them blood to drink.
>   It is what they deserve! (16:5b–6)

As soon as this angel affirms the justice of these plagues upon the bloodthirsty, another heavenly voice follows:

> Yes, O Lord God, the Almighty,
>   your judgments are true and just! (16:7)

The heavenly voices repeatedly reinforce John's message precisely when it grows most painful to hear.

In sum, John rhetorically constructs authority by framing his message as a direct revelation from the risen Jesus, condemning his opponents, and enlisting heavenly voices to proclaim his point of view and deflect potential objections.

SCRIPTURE

Another way Revelation reinforces its claims to authority is through its use of Scripture. Revelation's use of Scripture marks the book as a scribal and rhetorical project. As Steve Moyise writes, "Although there are no formal quotations from the Old Testament in the book of Revelation, there are more allusions and echoes to it than in any other New Testament book." The recognition of these allusions and echoes depends upon interpreters and the criteria they adopt, but Moyise estimates that the number of scriptural allusions in Revelation ranges from "several hundred to over a thousand."[13] Scholars debate

---

13. Moyise 2020, 85.

whether John meant to allude to scriptural passages according to their ancient contexts and meanings or perhaps did so "with a high degree of liberty and creativity" without concern for their literary contexts.[14] By all accounts, John engages Scripture with a high degree of intentionality. Garrick V. Allen demonstrates that John "often clarifies gaps or ambiguities" in his source material.[15] Allen's work has shown us that John accessed multiple versions of Zechariah, both in Hebrew and in Greek, and was aware of popular interpretive traditions concerning the book. More specifically, Allen demonstrates that John used these different versions of Zechariah in accordance with thematic and rhetorical aims. So too Moyise finds that Rev 1:12–18 weaves together "at least eight identifiable allusions" from Daniel, Isaiah, and Ezekiel.[16] Moreover, Rev 20–22 draws upon Ezekiel at least eight times in the exact same sequence in which the passages occur in Ezekiel.[17] One gets the impression that John was working with a library at hand.

As many Christians do today, John alludes to Scripture for multiple purposes. These include providing a broader context for readers to understand the images he uses as well as drawing insight from the passages to which he alludes. Here I am interested in the ways in which Scripture lends its authority to John's apocalypse and to his agenda.

Interpreters differ concerning how faithfully or creatively Revelation uses Scripture. Robert M. Royalty argues that Revelation "(mis)uses" the Scriptures to a unique degree and "attempts to con(trol) its audience."[18] In conflict with competing prophets concerning the meaning of Scripture, Revelation "tries to cover the tracks of its scriptural subtexts."[19] In other words, Royalty detects subterfuge in John's engagement with Scripture. Like other Jewish texts of its day, Revelation is "rewritten scripture, and yet it ends with a strict warning against writing."[20] It "swallows the biblical subtext," elevating John's voice above even that of Moses.[21]

David A. deSilva has engaged this question in a particularly productive way, often weighing constructive critiques of Royalty's argument and of my earlier work.[22] DeSilva finds that John produces fresh meaning from the texts

---

14. Beale 1999, 81, arguing against the latter possibility and for the former.
15. G. Allen 2017, 32, 168–215.
16. Moyise 2012a, 112.
17. Moyise 2001, 120.
18. Royalty 2004, 282–83.
19. Royalty 2004, 290.
20. Royalty 2004, 292.
21. Royalty 2004, 293.
22. DeSilva 2009, 147–64. See also Carey 1999; Royalty 2004.

he engages and "subtly invites these Scriptures to lend their authority to his own visions."[23] The Scriptures thus function for John "as a harmonious witness to his own voice," much like the heavenly voices that buttress John's vision.[24] DeSilva does not choose sides between whether John intends a "faithful" or "creative" use of the Scriptures on the grounds that John engages Scripture in ways that ancient readers would expect from authors interacting with authoritative sources. I largely agree and very much appreciate deSilva's explication of how Revelation draws upon Israel's Scriptures to shape its own message.

I suspect—and this is no criticism—that deSilva reads my argument alongside Royalty's because he perceives both as criticisms of Revelation that obscure its faithful engagement with Scripture and therefore its capacity to address contemporary audiences. DeSilva elucidates several relevant messages that John applies from the Hebrew Scriptures: that God alone is worthy of worship; that God indicts systems of domination; that the God of the exodus is a god of liberation; that God vindicates the faithful; that God rules over the cosmos; that God ensures shalom in God's own presence; and that God's patience has limits. I commend all these points not simply as correct but as examples of elegant theological exegesis. Where Royalty claims John twists and obscures Scripture, deSilva points out how deeply John draws from its streams.

But Royalty and I are not saying the same thing, and while deSilva cites the point I made earlier and am making here, he does not counter it. I argue simply that John insists upon the absolute authority of his vision; he has received it directly from God, and reader/hearers must heed it to receive the eschatological blessings.[25] The Scriptures indeed contribute to John's message and its presentation, but they also lend authority to John as a prophet who engages them deeply. And, as deSilva acknowledges, John's allusions to Scripture reinforce the authority of his visionary experiences.

Disgust

Another means by which John builds up his own authority involves debasing the status of his opponents. John dehumanizes his opponents—both those inside the assemblies and outside of them—often by deploying the rhetoric of disgust.[26] For example, the risen Jesus relates that he hates the Nicolaitans

23. DeSilva 2009, 148.
24. DeSilva 2009, 149.
25. Earlier, Carey 1999, 178.
26. Although I address this element in Carey 1999, see also Stephen D. Moore's much

(2:6). John associates other competing prophets with the biblical villains Balaam and Jezebel, both of whom led Israel into idolatry. As noted in chapter 1, the biblical Balaam and Jezebel both come to violent ends, and John applies particularly debasing imagery to the Jezebel he opposes, accusing her of *porneia* and depicting her as being thrown onto a couch or bed (2:22). Still another example of John's use of disgust is his employment of the term "synagogue of Satan" to demonize opponents who claim a Jewish identity that he rejects (2:9; 3:9). John also compares Rome to a monster that is inspired by Satan and characterizes it as the Prostitute who faces abjection and destruction—she drinks blood and filth (17:4–6).

Also notable is how John regards the Inhabitants of the Earth as worthy of torment and incapable of repentance. Although Revelation calls its audience to repent, the Inhabitants of the Earth apparently cannot do so; even in torment they still practice evil (9:20–21) and curse God (14:6–11). When they suffer the horrific judgments that Revelation pours forth, heavenly voices break out in song to celebrate God's justice (11:15–19; 15:3–4; 16:5–7).[27] From a theological perspective, the capacity to repent is fundamental to human identity. By depicting the Inhabitants of the Earth as being unable to repent, Revelation dehumanizes the vast majority of humankind.

If Sara Ahmed is correct to identify disgust with objects that are sticky, oozing from the boundaries that separate our bodies and the outside world, it matters that Revelation directs its reader/hearers to the Inhabitants of the Earth as they gnaw their tongues and lament their open wounds (16:10–11).[28] It also matters that the birds feed on their corpses (19:21). Scholars often refer to the dualistic dimension of apocalyptic literature in which supernatural and human persons are reduced to two classes: the good and the evil. Revelation tends to characterize John's opponents, especially the Inhabitants of the Earth, as less than human; they are unworthy of pity and incapable of repentance. John's audience stands under threat too; Jesus just might spit them out of his mouth (3:16), another disgusting image. Revelation builds its authority in part by evoking disgust toward John's opponents and justifying their suffering. Revelation's appeals to debasement and disgust include monsters, torture, dehumanization, and filth.

---

more evocative essays (2014) and Sarah Emanuel's examination of humor as a weapon in Revelation (2020).

27. There are more positive ways to interpret these songs. See Hansen 2014.

28. Ahmed 2014, 52; see also Lateiner 2017, 205; Marchal 2019, 118–19; Nussbaum 2004, 14, cited in Moore 2014, 170.

Researchers are just beginning to explore how ancient Greek and Latin authors characterize disgust, which does not appear in the ancient rhetorical handbooks.[29] To my knowledge, no one has yet tapped the links among disgust, authoritarian rhetoric, and Revelation, but it is worth noting that disgust is a hallmark of authoritarian discourse. "Projective disgust" occurs when communicators "project" things that elicit disgust upon other people in ways that stigmatize, marginalize, and dehumanize them.[30]

For example, Nazi propaganda promoted disgust toward Jews by diverse means. A June 1933 poster shows a muscular man throwing a Jew over a cliff with a caption that concludes, "You demon!" (*Du Ungeist*). One from 1934 draws a Jew with the body of a worm, while one from 1935 depicts the strangulation of a snake. A 1935 poster depicts a woman half-naked before a Jewish man who holds a bag of money, and the caption below the poster includes the words "Souls poisoned, blood infected." As late as 1944, a poster depicts a Jew as a worm under the caption, "Vermin" (*Ungeziefer*).[31]

Similar rhetoric has made its way into American political discourse—and not just on the margins. Donald Trump has referred to his political enemies as "vermin."[32] Meanwhile, American "family values" literature has applied similar rhetoric to queer folk. One Family Research Institute pamphlet compares same-sex intercourse to eating shit: "Medically speaking, it doesn't matter whether you pursue such activity for 'fun' or ingest waste because your salad wasn't washed—exposure to feces is unhealthy. Psychologically, to undo the hygienic training of childhood in pursuit of adult sexual pleasure literally 'turns all the rules upside down.'"[33] As these examples show, disgust is a powerful weapon—and a risky one. It can inflame the passions of sympathetic reader/hearers or turn them away.

Intuitively or scientifically, authoritarians have always known how to incite disgust by using metaphors concerning infection, invasion, insects, parasites, and bodily fluids. Disgust requires ideological fuel in order to be ignited.[34] Therefore, authoritarian rhetoric not only appeals to disgust but also generates it. As candidate and president, Trump has expertly wielded disgust as a means of building solidarity among his followers. According to him, immigrants are

---

29. Morales 2017; Lateiner and Spatharas 2017.

30. Introduction to Lateiner and Spatharas 2017, 23–24.

31. For these and other examples, see the German Propaganda Archive compiled by Calvin University (https://research.calvin.edu/german-propaganda-archive/sturmer.htm).

32. LeVine 2023.

33. Introduction to Lateiner and Spatharas 2017, 2–3; citing Family Research Institute 2009.

34. Hodson and Costello 2007; Shook et al. 2017.

infesting the United States. What's more, Trump has often described their purported crimes in revolting detail, going as far as to identify them as rapists. Such performances have often included Trump reciting one of his crowd favorites known as "The Snake," the story of a woman who rescued a snake from the cold only to have it kill her with a venomous bite. And women? In Trump's rhetoric, women who oppose him are nasty. They bleed from their "wherever." Trump directly and repeatedly has invoked the words "disgusting" and "disgusted."[35] These rhetorical appeals unified Trump's supporters.[36]

Disgust bears a particular affinity with social and political conservatism. In noting this, I mean not to stigmatize conservative people or opinions. The observation is necessary if we are to engage the relationship between disgust and authoritarian discourse in Revelation or elsewhere. (My own outlook trends toward very liberal but not always; I also respond to disgust.) The social psychologist Jonathan Haidt brought to public attention how persons inclined toward political conservatism generally have higher sensitivity to disgust than do their liberal neighbors.[37] A host of social scientific research, some of it conducted by Haidt himself, confirms the impression. For example, conservative attitudes map onto heightened sensitivity to body odor.[38] As noted above, one place where heightened disgust sensitivity and an affinity for authoritarianism mutually reinforce one another is in rhetorical opposition to transgender rights.[39] Remarkably, inducing disgust reactions heightens antipathy toward homosexuals in political conservatives, while it reduces prejudice among liberals.[40] These disgust responses resonate more powerfully in persons who are drawn toward right-wing authoritarianism and play out in negative attitudes toward issues like immigration, interracial marriage, and interracial adoption. These are all dispositions in which American Christian nationalists score highly in public opinion polls.[41]

The flip side of disgust is purity, the sense that things should remain in their proper places. Revelation promotes purity through the imagery of white garments, keeping one's clothes unsoiled (3:4), and coming out from the Prostitute (18:4).[42] Purity language shapes Revelation's discourse concerning women.

---

35. Mercieca 2020.

36. The journalist Thomas Edsall (2016) attempted to collate the work of contemporary research on the subject in real time.

37. Haidt 2012, 352.

38. Luiza et al. 2018.

39. P. Miller et al. 2016.

40. Terrizzi et al. 2010.

41. Whitehead and Perry 2020, 117.

42. Acknowledging Pippin (1992, 82) for naming the double entendre in 18:4.

Whether actual women like the so-called Jezebel or symbols like the Woman Clothed with the Sun, Babylon, and the New Jerusalem, John presents them only as either promiscuous, virginal, or motherly. Let us also not neglect the virginal men who follow the Lamb (14:1–5).

Revelation's recourse to disgust is a powerful rhetorical move that is also authoritarian. I am not arguing that Revelation is an example of modern authoritarian discourse, or that many modern authoritarians are directly influenced by Revelation. (Some surely are.) Nor would I position Revelation on a modern political spectrum from left to right. There are other ways to describe Revelation's appeal to the grotesque and the disgusting. We could identify it with "weapons of the weak," with postcolonial or resistance mimicry, or with the carnivalesque. I have used all these models in the past and view them as helpful. But the spell of authoritarianism weighs heavily upon the world we live in now. Christian millenarian readings of Revelation track strongly with authoritarianism, and as Revelation's modern readers, we should sensitize ourselves to that dimension of the book—disgust.

Revelation wields disgust as a weapon aimed primarily against those who hold power and status. The emperor, the emperor's gods, the emperor's representatives, and those who perform diplomacy and commerce on behalf of the empire (see Rev 18) all fall prey to Revelation's ridicule. In its own setting, Revelation's manipulation of disgust aims toward contempt of those who hold power. This is the rhetoric by which groups who perceive themselves as being oppressed assure themselves of their own royal status (1:5–6). As such, Revelation participates in a long tradition of Jewish and Mediterranean countertyranny invective meant to inspire the courage necessary for resistance by means of contempt.[43] It also targets those within the assemblies who may bear an affinity with those who bear authority and honor: "For you say, 'I am rich, I have prospered, and I need nothing.' You do not realize that you are wretched, pitiable, poor, blind, and naked" (3:17).

But this is a generous reading. Revelation also debases John's opponents. Many readers consider Balaam, the Nicolaitans, and Jezebel as false prophets who entice the saints to collaborate with idolatry. In so doing, we accept John's point of view without question. That choice is theologically driven. It does not represent historical judgment or literary sensitivity. In particular, let us consider what happens to Jezebel, whom John associates with *porneia* and whom Jesus will throw upon a bed to die. Interpreters and biblical translators argue that Jezebel's bed is a sickbed and that the scene does not entail sexual violence. Yet, John's association of Jezebel with the Prostitute includes intima-

---

43. Emanuel 2020, 114; see also W. Miller 1997, 220–24.

tions of *porneia* and sexual humiliation, and it strongly suggests divine rape.[44] One might query whether Revelation's sexualized debasement of Jezebel and the Prostitute indicates a measure of suppressed desire.[45]

We have noted that Revelation deploys disgust rhetoric most prominently against the empire, the emperor, and the elites who benefit from imperial commerce. In so doing, Revelation stands among a great crowd of ancient and global resistance discourses that turn disgust toward the ridicule of the powerful. One could see the potential for authoritarianism in any text that dehumanizes and debases its opponents, though we tend to excuse such discourse when it voices resistance to oppression. But Revelation also turns disgust against others who suffer from Roman domination, the Inhabitants of the Earth, and upon leaders among the churches and their followers who do not share John's point of view. Throughout the centuries, many Christian readers have deployed Revelation to demonize their enemies. Therefore, it is right to elevate disgust in our assessment of authoritarianism in Revelation.

Authoritarianism in an Egalitarian Mode

Revelation balances its authoritarian tone with egalitarian appeals. Modern authoritarian rhetoric often adopts an egalitarian posture. Authoritarian leaders seek to establish a psychological bond with their followers, albeit one in which "the . . . leader wields a privileged power wholly unlike the crowd that longs for identification."[46] Consider the 2018 speech of Viktor Orbán, the authoritarian prime minister of Hungary, celebrating the one hundred and seventieth anniversary of Hungary's failed 1848 revolution. Orbán attempted to unite all Hungarians by referring to them as "Dear Friends" fighting off enemy elites.

> We, the millions with national feelings, are on one side; the elite "citizens of the world" are on the other side. . . . On one side, national and democratic forces; and on the other side, supranational and anti-democratic forces. . . . We are up against media outlets maintained by foreign concerns and domestic oligarchs, professional hired activists, troublemaking protest organizers, and a chain of NGOs financed by an international speculator, summed up by and embodied in the name "George Soros."[47]

44. Pippin 1992; Warren forthcoming.
45. See Marchal 2019, 117–19.
46. Gordon 2018, 66.
47. Orbán 2018.

Orbán invites patriotic (that is, nationalist) Hungarians to identify with him as part of a society that is vulnerable to attack, beset by powerful and hostile enemies on the outside. George Soros, for example, is a Hungarian-American businessman who is extremely wealthy and very much engaged in global affairs. He is also Jewish, a villain in popular anti-Semitic conspiracy theories. Although Orbán locates his followers as holding majority status within Hungary, they are oppressed by "elite" "supranational" forces like Soros and a host of unnamed entities. Authoritarian rhetoric often takes such a popularist tone, building lines of solidarity while pitching the outside world as threatening and hostile.

Revelation performs similar egalitarian moves. John is a brother to the assemblies, one who participates in their distress (1:9). Together they inhabit a hostile world, one in which Jesus-identified people are subject to persecution from beastly and immoral authorities (13:7; 17:6). All society, represented by the Inhabitants of the Earth, poses a threat to them (6:10; 12:11; 20:4). Despite these difficulties, John and the assemblies own a common identity as rulers and priests through Jesus (1:5–6; 5:10; 20:6). John shares other status markers with his audience. John draws upon the common trope of presenting both himself and his audience as being enslaved to God (e.g., 1:1; 2:20)—a status they together hold in common with angels (19:10; 22:9). John writes to the assemblies as a true prophet (1:3; 10:11), who stands in opposition to Jezebel, and as a self-appointed prophet (2:20), unlike the Other Beast, who is a false prophet (16:13; 19:20; 20:10). But John also acknowledges other true prophets (10:7; 16:6; 18:20, 24; 22:6, 9). John potentially extends this status to all the assembly members, since they are called to bear witness to Jesus, and "The testimony of Jesus is the spirit of prophecy" (19:10). Rulers, priests, partners, siblings, (exalted) slaves, and prophets—all these markers of status are extended by John to those audience members who adopt his message.

As a faithful witness, John shares everything he has seen (1:2, 11), thereby elevating the assemblies almost to his own level of knowledge concerning "the things that must happen soon" (22:6). This knowledge is "faithful and true" (22:6). As a faithful witness, John also identifies himself with *the* singular "faithful witness," Jesus (1:5; 3:14; 19:11). Thus, John's authority as a faithful witness derives from that of Jesus, and he invites the Jesus followers of the assemblies to participate in his privileged perspective. But there is more. One believer, a certain Antipas, has suffered death. In the letter to Pergamum Jesus refers to him as "my faithful witness" (2:13). Likewise, the Lamb's followers emulate the example set by Jesus, John, and Antipas. They conquer the Beast "by the blood of the Lamb and the word of their testimony," even at the risk of their lives (12:11). All these associations identify John and his audience with Jesus's exalted status.

John also allows his audience to observe his own role in the narrative. Somewhat common among the literary apocalypses, this technique cements his egalitarian bond with his audience. John discloses occasions when heavenly figures correct him for showing fear or sadness (1:17; 5:5) as well as when he mistakenly bows in worship before angels (19:10; 22:8–9), reactions to heavenly beings that are easily relatable. By sharing his grief and sadness and by relating moments when he is rebuked, John signals his vulnerability to the audience. John even shares a moment of personal disgust. While he is not the only biblical prophet commanded to do something unpleasant, John is forced in Rev 10 to ingest a scroll. The taste transitions from sweet to bitter, just as he is warned (10:8–11). Despite his limitations and his comic moments, John faithfully performs the services to which he is called in sharing "whatever he saw" (1:2, my translation). But there are exceptions. John hears a song he cannot learn and thus cannot record (14:3). He once receives a task without telling us he has performed it (11:1–2). On another occasion, John is prohibited from recording what he has heard (10:1–4; see also 2 Cor 12:4 mentioned above). Thus, John cannot quite fulfill his promise to share everything; he must keep some things to himself.

Apocalyptic visionaries claim an extraordinary level of privilege. Like other such visionaries, John experiences things exceedingly few mortals can access. John's claims to divine revelation and authority could have elicited challenges from his reader/hearers. The egalitarian tone deployed by John softens those claims, but it does not eliminate them. John reaches out to his audience as a partner who faces common challenges and risks, shares their exalted status, and is vulnerable to his own embarrassing moments. Although appeals like these invoke egalitarianism, they are a common feature of authoritarian rhetoric.

Coming to Terms with Authority

Many commentators argue that we should not question John's authority but instead should read along with it. After all, John is relating a direct revelation from God. He courageously voices the truth within and against a hostile culture. When he draws upon Scripture, he underscores an authority that far transcends his own. Therefore, to question John's authority is to read against the grain of his own argument, with the result that we necessarily fail to understand his message.[48]

I would reply that when we take John at his word, we confuse what may or may not have been his intention with the demands of literary and rhetorical

---

48. Classically, deSilva 2009, 147–74.

analysis. In his own mind, John may very well have attempted to represent a divine perspective, even to record an authentic revelatory experience. If we seek to understand John—a decision that requires a series of other judgments regarding Revelation's authorship and authorial voice—we may then attempt to present his understanding of his world and of God's plan for it. When we do so, however, we have stepped outside the ordinary conventions of literary and rhetorical interpretation. Literary theorists have long recognized levels of discourse, relationships of authority that include one or more authorial voices alongside the other voices organized within their narrative. To take an obvious but challenging case, William Faulkner's *The Sound and the Fury* deploys three narrators who hold conflicting perspectives and closes with a more authoritative narrating voice that has access to more information than any single participant in the story world could possess. (It was also my mother's favorite novel.) That kind of plurivocal and multiperspectival approach was vanishingly rare in the ancient world. (Perhaps the Song of Solomon attempts it?) No one seriously proposes that John intentionally authorizes multiple, competing points of view. From an analytical perspective, we are left to discern how John wrangles all these perspectives to suit one larger rhetorical purpose—his own.

Further, we need not bind ourselves to notions of authority that force a choice between rejection and submission. This is not to deny that John requires submission. But we can imagine authority differently. We may identify authority in the voices John rejects as well as in John's perspective. We may imagine the arguments John's opponents would have advanced, arguments that apparently persuaded quite a few members of the assemblies. We may even locate authority in those assembly members who felt deep tension among the available options. And we may extend authority even to the Inhabitants of the Earth, who worship the Beast and torment the saints. In an era in which hate crime continues to escalate and citizens tolerate those who undermine human decency and democracy, the Inhabitants of the Earth could teach us a bit about our own implication in structures of domination and violence. As an interpreter, I am not ready to cast the Beast or the Prostitute in a sympathetic light or yield authority to them, but let us note that John depicts (and distorts) their perspectives too. The whole earth shows amazement before the Beast. John acknowledges his own amazement in the presence of the Prostitute (17:6–8). Whatever its dangers and offenses, John implicitly acknowledges that there is something compelling about the imperial system.

Engaging John's authority requires contemporary readers to take account of our own circumstances. We, too, live in an era where loyalties are clearly drawn, and people yield absolute authority to their own political and cultural outlooks. Many Christian nationalists aim to "take dominion over the seven mountains of culture." In such a context, Christians often deploy Scripture as a weapon with which to smash their opposition. Revelation provides a pointed case study for our divisive context: some read it as embodying the voice of the marginalized, while others claim it as a mandate for authoritarian nationalism. For these reasons, it is helpful to reimagine the perspectives of those John and other biblical authors seek to suppress.[49]

I read Revelation sympathetically because I understand Revelation as an example of counterimperial literature. It makes sense to imagine John as alarmed. He portrays Rome as a ravenous monster that derives its authority from Satan, and he presents the prevailing religious and cultural life of Roman Asia as incompatible with devotion to Jesus. John acknowledges division among the assemblies regarding how to follow Jesus in this context. He opens no room for compromise or accommodation: the threat is absolute.

But we are not done when we have sketched John's basic agenda. To read sympathetically does not rule out reading critically. It does not exclude imagining why other Jesus followers in the assemblies saw things differently. Nor does a sympathetic reading cut off discernment regarding how to appropriate Revelation in our own cultural contexts.

Many of Revelation's most vocal advocates have an affinity for authoritarianism. That is no accident, and it presents specific challenges to readers who reject predictive and exclusivist interpretation. These challenges "call for wisdom" (13:18). Revelation does not model a mode of authority that applies to every context. On the contrary, Revelation's mode of authority *always* comes with problems and should not be the norm. With Revelation, wisdom entails specifically contextual and communal discernment. I would propose three related questions.

- When is it appropriate to claim that one's point of view amounts to God's will?
- When is it appropriate to tolerate no moral or theological compromise or dissent?
- When is it appropriate to identify others with evil?

Whenever I encounter questions like these, I find myself confronted by Allan Boesak, a Black South African pastor and anti-apartheid activist. While in solitary confinement, he experienced "an angelic visitation" that deepened his en-

---

49. See the essays in Marchal 2021, in response to Wire 1990. Also, Concannon 2021.

gagement with Revelation, work that led to one of the most compelling studies of Revelation now available. He recalls the period as bringing him "close to the heart of that lonely, brave prophet on his island."[50] Of John's vision for the destruction of his enemies, Boesak writes: "If [Christ's] cloak is spattered in blood, it is the blood of his enemies, the destroyers of the earth and of his children."[51] This single quotation stands out among all the things I have read about Revelation, and it will appear elsewhere in this book. It also embodies answers to all three of the questions I have just posed. In the context of apartheid horror, Boesak does not shirk from claiming to be on God's side, recognizing no space for compromise, and perceiving his enemies as God's enemies. I cannot imagine looking Boesak in the eye and accusing him of being authoritarian or exclusive.

Almost surely, most people who have claimed Revelation as Boesak does have abused the text. But we also celebrate heroes of the faith who recognized their moments and named the stakes. Frederick Douglass was not wrong to describe the church of his day, whether promoting slavery or tolerating it, as "an abomination in the sight of God." Martin Luther King Jr. practiced love for his enemies and rejected retaliation, but he did not hold back from voicing his disappointment with the church or from identifying the wickedness of segregation. In his "Letter from a Birmingham Jail," King assesses "the white moderate" as a greater threat to civil rights than "the White Citizen's Counciler or the Ku Klux Klanner." Douglass and King were both considered extremists in their day and are revered as heroes now. Similarly, Dietrich Bonhoeffer, a prominent figure in the international peace movement, found himself obligated to participate in a conspiracy to assassinate Hitler.

It is unclear precisely how Bonhoeffer and Boesak related to the authorship of the Barmen Declaration (1934) and the Kairos Document (1985), two of three twentieth-century declarations of faith that have entered the canon of classic Protestant confessions, but they were closely associated with the movements and the people who produced them. Bonhoeffer endorsed the Barmen Declaration as an essential but limited step in defining a faithful church in Germany.[52] Boesak wrote a book devoted to applying the Kairos Document to contemporary crises, particularly the Israeli repression of Palestinians.[53] Each of those documents named a contemporary crisis as a fundamental test of faithfulness. The Barmen Declaration responds to

50. Boesak 1987, 14.
51. Boesak 1987, 124.
52. Marsh 2014, 223–25.
53. Boesak 2015.

the errors of the "German Christians" and of the present Reich Church Administration, which are ravaging the Church and at the same time also shattering the unity of the German Evangelical Church.

The Kairos Document confesses

that any teaching which attempts to legitimate such forced separation by appeal to the gospel, and is not prepared to venture on the road of obedience and reconciliation, but rather, out of prejudice, fear, selfishness and unbelief, denies in advance the reconciling power of the gospel, must be considered ideology and false doctrine.

Both documents name error for what it is: false and dangerous. Both do so concerning other members of the church.

Neither the Barmen Declaration nor the Kairos Document calls for violence against evildoers. King and the rest of the mainstream civil rights movement rejected violence as a means of achieving social change, as does Boesak. Bonhoeffer himself condemned violence but willingly became complicit in it. For his part, Douglass called for the recruitment of Black soldiers in the Civil War. If their dispositions toward violence differed from one another, none of these figures called for the torment or the eternal destruction of their foes. As clear as they were about the undeniable evils of their respective moments, Douglass, Bonhoeffer, King, and Boesak have not gone where Revelation sometimes goes.

Perhaps more aligned with Revelation's rhetoric is the Mississippi civil rights activist Fannie Lou Hamer. Aware that she did not speak standard English, Hamer credited her elocution to the poor education available to Black people in Mississippi. But in her 1964 speech in Indianola, Mississippi, Hamer turned her critical eye both inside to Black preachers and outside to White segregationists. And she used a particular kind of biting humor. Regarding the Black preachers, Hamer indicted their failure to exhibit the courage they claimed to inspire in their sermons. These preachers had failed to open their churches to voting rights meetings.

Every church door in the state of Mississippi should be open for these meetings. But preachers have preached for years what he didn't believe hisself. And if he's willin' to trust God, if he's willin' to trust God, he won't mind openin' the church door.[54]

54. Quoted in Houck and Dixon 2006, 787–88.

And,

> Preachers, preachers, preachers, is, is really shockin' to find them out. You know they like to read back in the corners and over the rostrum and say "what God has done for Meshach, Shadrack, and Abednego."[55]

And as for the White segregationists? Like John, Hamer puts their character right before the hearers' eyes.

> Some of the white people will tell us, "Well, I just don't believe in integration." But he been integratin' at night a long time. If, if he hadn't been, it wouldn't been as many light-skinned Negroes as it is in here.[56]

Hamer's rhetoric is not apocalyptic in the sense of deploying symbols like the Beast or tropes such as Jezebel. But it does resemble Revelation in taking supposedly respectable people and unveiling their true character in graphic, even comic, detail.

Interpreters have found ways to soften Revelation's glee in assigning torment and damnation to its enemies, especially the Inhabitants of the Earth. A classic case is embodied in the work of Adela Yarbro Collins, who assessed Revelation as "a partial and imperfect vision."[57] Without excusing Revelation, Yarbro Collins interpreted the themes of violence and retaliation as a therapeutic way for a community that perceived itself as oppressed to come to terms with its disempowerment and disillusionment. To some degree, she must be correct. Almost all of us enjoy a good revenge fantasy once in a while. Yet, whatever their dispositions toward violence, we do not observe Douglass, Bonhoeffer, King, or Boesak reveling in visions of their enemies suffering. Hamer, who was beaten and tortured just for seeking the right to vote, testified before her captors by singing in jail. She reached the spiritual space in which she rejected animosity. "It wouldn't solve any problem," she said, "for me to hate whites just because they hate me. Oh, there's so much hate, only God has kept the Negro sane."[58]

Historical change clarifies many things. All of the persons I have considered here faced criticism from other Christians. Yet, history has vindicated their

55. Houck and Dixon 2006, 789.
56. Houck and Dixon 2006, 788.
57. A. Yarbro Collins 1984, 172.
58. Marsh 1997, 22; citing McLaurin 1982, 13.

moral and theological clarity concerning slavery, Nazism, segregation, and apartheid. We should exercise caution before assigning such clarity to our own moral and theological judgments, especially before labeling those who oppose us as God's enemies. I would propose that we should absolutely refrain from wishing suffering and damnation upon anyone. Yet, among the books in the New Testament, Revelation most directly models what it can look like to identify evil, idolatry, exploitation, and deception for what they are and for brooking no compromise with them. We cannot step back into John's moment and say how we would assess things. Nor can we endorse all of John's vision. But we do need to discern, in community and with humility, when to hold our ground and name violence, dehumanization, exploitation, and deception as evil, trembling before God every step of the way.[59]

59. Multiple copies of Douglass's "What to the Slave Is the Fourth of July?" and of King's "Letter from a Birmingham Jail" are available online, along with translations of the Barmen Declaration and the Kairos Document.

Jesus in Relation to God and the Spirit

R EVELATION BEGINS AND ENDS WITH JESUS. Jesus authorizes its message as the "revelation of Jesus Christ" (1:1), and the book's hope for his imminent return and ongoing presence assures its audience (22:20–21). Apart from John's narrating voice, Jesus is Revelation's primary speaker and dominant character. Yet, Revelation's beginning and ending remind us that while Jesus may deliver its message, the message ultimately comes from God (1:1; 22:16), and it is God who enforces its truth. Moreover, when Jesus speaks directly to the seven assemblies in chapters 2–3, he calls each individual among those churches to "listen to what the Spirit is saying to the churches." Revelation's final set of blessings and admonitions features a call from the Spirit for reader/ hearers to come and receive the water of life (22:17). Revelation may focus on Jesus, but his relationships to God and, to a lesser degree, to the Spirit prove essential to his identity and to the message he reveals.

Theologically inclined readers often use Trinitarian language to make sense of these relationships between God, Jesus, and the Spirit. In so doing, they paddle against a significant current of critical biblical scholarship, which holds theological presuppositions at a distance (or suspends them outright) and values historical and literary evidence apart from "anachronistic" theological categories.[1] Some scholars do begin with Trinitarian assumptions and read biblical texts according to that rubric.[2] Others, attuned to the reality that few New Testament texts voice explicitly Trinitarian frameworks and aware that Trinitarian theology grew out of prolonged reflection on the New Testament and the life of the church, ask how a Trinitarian outlook might enhance interpretive insight.[3] It is not my aim to criticize any class of readers but to be

---

1. For example, Jeffcoat Schedtler 2023.
2. For example, Mangina 2010, 43.
3. For example, B. Smith 2022, 2.

transparent regarding my own interpretive approach. Although I am interested in Revelation's relevance for doctrine, I am open to the possibility that Revelation might surprise us. And I hope to read Revelation in life-giving ways.

Revelation has a way of blurring the relationships between God, Jesus, and the Spirit. In this chapter I am primarily interested in how Revelation depicts Jesus, its most compelling character, in relation to God and the Spirit. I do not propose to develop a full Christology or a fully adequate theological construction of the Trinity in Revelation. Other scholars who are more literate in the language of systematic theology than I have done so, and I will engage their work in this chapter. I am instead interested in a more narrowly focused question: How does Revelation interpret and present the figure of Jesus, particularly in relation to God and to the Spirit?

We will not begin to approach this question by presupposing an abstract or orthodox understanding of the Trinity and reading Revelation through that lens. For one thing, I do not regard myself as being sufficiently theologically competent to do so; I certainly haven't grasped the nuances of fourth-century or medieval debates about the Trinity. More importantly, I join most biblical scholars in certain assumptions. Like some other New Testament documents, Revelation presents God, Jesus, and the Spirit in relationship to one another but not in the rigorously formulated way sought by later ecumenical councils. One might read Revelation by first presupposing the creeds and what is known from patristic writers about the Trinity, and such a process is certainly enlightening.[4] However, that is not my goal here. It is appropriate to investigate these relationships in Revelation, but I aim to do so without reading the book into a creedal formula.

A WAY INTO THE QUESTION

One primary feature of Revelation has drawn my attention to this question regarding the relationship between Jesus, God, and the Spirit. Revelation frequently blurs or overlaps the boundaries that distinguish God, Jesus, and the Spirit from one another. This blurring occurs between Jesus and God more commonly than between Jesus and the Spirit or between God and the Spirit.

Blurring between God and the Spirit does occur at times. For example, John's vision derives in some sense from God (1:1). For this reason, most translations read Rev 1:1 as a "revelation *of* Jesus Christ" rather than as a "revelation *from* Jesus Christ," a decision based on context rather than demanded by Greek

---

4. B. Smith 2022, 2.

syntax. That choice is complicated by Jesus's declaration that he has sent the angel to bear the testimony to the churches (22:16). However, later in chapter 1 John experiences the vision because he was "in the spirit," taken by most commentators to connote *the Spirit*. This is what I mean by blurring. In some sense, both God and the Spirit receive credit for the vision, as does Jesus, yet they are treated as in some ways distinct.

As we can see, blurring occurs right from the beginning of Revelation. We have already noted that Rev 1:1 advances a hierarchical relationship between God and Jesus: God gives the revelation to Jesus, and Jesus delivers it to his followers (literally, the enslaved ones) through an angel.[5] Revelation 1:4–6 constitutes Revelation's formal greeting, which names John as the author and the seven Asian assemblies as its recipients before proceeding with a blessing of "grace and peace." Contemporary readers (and likely ancient ones) recall these words being used in Paul's standard greeting formula. But whereas Paul typically pronounces grace and peace "from God our Father and the Lord Jesus Christ," John adds something very different:[6]

> Grace to you and peace from him who is and who was and who is to come and from the seven spirits who are before his throne, and from Jesus Christ, the faithful witness, the firstborn of the dead, and the ruler of the kings of the earth. (1:4b–5)

Not only does John elaborate upon the identities of God and of Jesus Christ, using language that occurs elsewhere in Revelation, he adds something very confusing to contemporary readers: "the seven spirits who are before [God's] throne" (1:4; see also 3:1; 4:5; 5:6).

Commentators typically propose two mutually exclusive options for these seven spirits, if they explain their presence at all. One option is that the "seven spirits" point to the Holy Spirit. Brandon D. Smith reads the seven spirits as "an innovative element of including the Spirit in a type of greeting that often only included the Father and Jesus." By adding the Spirit to the traditional greeting we encounter in Paul, John extends the greeting from a Binitarian (i.e., Father and Son) to an "incipient trinitarian discourse."[7] Other commentators,

---

5. Revelation 1:1 offers notorious translation problems. The revelation could *come from* or *be about* Jesus Christ, and only context suggests that the one who delivers the revelation through an angel is more likely Jesus than God (see 22:16).

6. Rom 1:7; 1 Cor 1:3; 2 Cor 1:2; Gal 1:3; Phil 1:2; Phlm 3; cf. 1 Thess 1:1.

7. B. Smith 2022, 55; among others see Reddish 2001, 34; Moloney 2020, 46; J. Davies

however, regard the seven spirits as part of God's divine council of heavenly beings along with the twenty-four elders and the four living creatures, who first appear together at 4:4–5.[8] The notion of the heavenly assembly occurs several times in the Hebrew Scriptures, including 1 Kgs 22:19–23; Isa 6:1–9; Job 1:6; 2:1; and most notably Ps 82.[9] We might also note that Luke 9:26 alludes to the glory of Jesus, of the Father, and of the holy angels with no reference to the Spirit, with similar language occurring at 1 Tim 5:21.[10] Readers on both sides of the argument appeal to the importance of seven messengers or angels—the Greek word is *angeloi*—who deliver the seven messages to the assemblies and unleash the seven trumpets and seven bowls of judgment.[11]

The genre of commentary writing strongly encourages scholars to express definitive opinions. But are these options mutually exclusive? That would be the case with most texts. But Revelation is fond of blurring categories. For example, Revelation applies the term "faithful witness" to two characters and associates it with others. (Note that the same Greek root *martys* lies beneath our words for witness and testimony.) Jesus is the faithful witness (1:5; 3:14). So is Antipas, an apparent martyr (2:13), and so are others who suffer for their testimony (6:9; 11:7; 17:6; 20:4). Does this category apply to John, who testifies faithfully (1:2, 9)? Does it extend to all of Jesus's faithful followers (12:11, 17; 19:10)? Revelation identifies Antipas as "*my* faithful witness" (my translation) alongside Jesus, "*the* faithful witness," thereby opening the possibility that all who testify faithfully may participate in Jesus's identity. Revelation deploys this sort of blurring as a rhetorical device.[12] Such blurring applies to Jesus, his relationship to God, and, to a lesser degree, to the Spirit. Therefore, perhaps we should not assume that the opening blessing of Rev 1:4–6 must be *either* Trinitarian *or* something else.

Blurring between the status and identities of God and the Lamb occurs most prominently in Revelation's worship scenes. Worship constitutes one of Revelation's pressing concerns. Not only do God and the Lamb receive worship, so does the Beast. In Revelation God first receives worship in the heavenly throne room (4:8–11). Later, but in the same worship room scene,

---

2023, 36–37. For additional arguments, see Koester 2014, 216. Also, see Matt 28:19; 2 Cor 13:13; 1 Pet 1:2 for Trinitarian phrasing within the New Testament.

8. For example, Aune 1998, 1:33–35; F. Murphy 1998, 66–70; and Koester 2014, 216.

9. Mullen 2007, 2:145.

10. F. Murphy 1998, 69.

11. For more extended arguments, see Moloney 2020, 46; Beale 1999, 189–90; and Koester 2014, 216.

12. Carey 1999, 118–28.

the Lamb receives worship in response to its first appearance (5:9–14). Worship continues throughout Revelation, directed primarily toward God but also often toward the Lamb. After all, salvation and the kingdom belong to God and to the Lamb (7:10; 11:15; 12:10). After God and the Lamb receive worship together in 7:10, the same scene directs worship to God and to the Lamb alternatively (7:9–17). That's blurry. What makes worship blurry here is that it involves praise of both figures, just as the saints are marked with the names of both God and the Lamb (14:1), and just as the martyrs serve as priests to God and Christ and reign with them (20:6). (Only deities have priests.)[13] In the same scene both God and the Lamb are "worthy" to receive glory and honor and power (4:11; 5:11).[14] Commentators typically assume—often without argument—that the worship in Rev 22:3b–4 is directed specifically toward God, but the language is ambiguous:

> But the throne of God and of the Lamb will be in it, and his servants will worship him; they will see his face, and his name will be on their foreheads.

This reading has the advantage of conforming to v. 5 ("for the Lord God will be their light"), but it also stands in tension with the depiction of God and the Lamb sharing the throne as well as the Lamb's followers bearing both his name *and* the Father's on the foreheads (14:1). In any event, both God and the Lamb receive worship in Revelation, sometimes together. This is why Richard B. Hays describes Jesus in Revelation "as sharer in the identity of God."[15]

Another telling example of Revelation's blurring involves the language of Alpha and Omega, the first and the last. As God's voice declares at the beginning of the book, "I am the Alpha and the Omega, . . . who is and who was and who is to come, the Almighty" (1:8).[16] Later in the same chapter Jesus says, "I am the first and the last" (1:17). As the book nears its conclusion, the one seated on the throne self-identifies with the words "I am the Alpha and the Omega, the Beginning and the End" (21:6), but Jesus soon proclaims a few verses later that "I am the Alpha and the Omega, the First and the Last, the Beginning and the End" (22:13). According to Richard Bauckham, Rev 1:8 and 21:6 comprise the book's only examples of direct speech from God.[17] The placement of these state-

---

13. B. Smith 2022, 134–35.
14. Hays 2012, 76.
15. Hays 2012, 70.
16. I have modified the NRSVue's punctuation in order to convey my impression concerning the speech attributed to God here.
17. Bauckham 1993b, 25–27.

ments from God and from the risen Jesus seems strategic, a matter of literary design and theological significance. Collectively, they "reveal the remarkable extent to which Revelation identifies Jesus Christ with God."[18]

Perhaps the most striking instance of blurring between Jesus and the Spirit occurs in the seven letters to the assemblies in Rev 2–3. The risen Jesus instructs John to "Write in a book what you see and send it to the seven churches" (1:11). Each letter presents itself as the dictated words of the risen Jesus: "And to the angel of the church in X write Y." Within the seven letters, Jesus speaks in the first person, yet the final or penultimate sentence of each letter invokes the Spirit in language suggesting that the Spirit is its true author: "Let anyone who has an ear listen to what the Spirit is saying to the churches." We may differentiate between the activity of Jesus and that of the Spirit. For example, one could propose that Jesus dictates the letters, which call reader/hearers to heed the Spirit as it continues to address the assemblies. But in this pattern, I perceive blurring. Both the risen Jesus and the Spirit function as the authors of the seven letters.

Blurring between God and Jesus is more prominent than the other examples mentioned above. Although I am sure the observation goes back many decades, I first encountered this reality through an essay by Richard B. Hays, who identifies "proto-Chalcedonian Christology" in Revelation.[19] Particularly fascinating to me is the prominence of a throne. Revelation 4:3 depicts one figure seated upon the throne, connoting God and alluding to the divine throne in Isa 6 and Ezek 1. Revelation 4 and 5 set one continuous scene that unfolds in the heavenly throne room. In that scene, we encounter the Lamb, Revelation's most prominent symbol for Jesus, who stands between this throne and the other heavenly beings. The basic scene challenges our visual imagination: God sits on the throne, and Jesus, who receives authority from the Father (2:28), stands adjacent to it. Just prior to this grand heavenly scene, the risen Jesus has assured his followers in Laodicea:

> To the one who conquers I will give a place with me on my throne, just as I myself conquered and sat down with my Father on his throne. (3:21; see also 22:3)

Now we have blurring. How many thrones do we have here: one or two? (The heavenly throne room features twenty-four thrones in addition to "the" throne.) Jesus shares his throne with his faithful followers, and his Father

---

18. Bauckham 1993b, 55; see also McGrath 2009, 74–75; Hays 2012, 75; B. Smith 2022, 94–95.
19. Hays 2012, 81.

shares a throne with him. We would generally be inclined to distinguish two thrones, one properly belonging to God, which is the prevailing pattern in Revelation, and one belonging to Jesus. However, we encounter another surprise at Rev 7:17. Prior to v. 17, John describes God being on the throne and the Lamb being close by. But now we encounter peculiar language: "the Lamb *at the center of* the throne" (7:17, literally, *in the midst of* the throne).

One can imagine after reading 7:17 how Richard Hays construes a "proto-Chalcedonian Christology" from this blurring. Revelation recognizes the distinctive persons of God, Christ, and the Spirit, but the blurring suggests the mystery of oneness in differentiation. At the same time, Revelation's blurring is, well, blurry. If John wants to equate Jesus with God, he passes on clear opportunities to do so, and sometimes he gives a contrary impression.[20] Although some would deny subordinationism in Revelation, I agree with those who "have noticed varying levels of subordination and divine agency" attributed to Jesus.[21] After all, Jesus receives both John's revelation (1:1) and his own authority from the Father (2:28).

Justin P. Jeffcoat Schedtler has surveyed evidence concerning throne sharing in the ancient Greek and Roman worlds.[22] The ancients commonly depicted thrones being shared between multiple deities or exalted mortals and even between mortals and deities. Yet, not all deities are alike. When *Dikē* (Justice) sits upon the throne of Zeus, that word picture does not imply equality between the two. Nor does it suggest equality when an epitaph depicts a deceased mortal as enthroned with a deity—surely an honor, even a recognition of divinity, but one that does not entail equality. Ancient Jewish literature rarely depicts mortals sharing heavenly thrones, likely a reflection of their recognition that although heaven might be densely populated, Israel's God nevertheless held uniquely exalted status.[23] So when God calls David to "Sit at my right hand" (Ps 110:1), this throne sharing does not suggest a common status. As time passed, other later Jewish texts, notably the Similitudes of Enoch, begin to imagine messianic figures who sit on the divine throne and dispense judgment. From this review of the literature, Jeffcoat Schedtler determines

20. B. Smith 2022, 8, citing McGrath 2009, 72. For Smith's valuable summary of research regarding Revelation's Christology in terms of high/low, see B. Smith 2022, 7–11.

21. B. Smith 2022, 8; citing McGrath 2009, 71–80, and Adela Yarbro Collins in A. Yarbro Collins and J. Collins 2008, 189. McGrath and A. Yarbro Collins argue that the elevation of Jesus to the throne and the direction of worship toward him do not necessarily indicate his divine status. For a denial of subordination in Revelation, see Hoffmann 2005, 168.

22. The discussion in this paragraph draws heavily from Jeffcoat Schedtler 2023, 82–102.

23. Fredriksen 2018, 147–48.

that Jesus's enthronement in Revelation indicates his status as God's "heavenly vice-regent," an exalted status but not one that implies equality in the way developed by Trinitarian theology.[24] Jeffcoat Schedtler's work, combined with a few decades of research into messianic and Son of Man thinking, opens a path for imagining Jesus's exaltation without necessarily rushing toward fully developed Trinitarian discourse.[25] At the same time, Revelation does blur the relational boundaries among Jesus, God, and the Spirit.

Ruben A. Bühner adds an important dimension to our reflection. Although the Lamb may be differentiated from and subordinate to God, Revelation consistently exalts the Lamb above other heavenly beings.[26] Those beings and mortals who reside in heaven sing or shout praises to the Lamb on several occasions, sometimes singing to God alone and sometimes offering common praise to God and to the Lamb (5:13–14; 7:10; 11:15; 12:10; see also 7:15–18). In the ancient world, choruses like these contributed to political demonstrations, whether as an offering of praise to the emperor and to Rome or simply as an act of praise to a great ruler.[27] Revelation, however, often directs praise to God and to the Lamb together. Consider this example: "Salvation belongs to our God who is seated on the throne and to the Lamb!" (7:10). Here what differentiates God from the Lamb is God's throne. Salvation belongs to both. And in the very same scene, it is the Lamb at the *center* of the throne and not simply alongside God (7:17). Again, any differentiation between the two is blurry.

Accustomed to think in monotheistic and Trinitarian terms, Christian readers (and even scholars) struggle to imagine a portrait of Jesus as fully divine but not quite sharing equal status with "God." Yet, we encounter precisely such figures in the apocalyptic literature of ancient Judaism. One such category, the Son of Man, figures more prominently in Revelation than some readers acknowledge and merits attention in this light.

SON OF MAN

Some readers maintain that Revelation does not make much of Jesus's messianic identity, noting that Revelation uses the term Christ (i.e., Messiah) only eight times and "one like the [or a] Son of Man" twice. Indeed, it is an error

24. Jeffcoat Schedtler 2023, 101.

25. For example, Stuckenbruck 1995; Hoffmann 2005; Hurtado 2005; A. Yarbro Collins and J. Collins 2008; Boyarin 2012; and Bühner 2021.

26. Bühner 2021, 127–30; see also B. Smith 2022, 92–96.

27. Hansen 2014, 50–56; Friesen 2001, 104–13, 196–97. Especially evocative is Jenkins 2023, 32–33.

to place too much weight upon specific titles without assessing their role in a larger literary work. The Lamb constitutes Revelation's dominant symbol and primary representation of Jesus from chapter 5 through chapter 22. However, the Lamb only makes sense as an expression of messianic Christology. As Jeffcoat Schedtler expresses it: "The Lamb's status as God's royal messiah is revealed throughout Revelation by the use of royal and messianic epithets, narrative sequences in which his royal character is exhibited, and symbolic imagery denoting his position as viceregent of God."[28]

We might make similar arguments concerning the phrase "one like the Son of Man" (1:13; 14:14). Although it occurs only twice in the book, one of those instances involves Jesus's initial appearance, which shapes expectations for the rest of the book. This appearance echoes a passage in Daniel that influences several other messianic passages in Jewish apocalyptic texts. To underscore the significance of Dan 7 for Revelation, John alludes to this scriptural text over two dozen times, with ten of those instances referring specifically to 7:9–14.[29] Revelation's adoption of the Son of Man is no minor detail.

DANIEL 7:9–14

As I watched, thrones were set in place, and an Ancient One took his throne; his clothing was **white as snow** and the **hair of his head like pure wool**; his throne was **fiery flames**, and its wheels were **burning fire**. A **stream of fire** issued and flowed out from his presence. A thousand thousands served him, and ten thousand times ten thousand stood attending him. The court sat in judgment, and the books were opened. I watched then because of the noise of the arrogant words that the horn was speaking. And as I watched, the beast was put to death and its body destroyed and given over to be burned with fire. As for the rest of the beasts, their dominion was taken away, but their lives were prolonged for a season and a time. As I watched in the night visions, I saw **one like a human being** [literally, one like a Son of Man] coming with the clouds of heaven. And he came to the Ancient One and was presented before him. To him was given dominion and glory and kingship, that all peoples, nations, and languages should serve him. His dominion is an everlasting dominion that shall not pass away, and his kingship is one that shall never be destroyed.

---

28. Jeffcoat Schedtler 2023, 82.

29. As indicated in the apparatus to the fifth edition of United Bible Societies, *Greek New Testament*.

Jesus in Relation to God and the Spirit

REVELATION 1:13-16

and in the midst of the lampstands I saw **one like the Son of Man**, clothed with a long robe and with a golden sash across his chest. **His head and his hair were white as white wool, white as snow;** his eyes were like a **flame of fire;** his feet were like burnished bronze, refined as in a furnace, and his voice was like the sound of many waters. In his right hand he held seven stars, and from his mouth came a sharp, two-edged sword, and his face was like the sun shining with full force.

One quickly discerns not only Revelation's appropriation of Dan 7 but also an important misfit between the two. The depiction of the one like a Son of Man (henceforth "Son of Man") in Rev 1 relies almost exclusively upon Daniel's portrayal of the Ancient One (or Ancient of Days) rather than upon Daniel's one like a Son of Man.[30] The images of intense whiteness and fire combine with the woolly hair to bond the connection. Daniel's Ancient of Days sits on a throne, has hair like white wool, and is associated with flames, as is Jesus in Revelation (Dan 7:9; see Rev 1:14-15). In these respects, Revelation's word picture provides another key instance of blurring between the God-image of the Ancient One and the messianic image of the Son of Man.[31]

John's other reference to the Son of Man depicts Jesus as a heavenly judge who rides a cloud (14:14-16; see also 1:7). Once again, John builds upon Daniel's language, where it is the Son of Man and not the Ancient of Days who rides the clouds. Remarkably, here the Son of Man receives what appears to be a command from one of the angels: "Use your sickle and reap." The cloud imagery and its resonance with Daniel's Son of Man are significant: they point to Jesus's deity. As Daniel Boyarin puts it, "Clouds—as well as riding on or with clouds—are a common attribute of biblical divine appearances."[32] This applies to Yahweh in the Jewish Scriptures; "He who rides upon the clouds" (Ps 68:4) also makes the clouds his chariot (Ps 104:3; see also Deut 33:26). And this is true of other ancient deities in the ancient Near Eastern and Mediterranean worlds, most notably Baal and Zeus.[33] It looks as if there are two deities in Dan 7, each with his own throne, and the same can be said regarding Rev 14.

30. David Aune (1998, 1:90–91) notes that two Greek manuscripts of Revelation include "Son of Man" before the Ancient of Days in Dan 7:9.
31. Numerous commentators observe angelic (or angelomorphic) dimensions in Revelation's presentation of the Son of Man. See the discussions in Stuckenbruck 1995; Hoffmann 2005; Bühner 2021, 178–81; and Aune 1998, 1:92–93.
32. Boyarin 2012, 39–40.
33. Weinfeld 1973; Boyarin 2012, 36–46.

This reading runs counter to those that regard the Son of Man as a messianic but (merely) mortal figure. But it is consistent with portrayals of the Son of Man in Jewish apocalypses like the Similitudes of Enoch (1 En. 37–71) and 4 Ezra (2 Esd 3–14). It appears that Dan 7 started a tradition, according to which Yahweh reigns alongside a younger deity, the Son of Man. The Similitudes, 4 Ezra, and Revelation do not align on many particulars, but they do draw upon Dan 7, and the Similitudes and 4 Ezra present this heavenly figure as having existed prior to creation, overcoming evil, and installing an age of peace and justice. The Similitudes blur language associated with the Son of Man and the Messiah (see 1 En. 48), but both figures execute justice and reign before the "Lord of Spirits." 1 Enoch 46:1–5 even draws on Dan 7 in ways very similar to Rev 1:13–16.[34] Moreover, the Son of Man presented by the Similitudes is more than a mere mortal; he has been "hidden" from the beginning (62:7).[35] Although it does not use the phrase "Son of Man" in extant manuscripts, 4 Ezra 13 likewise draws upon Daniel in describing a preexistent figure who rides upon the clouds, overcomes the forces of evil, and judges the earth. He gathers all the tribes of Israel, even the nine tribes destroyed by the Assyrians. (We may recall that Rev 7:4–8 and 21:12 show concern for all twelve tribes.) Fourth Ezra 13:32 even depicts God referring to this "man" as "my Son," a term also applied to the Messiah (7:29).[36]

Alongside the Similitudes of Enoch and 4 Ezra, Revelation's depiction of Jesus as the Son of Man participates in a tradition of messianic reflection on Dan 7. Although Revelation only uses the term Son of Man in chapters 1 and 14, both passages identify Jesus as an eschatological Messiah who overcomes evil. Moreover, Rev 1:13–16 and 14:14–16 contribute to the book's pattern of blurring the representations of God and of Jesus. The first passage associates Jesus with the attributes Daniel assigns to the Ancient of Days, while the second echoes Daniel's language of riding on the clouds. As a result, the term Son of Man functions as messianic language in Revelation, just as it does in the Similitudes of Enoch and 4 Ezra.

~~Lion~~-Lamb

Revelation primarily designates Jesus as the Lamb.[37] The term occurs over twenty-five times, the first of which (5:6) is critical to Revelation's presentation

---

34. See the discussion in Boyarin 2012, 77–81.

35. A. Yarbro Collins and J. Collins 2008, 89–90.

36. A. Yarbro Collins and J. Collins 2008, 97.

37. Whitaker (2023, 40) uses "~~lion~~-lamb," as have I (Carey 2022, 38), but we construe the juxtaposition differently.

of Jesus and to other dimensions of the book's meaning. Revelation uses Jesus's name fourteen times but rarely in reference to his own agency. It introduces Jesus as "Jesus Christ" or "Jesus the Messiah" (1:1–5), and it only occasionally refers to Jesus by name elsewhere. With the exception of Revelation's conclusion, other references to Jesus refer to the "testimony of Jesus" or the "faith of Jesus." (A better-known instance of this problem involves Paul's use of *pistis Iesou*; some translate the phrase as faith *from* Jesus, others as faith *relating to* Jesus.) Revelation 1:9 links the testimony of Jesus with "endurance in [or of] Jesus." I will argue in chapter 9 that Revelation uses endurance (*hypomonē*) to indicate a form of active resistance embodied primarily in testimony to Jesus at the risk of one's life (see 12:11; 13:10).[38] In short, apart from its opening and closing chapters, Revelation uses Jesus's name only in relationship to testimony or faith.

We first meet the Lamb in chapter 5. After the risen Jesus dictates the messages to the seven Asian assemblies, a voice summons John into the heavenly throne room, where he finds himself "in the spirit" (4:1–2; see also 1:10–11). He encounters a set of heavenly beings who worship God, the one seated upon the throne, and then sees a scroll "sealed with seven seals" (5:1). John has not told us yet, but this scroll contains the fate of the cosmos. John weeps greatly because no one is declared worthy to open the scroll. Then John hears a comforting word:

> Do not weep. See, the Lion of the tribe of Judah, the Root of David, has conquered, so that he can open the scroll and its seven seals. (5:5)

"Lion of Judah" and "Root of David" are messianic terms. Lion of Judah alludes to Gen 49:9–10, where the patriarch Jacob blesses his son Judah as "a lion's whelp" who possesses both the scepter and the royal staff. Justin P. Jeffcoat Schedtler points out that 4 Ezra identifies the Messiah as "a creature like a lion" who descends from David and rules in the last days (4 Ezra 11:37–46). The phrase "Root of David" alludes to Isa 11:1–10, where it executes justice through violence. John has prepared his reader/hearers for an end-time Messiah who "carries out the eschatological judgment of the enemies of God and the restoration of God's people."[39]

But, as mentioned earlier, the Lion does not appear. Indeed, Revelation never presents Jesus as a lion from this point onward. Instead, John sees a Lamb, "standing as if it had been slaughtered, with seven horns and seven

---

38. Carey 2018, 204–06.
39. Jeffcoat Schedtler 2023, 44.

eyes" (5:6). The slaughtered yet standing Lamb almost surely points to Jesus's crucifixion and resurrection. Although the Day of Atonement ritual in Lev 16 involves a slaughtered bull rather than a lamb, elsewhere in Leviticus lambs serve as guilt offerings in connection with rituals of purification (14:10–32) among other sacrificial purposes. As Jeffrey S. Siker points out, the New Testament has a way of blending the Passover sacrifice of a lamb with the Day of Atonement ritual, as in John 1:29.[40] I am more inclined to read the Lamb in a Passover context, a victim whose blood brings liberation rather than forgiveness (Rev 1:5).[41] Without suggesting a literary relationship—but not quite ruling one out either—I note how the image resonates with Paul's interpretation of the cross as demonstrating strength through weakness (1 Cor 1:22–25).

The point of controversy involves the nature of the Lion-Lamb relationship. Is Revelation's Jesus a Lion-Lamb or a ~~Lion~~-Lamb? That is, should we interpret the Lamb as being lion-like, or does the Lamb image strike out the Lion? Many interpreters read the two symbols together rather than apart and for good reason. Robyn Whitaker identifies Revelation's lamb not as "a cute, fluffy little lamb skipping through green fields" but as the conquering ram of Dan 8:3 and 1 En. 90, a symbol of victorious resistance (see also T. Jos. 19:8–12). She points out that Revelation uses the Greek word *arnion* that is translated "ram" in other contexts.[42] Many interpreters maintain that the Lamb conquers through death and resurrection, but elsewhere in Revelation Jesus kills with a sword that protrudes from his mouth and wears a robe drenched in blood (19:11–21; see also 1:16; 2:12, 16). Moreover, Jesus is not directly identified as a Lamb in this great battle scene, but the larger context introduces it as the grisly "marriage supper of the Lamb" (19:9).

Yet, I regard the Lamb as a displacement of the Lion rather than understand the two images as a compound metaphor. The interpretation of the Lamb image does not "settle" the problems of violence and conquest in Revelation. Nevertheless, I agree with interpreters who regard the Lamb, Revelation's dominant image, as displacing the Lion.[43] I have two primary reasons for this. First, we have observed that, after 5:5, no actual lion appears again in Revelation. Instead, it is all Lamb all the time. John "sustains the [lamb] metaphor through-

40. Siker 2011.

41. Huber with O'Day 2023, 74–75. See also Bowden 2021, though Bowden does not account for the ways early Christian reflection on Jesus's death appropriated Jewish sacrifices or the relevance of 4 Macc 17:20–22.

42. Whitaker 2023, 40–41; Jeffcoat Schedtler 2023, 45.

43. Note especially Bauckham 1993a, 174–98, 215; Howard-Brook and Gwyther 1999, 207–9; Johns 2003; Kraybill 2010, 134–36; and Grimsrud 2022, 68–75.

out the book."[44] The most significant instance of lion imagery occurs when John describes the Beast as having a mouth "like a lion's mouth" (13:2; cf. also 4:7; 9:8, 17; 10:3). That image alludes to Dan 7:4, part of a passage that is critical to Revelation. Daniel 7 refers to empires that oppress Israel, just as the Beast persecutes the saints in Rev 13. Revelation's lion imagery connotes "ferocity, destructiveness and irresistible strength."[45] Moreover, the Beast stands as the Lamb's direct antagonist, mimicking the Lamb's features in perverse ways.[46] Thus, the Lamb is decidedly unbeastlike.

Second, although the Lamb's primary characteristic is its conquest of evil, Revelation presents Jesus's faithful but vulnerable death precisely as a vehicle for that conquest. Jesus is first introduced as "the faithful witness, the firstborn from the dead, and the ruler of the kings of the earth," one who demonstrates love and liberates the saints by his blood, and one whose very conquest reminds the world that it has "pierced" him (1:5–7). Jesus's faithful witness indicates his faithful life that led to execution, a pattern to be emulated by his followers (12:10–11). Some argue that the juxtaposition of the Lamb and the Beast constitutes Revelation's primary way of revealing divine power.[47] I would agree. However, even if Revelation critiques violence and envisions its end, Paul Middleton reminds us that violence ends *only after* "Rome crumbles when faced with the true might of God, the Lamb, and his saints in a day of wrath and judgement."[48]

A Word of Caution

Some commentators explain Revelation's Lamb imagery in ways that are misleading and prejudicial toward Judaism. Scholars are growing more sensitive to this potential, but it remains the case that important interpretations participate in this trope. The pattern works this way: one explains that Jews expected a violent and revolutionary messiah, offering ancient textual samples as evidence; then one points out how the Lamb accomplishes liberation without violence. This argument plays into a larger trope, according to which Jesus was not the violent Messiah Jews expected.

The harm consists in pitting a supposedly nonviolent Jesus against a supposedly violent Judaism. The pattern labors in tandem with the worn-out con-

---

44. Johns 2020, 227.
45. Bauckham 1993a, 182.
46. Carey 1999, 153–54; deSilva 2009, 112–13; and Whitaker 2015, 193–96.
47. Grimsrud 2022, 68–75.
48. P. Middleton 2018, 237.

trast between an allegedly violent "Old Testament" God and an allegedly loving "New Testament" God. Such interpretations celebrate Christianity (which is fine) by denigrating Judaism (which is wrong and dangerous).

This interpretive pattern is misleading on several levels. First, Revelation is a profoundly Jewish book in the first place. Nothing in Revelation suggests that following Jesus alienates the saints from Judaism. On the contrary, Rev 2:9 and 3:9 use extreme language precisely in an attempt to claim "true" Jewish identity.[49] Second, no single messianic aspiration defines ancient Judaism. We have no idea how prominent messianic expectation was among Jews in John's contexts. Ancient Judaism was just as fluid and diverse as any other widespread cultural or religious phenomenon. For John J. Collins, "Jewish messianic expectation," however widely it was expressed, "was never uniform."[50] Judaism owned no "reified messianic idea," as Matthew V. Novenson attests.[51] Nor should we read messianic notions as accounting for a perceived split between Jesus assemblies and synagogues.[52] For all these reasons, we do far better to read Revelation within a pluralistic Judaism rather than over against an imaginary monolithic version of it.

An "Upside-Down" Trinity?

The recent television series *Stranger Things* features a realm called the Upside Down. The Upside Down relates closely to the world above. It has similar features, all diminished and distorted. Time works differently there from the way it works in the mundane world. Deadly monsters emerge from the Upside Down to wreak destruction on the above world. One might say the Upside Down represents the evil (or at least destructive) counterpart to the conflicted realm of ordinary human affairs. Likewise, the Jordan Peele film *Us* depicts an underground world known as "the Underpass." There reside doppelgängers (actually clones) of the aboveground inhabitants, who wish to break the "tethers" that bind them to those who reside above by killing them. The notion of a shadow dimension that poses a threat to humankind scarcely originated with these projects, but it may enlighten our theological engagement with Revelation.

---

49. See Marshall 2001, 123–27; Frankfurter 2001; Emanuel 2020, 25–35.

50. J. Collins 2007, 19; see also Stuckenbruck 2007, 112, who notes that beyond Jewish Messiahs functioning as end-time deliverers and judges, "diversity takes over" among ancient Jewish texts in their expressions of messianic hope.

51. Novenson 2015, 41.

52. Reed 2022, 217–53.

We have discussed how Revelation blurs the distinctions between God, Jesus, and the Spirit. In opposition to them, it pits what Robyn Whitaker characterizes as an evil trinity: the Dragon, the Sea Beast, and the Land Beast.[53] Theologian Joseph L. Mangina goes even farther: "together the dragon, beast, and false prophet constitute an entire demonic Trinity parodying God, the Lamb, and the Spirit."[54] All three of these figures meet their end in the lake of fire (19:20; 20:10). Whitaker does not explore how her metaphor might relate to the presentation of God, Jesus, and the Spirit, but that set of relationships could strengthen the case for a Trinitarian-inflected reading of Revelation. As we saw in chapter 1, Revelation juxtaposes the Lamb and the Beast in significant ways. One of these points of comparison involves how both figures receive authority from what I call sponsors: the Lamb receives authority from God (2:28), and the Beast receives it from the Dragon or Satan (13:2). Both figures also receive enthronement (7:17; 13:2). While the Spirit testifies to Jesus, the Land Beast testifies to the Beast and its powers. It is as if the Dragon, the Beast, and the Other Beast serve as doppelgängers over and against God, the Lamb, and the Spirit.

I would not present Revelation's posturing of God, the Lamb, and the Spirit over against Satan and the two beasts as a definitive indication of Trinitarianism and certainly not of the formulized Trinitarianism of later Christian orthodoxy. But these contrasts between three divine agents and three evil ones hint toward incipient Trinitarian imagination.

MARKING THE GOD-LAMB

This chapter does not present a full or systematic Christology of Revelation or attempt to develop a thorough Trinitarian reading of the book. Instead, I have attempted to interpret Jesus as Revelation presents him, that is, in relationship to God and to the Spirit. I have drawn repeatedly on the image of blurring, calling attention to the ways in which Jesus's identity transgresses neat boundaries that would differentiate Jesus from God and from the Spirit. Yet, while it may be possible to read Revelation according to a Trinitarian rubric, we should also recognize the subordinationist dimensions of Jesus's relationship to God.

We might conclude that Revelation inconsistently presents the relationship between God and Jesus. In my view, the language of blurring more adequately (1) addresses Revelation's theological outlook and (2) resources our contemporary theologizing. Decades ago, scholars regarded a text's thematic tensions as

---

53. Whitaker 2023, 82.
54. Mangina 2010, 166; see also Gorman 2011, 116, 123–27.

signs of sloppy editing; we assumed ancient editors incorporated multiple ear-lier sources but did not seek the kind of unified perspective we treasure today. However, Revelation communicates its theology through symbols that reflect against one another rather than in abstract discursive sentiments. Readers who bring our contemporary theological preoccupations do well to account for this blurring rather than to force Revelation into modern analytical categories. Perhaps it is enough to affirm with Thomas B. Slater that, among other things, Revelation communicates that "Christ [is] Lord of the cosmos with whom God Almighty shared divine honors."[55]

In my view Michael J. Gorman synthesizes these patterns about as well as anyone might. The Lamb participates "in God's identity and reign, making him worthy of worship as the slaughtered Lamb, *and only as such*." He is "the true face of God."[56] When we say that Revelation's Jesus participates in God's identity, we also mean that the Lamb shapes our understanding of who God is and how God works in the world.[57] Gorman's assessment does not amount to a precisely Trinitarian form of accounting for Jesus's divinity, as it includes a qualification: the Lamb is worthy of worship precisely because of its deeds. (The same might be said of the worship directed toward God in Revelation based on a reading of the hymns.) Revelation presents the Lamb as God's singular agent in the world, one who reigns by means of his faithful witness, his death and resurrection, and his conquest of idolatry, oppression, and wick-edness. For all these reasons the Lamb is exalted to share the heavenly throne and to receive worship.

The rub occurs *after* we conclude that Revelation presents God as Lamb-like. In Revelation, the Lamb's identity blurs with that of God to the degree that the Lamb shapes Revelation's portrayal of God. But do we agree with Revelation? Do we worship this Lamb-God?

Some of the questions discussed here receive fuller treatment in other chap-ters. There is much to commend in the Lamb. The Lamb is God's faithful wit-ness (1:5), a status he shares with all the saints. The Lamb's death bestows free-dom from sins and an exalted status upon the saints (1:5-6; 5:9-10), extending opportunities for repentance when they fall short. The Lamb has the authority to unseal the scrolls and unleash heaven's final victory over the Dragon, the two beasts, and the Prostitute, all of whom represent violence, exploitation, and idolatry. The Lamb's marriage arouses great celebration. The Lamb's light

---

55. Slater 2019, 39.
56. Gorman 2011, 111.
57. Gorman 2011, 111.

illuminates the New Jerusalem, a city that excludes wickedness but welcomes all sorts of people (21:22–27; see also 22:3). No wonder the saints long to see the Lamb's face, a reality they will experience when they reign together with him (22:4–5). The Lamb loves the saints (1:5).

Yet, the Lamb is fearsome, even to John (1:17). Notoriously, his initial appearance is more than artists can handle. With its "accumulation of images," his description is best approached as an imaginative experience rather than a discursive description and tends to "overwhelm the reader/hearer."[58] Although John is corrected for falling down before this intense Jesus, we readers have reason to understand why he might do so. The letters to the seven assemblies continue to present Jesus as a threatening figure. Although the letters include congratulations and opportunities for repentance, five of the seven include direct threats. The most intense warnings in these letters apply to persons or groups identified as standing in rebellion. Most scholars understand these figures as Jesus followers whom John opposes. Setting aside the question of who is on the right side, the churches hear that these opponents face a Son of Man who will make war against them with the sword protruding from his mouth (2:16) and that he will throw one female prophet upon a bed and strike her children dead (2:22–23). His warnings apply to all the saints in the churches: "I will give to each of you as your works deserve" (2:23). Only those who conquer will avoid having their names erased from the Lamb's Book of Life (3:5). Despite Jesus's explicit love for the saints (1:5; 3:9), he remains a threatening figure.

Although the Lamb shares status with the saints, the saints bear the marks of enslavement to him, as his name is tattooed on their foreheads (14:1; 22:4; see also 7:3; 9:4). Only the risen Jesus knows the name inscribed upon himself (19:12), suggesting his superior status. However, it appears that the name(s) Jesus bears is his own (19:13, 16). The ancients, including biblical writers, commonly used enslavement as a metaphor for loyalty and service. As today, elites identified as servants of the people. Metaphorically as well as socially, an enslaved person's status depended upon that of their "owner." As Bob Dylan sang, "You gotta serve somebody"; surely one is better off bearing the marks of the Lamb than of the Beast (e.g., 13:16–17; 14:9–11).[59] Revelation's indications of solidary between the Lamb and the saints have their limits.[60]

The Lamb acts with divine authority to conquer the forces of evil. The Lamb stands as God's singular agent, "the ruler of the kings of the earth" (1:5) who

---

58. Reddish 2001, 41.
59. See Huber with O'Day 2023, 202.
60. Carey 1999, 118–28.

participates in the divine identity. Revelation depicts the Lamb/Son of Man as slaughtering its enemies with the sword that protrudes from its mouth. Although some interpreters insist the sword is a metaphorical reference to the Lamb's testimony and that the blood soaking the Lamb's garments is the Lamb's own, Revelation rejoices in vengeance and bloodshed. I do not regard the problems of Revelation's violence and its desire for violence resolved. At the same time, we should heed what Revelation says explicitly: the Lamb has already conquered prior to its first appearance, when it stands although it bears the marks of its own slaughter (5:5). The Lamb, therefore, conquers by means of its faithful witness, death, and resurrection (1:5; 5:9). The Lamb's followers likewise conquer by risking their lives with their own testimony (12:11). Many readers (myself included) cringe at the language of conquest. That is largely because we inhabit cultures that have practiced conquest and colonization. But for those who understand what it means to be dominated, oppressed, and dehumanized, conquest sounds like relief. Whether or not we can follow along, we should recall Allan Boesak as he reads Revelation amid the violence of Apartheid: "If [Christ's] cloak is spattered with blood, it is the blood of his enemies, the destroyers of the earth and of his children."[61]

I write during a period of sharp political polarization, especially but not only in the United States. For the first time I can remember, authentic demonization is active in our public discourse. All sides are quick to describe the others' actions and motives as "evil." That's not entirely novel. But an influential stream of right-wing Christian nationalism known as the New Apostolic Reformation explicitly describes its opponents as satanic, demonic, or controlled by demons and subject to spiritual warfare.[62] This movement seeks "dominion"—think of conquest in Revelation—over "seven mountains of culture" that include religion and politics.[63] In the wake of the January 6 insurrection, the lines between spiritual warfare and literal blood shedding are vanishingly thin. A "Rally for Revival" that occurred January 5, 2021 at the Freedom Plaza, less than two blocks from the White House, was actually a Christian nationalist demonstration preparing for what would happen the following day. There a preacher named Ken Peters declared: "We are not just in a culture war, we are in a kingdom war. This is the Kingdom of Darkness versus the Kingdom of Light."[64] A prominent apostle named Ché Ahn also

61. Boesak 1987, 124.
62. Gagné 2024, 47–70.
63. Christerson and Flory 2017, 91–101; Gagné 2024, 18–26.
64. Seidel 2022, 22.

proclaimed: "We're going to throw Jezebel out and Jehu's gonna rise up, and we're gonna rule and reign through President Trump and under the lordship of Jesus Christ."[65] Bible readers recognize both Jezebel and Jehu from 1 and 2 Kings, where Jezebel promotes idolatry in Israel and the prophet anoints Jehu to be Israel's (relatively) righteous king. Jehu sees to Jezebel's execution. But Ahn also has Revelation in mind, where (1) John condemns a competing prophet he calls Jezebel (2:20–23), and (2) the Beast receives its power from Satan (13:2; see 12:9). In the idiom of the New Apostolic Revelation, Ahn characterizes unnamed forces arrayed against Donald Trump as having "the Spirit of Jezebel," making them fit for defeat and annihilation.[66]

One can readily track how the Lamb's conquest can inspire resistance to evil—*but whose evil?* Revelation has long appealed to communities that perceive themselves as being oppressed, but its appropriation is open to any interpretation that can persuade other people. Christian nationalists who seek dominion claim victory, and so do those who hear Revelation as "a call to nonviolent arms against any and every human person or people who would position themselves as lord over the destinies of others."[67] In this sense, Revelation's Jesus reveals as much about his interpreters as it does our world.[68] I am not suggesting epistemological relativism, as if there are no grounds for discriminating among interpretations. Instead, I believe readers must be held accountable for how we use texts, not least Revelation.

65. Seidel 2022, 23.
66. Gagné 2024, 61–63.
67. Blount 2009, xi.
68. Blount 2005, 26–36.

Does Revelation Have an Eschatology?

R EVELATION FEATURES VISIONS OF the heavenly throne room, end-time catastrophes, conflict with Satan and his minions, resurrection and judgment, and finally a New Jerusalem where the saints dwell in perpetual light. Thus, we might expect that Revelation would play a leading role in shaping our theological imaginations on eschatological matters, such as the fundamental nature of the world; death, judgment, and the afterlife; and the ultimate direction of history. Yet, the deep rift between fundamentalist evangelical Christianity and the academic theologies that shape ecumenical churches is particularly visible when it comes to eschatology. Bible prophecy teachers generate end-time scenarios that outsiders mock as ludicrous, and ecumenical Christianity responds by minimizing Revelation and eschatology along with it. Even ecumenical theologians who address eschatology rarely place Revelation at the center of the conversation. This chapter attempts something that is surprisingly rare: an exposition of and theological engagement with Revelation's outlook toward classical eschatological topics.[1]

Bible prophecy teachers notoriously spin out detailed end-time scenarios built around their interpretations of Revelation. Thus, popular discourse associates Revelation with eschatology more strongly than any other book of the Bible. When Christian bookstores were still common, many included large "Bible prophecy" sections filled with selections that interpreted Revelation as resourcing detailed scenarios for the end times. Such books still appear regularly, applying what we might call a jigsaw puzzle approach to the Bible and the end times. In this approach, passages from diverse biblical books must somehow fit into a unified whole. The task of the interpreter is to make those pieces fit together. Revelation occupies a critical position for these interpreters,

---

1. This chapter relies in part upon Carey 2021, 243–53.

who assume the book lays out a discernible sequence for end-time events with chronological clues.

Professional theologians engage eschatology differently. Theologians who address eschatology seriously neither expect canonical uniformity nor privilege Revelation the way popular Christianity does. Regarding eschatology, Jürgen Moltmann may be the most influential theologian of recent decades. His classic *Theology of Hope* and more recent *In the End—The Beginning* scarcely mention Revelation. When Moltmann addresses revelation as a theological topic, he means how God reveals God's ways to mortals.[2] J. Richard Middleton and Philip G. Ziegler work more directly with and through biblical texts. Revelation figures prominently in Middleton's work, which mainly deals with the New Testament Gospels and Pauline literature, while Ziegler's work is far more deeply engaged with Paul.[3] I do not mean to overlook Catherine Keller's profound engagement with Revelation, though Keller does not attempt anything like a reconstruction of Revelation's eschatological outlook.[4] Nor should we overlook theologians who read Revelation closely. But it is rare to encounter theologians like Michael Battle, who ground their eschatological reflections as being in alignment with Revelation.[5]

Revelation's academic commentators rarely pause to assess the book's eschatological outlook, except when they must slow down and explain concepts like the first and second resurrection and Christ's thousand-year reign that *precedes* the final conflict with Satan and his allies (20:1–10). Scholars affiliated with some Christian institutions may be obliged to explain their theological approach to Revelation, especially how it relates to the end times.[6] Then again, even a basic explication of Revelation's theological interests is rare among academic commentaries.[7] Biblical scholarship's tendency to emphasize literary, historical, and cultural themes without speaking directly to theological concerns is so pronounced that two prominent scholars once declared, "there has been to date [2012] no fresh theological reading of Revelation" that takes account of recent research on Jewish and Christian apocalypticism.[8] That assessment reflects a narrow construal of theology, but it is fair to say that eschatology has been a relatively rare focus for Revelation's academic readers.

---

2. Moltmann 1967 and 2004.
3. J. R. Middleton 2014; Ziegler 2018.
4. Keller 1996, 2005, and 2021.
5. Battle 2017.
6. E.g., Wall 1991, 32–39; Beale 1999, 44–49; Yeatts 2003, 25–26; Tonstad 2019, 26–29.
7. For an example, see Reddish 2001, 22–26.
8. Hays and Alkier 2012, 4.

REVELATION'S DISTINCTIVE FEATURES

Revelation does advance a point of view on the most basic eschatological questions, but it does not offer comprehensive information in a discursive way. As an ancient apocalypse, it also presents important challenges for contemporary readers who wish to engage the book theologically. These include Revelation's symbolic and poetic mode of presentation, contemporary readers' interaction with an ancient Mediterranean cosmology and worldview, and the book's apparent cyclical or nonlinear, narrative structure. The first two challenges overlap significantly because it is often difficult to discern when to construe Revelation's images "literally," as expressions of what John intends his reader/hearers to believe about ultimate things.

For example, the New Jerusalem features transparent golden streets (21:21). Imagine we could time travel and interview John. Does he intend this imagery to connote unimaginable splendor? (Gold does not resemble "pure" glass.) Might the imagery indicate that the grandeur of Roman cities cannot compare to the holy city inherited by the saints? Both possibilities might apply at once. Or does he expect a future city just like the one he describes? Given the symbolic nature of Revelation and other ancient apocalypses, I believe a figurative reading most likely accounts for John's intent. But countless readers throughout history have expected to walk golden streets in "heaven." If that is what John wanted to convey, many contemporary readers will struggle to find such imagery meaningful or encouraging, at least not in isolation from the New Jerusalem's overall description. In the abstract, many of us would find little attraction in golden streets.

Most readers recognize that many of Revelation's images are symbolic. The desire to decode those symbols is at once understandable and near universal. Scholarly readers often pair the Beast's seven heads with specific Roman emperors, while Bible prophecy teachers provide modern-day "fulfillments" for Revelation's symbols. For example, Hal Lindsey's Cold War bestseller *The Late Great Planet Earth* identified Gog and Magog (Rev 20:8) as the Soviet threat and the armies from the east (9:14–16; 16:12) with communist China.[9] Biblical scholars typically rule out such futuristic readings without discussion. But then what do we do with the great battle in which the Messiah finally defeats the Beast and its allies (19:17–21)? Bible prophecy teachers expect that a literal global conflict will prepare the way for Jesus's reign. Scholars interpret the scene as a standard motif among the historical apocalypses. In symbolic language it expresses John's

9. Lindsey with Carlson 1970.

actual hope that God will eliminate those who oppress God's people. From a literary and historical perspective, we have exhausted the conversation. But if we are reading Revelation theologically, we must reckon with the apparently failed hopes expressed by biblical authors. That is, John expected that the demise of the Roman Empire would usher in Jesus's reign on earth. That did not occur, or at least certainly not "soon" enough from John's perspective. Dare we hope that evil will come to an end, basing our hopes to some degree on Revelation?

Readers must also account for what we might call Revelation's mythological cosmology. Perhaps John did not imagine a literal abyss reserved for the devil or a lake of fire as part of a cosmic geography. And perhaps he did. But he almost certainly envisioned God living in a heavenly realm that is "up there" in the sky (4:1; 20:1; 21:2). He takes quite seriously the existence of Satan and demons who oppose God and God's people. And he believes bodies that have been lost at sea can be reconstituted in a great resurrection. Many contemporary people would find all of these assumptions quite anachronistic.

Many readers choose to translate such anachronistic elements into categories modern people can appreciate. The classic case is Rudolf Bultmann, probably the most influential New Testament scholar of the twentieth century.[10] Bultmann called for "demythologizing" biblical concepts, suggesting we translate miraculous healings, exorcisms, and demons into the categories of existentialist philosophy. He was particularly concerned with Jesus's apocalypticism and with hope for God's dramatic intervention in history that never occurred. He argued that biblical eschatology confronts human beings not with an end-time crisis but with an existential one shaped by our own finitude. Bultmann named an essential problem, though I would recommend a different path. We should not simply "translate" Revelation and other New Testament texts into a framework we have already chosen. Rather, we should read through these elements to discern how they functioned in their own cultural moment.

Finally, Revelation is a narrative that guides readers through a sequence of scenes. The book includes three series of judgments: the seals, trumpets, and bowls. Revelation's "predictive" readers generally look to these as a literal sequence of end-time events that remain in our future. We have already affirmed that Revelation speaks to its own time and place, specifically to those seven assemblies of Jesus followers in Roman Asia, and that it does not "predict" events that lie in our historical future. Other factors complicate the assumption that these judgments represent a sequence of events. First, these judgments often draw from biblical antecedents and from John's own cultural moment, that is,

---

10. Bultmann 1958.

some look to the sacred past, and others address conditions contemporary to John and his reader/hearers. For example, the first trumpet judgment involves a plague of "hail and fire, mixed with blood" (Rev 8:7), echoing the "thunder and hail, and fire" of Exod 9:23.[11] But violence, famine, and disease were ordinary occurrences in the ancient world, as they have been throughout history (Rev 6:8). Micah D. Kiel reads accounts of environmental devastation in 1 Enoch and Revelation as describing the experiences of suffering communities confronted with imperial violence and degradation of the environment.[12] Revelation frequently refers to the (Mediterranean) sea, from which the Beast emerges (13:1) and in which Rome conducts commerce (18:15–19). But it also depicts plagues poisoning the sea, rivers, and streams as well as killing wildlife and causing harm to humans (8:8–11; 16:3–5; see also 7:3; 12:12). In these plagues, Kiel perceives a response to Rome's domination of the sea fused with Jewish creation mythology.[13] These plagues touch a tender spot for contemporary readers, who confront the effects of climate change, pollution, and overfishing in our seas and streams. But they may not represent "predictions" of future events on John's part.

Second, the plagues are somewhat repetitious. In chapter 8, a third of the water creatures die, while "every living thing in the sea" dies in chapter 16. One may perceive a sequence in these developments: chapter 16 intensifies chapter 8's poisoning of the waters. But other plagues appear simply to echo one another. For example, compare the sixth seal with the fourth trumpet.

REVELATION 6:12–14

When he broke the sixth seal, I looked, and there was a great earthquake; the sun became black as sackcloth, the full moon became like blood, and the stars of the sky fell to the earth as the fig tree drops its winter fruit when shaken by a gale. The sky vanished like a scroll rolling itself up, and every mountain and island was removed from its place.

REVELATION 8:12

The fourth angel blew his trumpet, and a third of the sun was struck, and a third of the moon, and a third of the stars, so that a third of their light was darkened; a third of the day was kept from shining and likewise the night.

11. A. Yarbro Collins 2021, 191.
12. Kiel 2017, 50.
13. Kiel 2017, 79.

These plagues are scarcely identical, but it is difficult to make sense of a sequential development from the first to the second.

Let us examine another example of judgments that seem to reinforce one another but do not necessarily track a chronological development. The fifth bowl judgment, which is next to last among the seals, trumpets, and bowls, brings a portentous development: darkness envelops the Beast's realm (16:10–11). But the sixth and final bowl judgment brings armies from the East to gather for the great battle at Harmagedon (16:12–16). This event recalls the sixth trumpet judgment, in which a massive demonic army comes from the East to inflict pain on humankind (9:11–21). Both judgments refer to the Euphrates River as a boundary that restrains these armies. Although we cannot rule out chronological development in these sets of judgment, we also discern patterns of repetition and reinforcement. They ought not be read directly as a sequence of events in time.[14] As Robyn J. Whitaker puts it, "If we were to read these [judgments] as descriptions of literal or chronological events (which I don't think they are), then the earth would be destroyed several times over."[15]

If we wish to discern eschatology in Revelation, we must account for these factors. We should not confuse Revelation's poetic and symbolic language with descriptions of actual states of affairs in the heavenly realm or in our future. We will encounter ideas few modern Western readers can integrate in a straightforward way. And we should not assume that Revelation lays out a chronologically precise sequence of events—or even tries to.

The Domain of Eschatology

The term "eschatology" points to the ultimate things. In theology, eschatology refers primarily to three subject areas. The first is often neglected: how do we imagine *ultimate reality* or *cosmology*, that is, those things that transcend and may determine the world we experience with our senses? This field can be hard to define, but it includes questions such as the nature and variety of supernatural beings and those of heavenly or hellish and other otherworldly regions. Jewish apocalyptic literature developed intensive speculation concerning good and wicked angels, places of temporary and eternal reward and punishment, and even astrological and meteorological phenomena and their origins. The apostle Paul claims to have visited the third heaven (2 Cor 12:2). This claim likely sounds bizarre to a modern Christian who knows their Bible

---

14. For a helpful and somewhat different assessment, see Koester 2014, 112–14.
15. Whitaker 2023, 49.

pretty well but is unaware that several ancient apocalypses describe multiple levels of heaven.

A second field of eschatology involves the ultimate *course of history*. Ancient prophets declare what God is doing or about to do in the world. But when someone claims to describe history's final resolution, we have moved into the realm of eschatology. Ancient Jewish and Christian eschatology foregrounds belief in a final blessed state in which wickedness and oppression no longer operate and the righteous dwell in peace and equity. These hopes often take a political tone, in which Israel's imperial oppressors meet violent ends and divine glory comes upon Zion. Still, ancient Judaism and Christianity describe this future in diverse terms.

Some Christian movements debate this question intensely, and their positions can influence public affairs. This is not the place for a detailed survey of popular eschatologies, but let us consider the difference between *postmillennial* and *premillennial* understandings of history. Postmillennialists expect that history will improve to the point that the kingdom (or reign) of God may be manifest on earth. Many early nineteenth-century revivalists such as Charles Grandison Finney held this view, and it motivated them to pursue progressive social change. But a wave of premillennial theology came ashore near the middle of that century. Premillennialists expect that the world will devolve into chaos before God dramatically intervenes to bring about Jesus's millennial reign. A prominent voice for this view was the evangelist Dwight L. Moody, and premillennialism has dominated American fundamentalism until recently. Premillennialists have typically resisted grand attempts to reform society or build international cooperation because they do expect the world to deteriorate rather than improve. Contemporary American Christian nationalism contains advocates for both views. One set holds that Christians must exercise dominion over the centers of cultural influence in order for Jesus to return (a postmillennial outlook), while the other scans the news for ominous developments that portend the final crisis (premillennial). These are just two of many, often highly refined systems of end-time belief that are popular in North American Christianity.

Eschatology often addresses a third interest: *death and what lies beyond death*. Ancient Judaism held room for remarkably varied understandings of this question. Sadducees apparently denied the existence of an afterlife altogether. Pharisees believed in a resurrection; people truly die but are raised from the dead at the last day. Jesus apparently shared their opinion. Some Jews believed that we enter eternal life (or torment) as soon as we die, while others held that we migrate into an intermediate state that may or may not include punishment, and still others maintained that only the righteous will experience an afterlife. Afterlife concerns bear upon the theological topic of anthropology, the question of what constitutes a human being. For example, it matters whether or not we believe humans possess immortal souls, a notion that is prevalent in popular Christianity but does not precisely reflect most early Christian teaching.

These eschatological topics were not unique to ancient Judaism and Christianity. People and ideas traveled widely in the ancient world, and cultures exerted significance on one another. In the past, theologians tended to frown upon syncretism, that is, the ways Judaism and Christianity borrowed from and adapted diverse cultural influences. Now we appreciate that no "pure" form of either religion ever existed apart from cultural pluralism. And where scholars formerly sought to pin down the "pagan" sources that shaped specific Jewish and Christian beliefs, we now accept that while we may identify some such sources, cultural influence is a messy process that rarely follows a simple path.

Revelation reflects rapid and profound developments in Jewish eschatology. These developments are rarely discussed in church settings, but they are fundamental for understanding the New Testament in general and Revelation specifically. Let us imagine a near-ideal reader of a Protestant Bible, one who understands and remembers everything they encounter. This person would read what we call the Old Testament, finish Malachi, and turn the page to encounter the New Testament as they enter the world of Matthew. Now our reader meets a series of fully developed concepts, for which they were scarcely if at all prepared. Our reader finds Jesus identified as *the* Messiah or anointed one, not one of many persons potentially anointed for a divine purpose but a singular agent who enacts God's reign among mortals. A devil and his demonic minions torment humankind. God raises Jesus from the dead, never to die again, and references to a future resurrection appear frequently. At some point after people die, they face a final judgment that separates the righteous from the wicked and assigns to them either a blessed or a cursed eternal state.

Without these ideas—Messiah, Satan and the demons, resurrection, and a final judgment—we could scarcely imagine the New Testament. But none of them find clear expression in the Jewish Scriptures. We may identify signs of their emergence and possible development, but nothing prepares our reader for the world of Matthew and the rest of the New Testament. Indeed, these ideas remained controversial even in the time of Jesus and beyond. But they are central to Revelation and almost all the other New Testament books.[16]

16. I develop this thought experiment somewhat more fully in Carey 2016, 2–5.

WHAT'S ULTIMATELY REAL?

John sets his story within a cosmological framework. That is, Revelation reflects ancient Jewish construals of ultimate reality, while it may offer some innovations. The book assumes that a realm exists in the sky (or heaven), where God and the risen Jesus reside along with other supernatural beings and exalted martyrs. Once John encounters the risen Jesus and records Jesus's messages to the seven assemblies, he receives a call to go "up" to heaven (4:1). This sort of cosmological journey appears in several ancient Jewish and Christian apocalypses. From that point on, John observes things from his heavenly vantage point. From time to time, however, John seems to move back and forth between heaven and earth, an impression somewhat encouraged by modern translations. For example, he receives a command to measure God's temple, a task that may imply visiting the holy city (11:1). He also observes angels "coming down" from heaven (10:1; 18:1; 20:1) as well as the New Jerusalem "coming down" from heaven (21:2, 10). The Greek root translated "coming down" (*katabainō*) does not imply that John is watching from below or from above; it could just as easily be translated "going down." "Descending" would be a preferable translation.[17] The entire vision is consistent with John's heavenly vantage point, but it assumes interaction between a heaven above and the earth "down here."

Modern translations also obscure that Greek, much like Hebrew, does not distinguish between "sky" and a realm called "heaven." Ancient peoples frequently associated deities with the sky. Although God and other heavenly beings reside in a space mortals cannot observe—at least not without the kind of help John receives—their journeys from heaven to earth and back make more sense when we imagine continuity between earth and sky. As Craig Koester observes, many ancient texts imagined doors and other means by which mortals and supernatural beings might pass from one realm into the next.[18]

The primary thing to appreciate about this heavenly realm is that it interacts with earth. In Revelation, some things happen in heaven and affect affairs on earth, while some earthly events, such as Jesus's crucifixion and resurrection, make possible other developments in heaven.[19] From heaven, John observes things on the ground as well as in the sky. Heavenly beings pass back and forth between sky and earth, and they can pour judgments down upon the earth. When judgments devastate nature and humanity, heavenly beings not only

17. As in Aune 1998, 2:557.
18. Koester 2014, 359.
19. Caird 1993, 61.

watch but also respond by praising God. This is not to say that God and the heavenly beings who serve God exercise direct control over all or even most earthly events. The Beast and the Prostitute perform wicked deeds, mortals express hostility toward the Lamb's followers, and even some among the seven assemblies fail to comply with God's will. But heavenly beings do interact with mortals, and ultimately they determine the earth's fate.

Generally speaking, heaven is not where Lamb followers go when they die. Martyrs apparently do (6:9–11; 20:4–6), and they constitute a notable exception. In contrast, the New Jerusalem comes down to earth from heaven, as do God and the Lamb. This factor is significant for our discussion of afterlife hope. The New Jerusalem motif alludes to the visions of a renewed Zion in Isa 65–66, a passage that involves proto-apocalyptic imagery but grounds its hope on this planet rather than in the sky.

Although God receives worship in the heavenly throne room, conflict does occur in the heavens. There the Dragon confronts the Woman Clothed with the Sun, having pulled down a third of the stars with its tail. The archangel Michael leads a band of angels in fighting against the Dragon and its angels, casting the Dragon down to earth (12:1–17). Thus we learn that the cosmos includes good and evil supernatural agents. We should not expect that Revelation provides a complete or consistent map of the cosmos or a census of its supernatural inhabitants.[20] Revelation does not attend to the Dragon's supernatural accomplices with the same detail it describes the heavenly beings who serve God. However, with the Dragon roaming the earth, those evil beings make war against God's people and supposedly wreak destruction in other ways (12:17).

Thus, although heaven is where God and God's supernatural allies reside, it is also a site of conflict, just as the world is. Until John's vision attains its resolution as narrated in chapter 20, mortals will be subject to violent outbursts from the devil and his allies.

Many contemporary readers cannot force their imaginations around a heaven "up" somewhere that houses God's throne room or a devil who actively combats God's work. But we do understand a world in which powerful forces frustrate our attempts to resist evil and elude our efforts to identify or resist them. To take one common example, contemporary communications amplify the most extreme voices in our societies, forcing the worst political candidates upon us, alienating us from one another, and making it all but impossible to negotiate mutually acceptable policies. We can identify human beings who study psychology and craft the algorithms that fuel these outcomes, but some-

20. McDonough 2008, 178–79.

how we fail to discern how to collaborate in ways that address climate change, inequality, and despair. Many of us continue to believe in a God who does not simply "fix" things in a mechanistic way but remains active to foster love and dignity. And while we may no longer believe in a Satan or his demonic minions, Revelation provides language with which we can imagine powerful systems that give strength and authority to beastly outcomes (13:3).[21]

While Revelation provides a framework for understanding pervasive evil, that same cosmological reality can nurture hope for salvation. By aligning themselves with God and the Lamb, the saints contribute to victory, evil's final destruction. This imaginary framework lends meaning to ordinary acts of faithful resistance and to heroic ones. Two thousand years removed from John's world, followers of Jesus still face evil we cannot quantify and explain. It remains a challenge to believe our actions matter on a grand scale. In part, Revelation's conviction that faithful behavior matters on a cosmic scale confronted John's reader/hearers in the seven assemblies, and it remains challenging today.

History's Ends

Revelation describes history's ultimate resolution. The Lamb defeats Satan, the Beast, and their mortal and supernatural allies. This conquest occurs in three stages. First, the Lamb conquers the Beast and the Other Beast, and they are thrown alive into a lake of fire (19:20). Second, after being bound for a thousand years, Satan is somehow released for a final rampage and a second great battle. Revelation describes his temporary release as somehow necessary but does not explain why (20:3). Finally, Satan is cast into the same fiery lake forever. Revelation sometimes uses the passive voice to describe what happens to the two beasts and to Satan: they are "thrown" into the lake of fire (19:20; 20:10), and Satan is "loosed" upon the earth (20:7). We are to understand that God and God's agents perform these actions, just as an angel binds the Dragon for a thousand years and throws him into an abyss (20:1–3).

This is a supernatural drama, but it includes mortals at war (16:12–16; 19:11–21; 20:7–10). Although mortal kings and their armies fight against the Lamb, we never hear of mortals fighting on the Lamb's side in these passages. In the final battle, the nations approach "the camp of the saints and the beloved city." But these saints never join the battle because God fights on their behalf

---

21. Philip G. Ziegler's 2024 Annie Kinkead Warfield Lectures at Princeton Theological Seminary, "God's Adversary and Ours: A Brief Theology of the Devil" (March 18–21), have helped me articulate this response. I look forward to their publication.

(20:9). The motif of God fighting on behalf of God's people goes back to the Hebrew Scriptures and appears in other early Jewish apocalyptic texts, not least the Qumran War Scroll (1QM). As Richard Bauckham points out, the saints contribute to the Lamb's victory through their witness (Rev 12:11) but not by deploying bows, spears, or swords. Bauckham notes Jewish texts like Daniel, 2 Maccabees, 4 Maccabees, and the Testament of Moses that describe martyrdom as the means of resistance and conquest.[22]

Revelation's especially close relationship to Daniel shapes its strategy for resistance. Revelation draws upon Daniel's vision of a series of beasts confronted by the Ancient of Days and by one like a Son of Man (Dan 7:1–28; see also Rev 1:13–20; 13:1–18). Daniel also contains the image of Michael, an angelic prince who fights on behalf of God's people (10:13, 21; 12:1; see Rev 12:7). These images all resonate with Revelation. For its part, Daniel responds to the Seleucid Empire of Antiochus IV Epiphanes, who suppressed observance of fundamental Jewish practices and imposed Hellenistic observances on the Judean population. Daniel reflects the circumstances of an active and eventually successful revolt, but it does not call its own audience to take up arms. Anathea Portier-Young's characterization of that book resonates with Revelation's call to faithful witness as a means of conquest. "The authors of Daniel resisted with language and symbol, limiting and even negating the power of Antiochus by writing, proclaiming, and teaching an alternative vision of reality.... They also presented their readers with a program of active nonviolent resistance."[23] Like Revelation, Daniel assures its audience that faithful witness will contribute to Antiochus's downfall, while eschatological reward awaits the righteous who die as martyrs.[24]

Despite its reliance on divine agency, Revelation envisions very earthly and historical consequences. Rome is done away with; the Beast is conquered, and Babylon is leveled. Human rulers and armies meet their doom, as do the rest of the Inhabitants of the Earth. Only the saints are left to inhabit the New Jerusalem. This vision ultimately leaves history behind when the former heavens and earth yield way to a new creation and a New Jerusalem.

Revelation expresses the conviction that the present time is marred by wickedness and oppression. From its own location in time, it interprets the present moment as history's ultimate crisis. And it envisions a resolution in which wicked empires and evil forces are vanquished and God's new realm

---

22. Bauckham 1993, 236–37.
23. Portier-Young 2011, 277.
24. Portier-Young 2011, 276.

allows the saints to enjoy God's presence forever. These convictions are common among the Jewish historically oriented apocalypses.

Revelation's final great vision of the New Jerusalem requires the dissolution of the first heaven and the first earth and the descent of a new heaven and a new earth (21:1). Many readers would reject this language as being escapist. In a world threatened by climate change, hope for a new heavens and earth offers little motivation for responsible social action to preserve the planet as a context in which creatures, including humans, can thrive. But this language comes from Isa 65:17; 66:22, which is committed to a vibrant existence on Zion. Isaiah's vision reveals joy and delight (65:18), houses and vineyards (65:21), bodies that "flourish like the grass" (66:14), and gentiles flocking into the holy city and even becoming priests (66:20–23). The New Jerusalem displaces the world evoked in Revelation's many plagues, a world marred by war, famine, and environmental devastation, and presents a realm of peace and abundance. The New Jerusalem is an aspiration, not an escape.

Again, modern people may question the credibility of all these convictions. Evil and oppression are always around somewhere. Periods of crisis come and go. So why should we expect these realities to change? And why should people regard their current crisis as inaugurating history's final resolution? The reply that Jesus announced and enacted God's reign on earth, expecting its imminent fulfillment, will not persuade even some Christians.

Christian hope is not the same thing as empty optimism. It is a common thing to meet a romantic interest and feel a rush of optimism. But hopefully, we do not enter a lifelong commitment to another person without having experienced them well enough to have grounding for our hope. Likewise, theological hope grounds itself in the experience of God, in the assembly of God's people, and in our sacred stories. Revelation follows precisely that model, constantly looking back to Israel's Scriptures and to the story of Jesus to shape its vision. The river that flows through the New Jerusalem echoes the Gen 2 creation account, as does the tree of life (2:7; 22:1–2).[25] The 144,000 who bear God's seal (7:3–8) and the twelve gates of the holy city (21:12) recall the formation of Israel. The song of Moses in Rev 15:3–4 may not resemble Exod 15, but John frames it to link Israel's exodus deliverance with the heavenly worship he describes.[26] Temple imagery appears frequently in Revelation, while the New Jerusalem renews the hopes for an idealized Zion expressed in Ezekiel and Isaiah. The slaughtered yet living Lamb bears Jesus's reign into the world of John's audience,

25. Moyise 2012b, 39.
26. Moyise 2012b, 39.

while even the New Jerusalem's twelve foundations honor the twelve apostles (21:14). In short, Revelation grounds its future hope in the shape of what God has already accomplished in creation, Israel, Jesus, and the church.

DEATH AND BEYOND

The Jesus of Revelation is the crucified and risen one who reigns from heaven. Revelation introduces him as "the faithful witness, the firstborn of the dead, and the ruler of the kings of the earth" (1:5). When he speaks, he declares, "I was dead, and see, I am alive forever and ever, and I have the keys of Death and of Hades" (1:18; see also 2:8). When Jesus appears as the Lamb, Revelation's prevailing symbol, it stands "as if it had been slaughtered" (5:6, 9). Jesus's identity as the crucified and risen one proves essential for understanding both his identity and the promises he extends to his followers.

We could imagine life after death in many ways. Jews and Christians have done so for a long time.[27] Many people, Christians included, imagine that we are created with immortal souls that must exist somehow after death. That may be the hope expressed in Luke's Gospel, where Lazarus and the rich man enter immediately into another realm of existence upon their deaths (Luke 16:19–31), and later Jesus assures one of those crucified alongside him, "today you will be with me in Paradise" (23:43). However, the Apostles' Creed and the Nicene Creed do not articulate belief in an immortal soul. The Apostles' Creed confesses "the resurrection of the body and the life everlasting," while the Nicene Creed anticipates "the resurrection of the dead and the life of the world to come." The notion that people have immortal souls that continue beyond death became prevalent among Christians by the fifth century, and it has some representation in the Bible. But the dominant view among New Testament authors is resurrection.[28] Revelation's primary hope involves resurrection, though it offers a particular vision for the martyrs.

Christian resurrection hope is grounded in the resurrection of Jesus. Revelation shares this view by foregrounding Jesus's own identity as the risen one. Jesus's resurrection is unique within the Bible. Other persons, like Lazarus in John 11, rise from the dead, but they will die again. (The bizarre story in Matt 27:52–53 of the dead leaving their tombs when Jesus dies marks a likely exception.) The emergence of apocalyptic literature provides a key grounding for understanding how Jesus's resurrection is unique and how it relates to hope

27. See Bauckham 1998. Carey 2023 addresses biblical afterlife hope in detail.
28. N. Murphy 2011.

for humankind. Within biblical traditions, resurrection hope first appears in apocalyptic literature, specifically Dan 12:1–3. Jesus's resurrection poses a special problem because resurrection constitutes an end-time event in Daniel and other Jewish apocalyptic texts, which did not entertain the notion of resurrection for a solitary individual. Paul identifies Jesus as the firstfruits from the dead (1 Cor 15:20, 23); that is, Jesus's resurrection is an eschatological event that promises the resurrection of all God's people. This is what Paul means when he writes, "since we believe that Jesus died and rose again, even so, through Jesus, God will bring with him those who have died" (1 Thess 4:14). For Paul, and apparently for John, Jesus's resurrection ensures the future resurrection of all the saints. He is the "first-born of the dead" (1:5).

Resurrection entails several other realities. First, death is real. We do not escape it. God, the God of the living (Mark 12:27 parr.), offers our only hope for life. Second, the dead are just that, dead, until the final moment of resurrection when God restores them to life (1 Cor 15:42–57; 1 Thess 4:13–18). And third, resurrection entails some measure of continuity and discontinuity with respect to our current lives. We remain that person who once lived, but we are somehow transformed by God's power. No wonder Paul calls it a mystery (1 Cor 15:51).

Revelation 20:4–6, 11–15 provides the critical site for our reflection. Remarkably, the passage features two resurrections. The first occurs prior to Jesus's thousand-year reign known as the millennium, and it includes only martyrs. Revelation 20:5 informs us,

> (The rest of the dead did not come to life until the thousand years were ended.) This is the first resurrection.

The martyrs are special, "blessed and holy" (20:6). They reign with Christ throughout the millennium.

The rest of humankind awaits a second resurrection that leads to judgment (20:11–15). The passage assumes that the dead who participate in the second resurrection are truly dead. Not only do Death and Hades return their dead, but even the sea returns those who have perished in it.[29] In other words, their bodies matter in Revelation's eschatological calculus.

Revelation elsewhere yields the impression that the martyrs enter heaven immediately upon their deaths. This is especially clear in Rev 6:9–11, where

---

29. Bauckham 1998, 280–81 reads Rev 20:13 differently, arguing that the sea functions as "simply another synonym for Sheol," but he does agree that Revelation envisions death "giving back" all persons in the resurrection.

the martyrs cry out for vengeance from a location underneath the heavenly altar. They are instructed that they must wait until the full complement of martyrs is fulfilled. (Contrary to many translations, Rev 6:11 does not use the term "number.") Scholars do not agree on the identification of the two groups in 7:1–17, but I see both the 144,000 and the innumerable multitude as most likely martyrs.[30] Revelation describes the 144,000 as those "who have been redeemed from the earth" and the "firstfruits" of humankind (14:3–4).[31]

The notion that martyrs receive immediate access to God's presence is not unique to Revelation, but it is underappreciated. Paul writes Philippians from prison, aware that he may not survive the ordeal. In chapter 1 he voices the expectation that he could "depart and be with Christ" (Phil 1:23), a hope that seems to stand in tension with his expectation that he may "attain the resurrection of the dead" (3:11). This tension lessens greatly if we take seriously the likelihood that Paul expects he may die as a martyr who would receive immediate transition into God's presence. Paul is not alone in this view. We encounter similar ideas in 4 Macc 17:17–18 and hinted toward in some early Christian literature.[32] Tertullian eventually adopted this view, namely, that the martyrs and only the martyrs reside in God's presence before Jesus's return.[33]

Revelation imagines three afterlife fates. Martyrs enter into God's presence immediately upon their deaths and judge the world during the millennium of Jesus's rule. Everyone else remains dead until the second resurrection, when they all rise to face judgment according to their works, as recorded in the books. One "additional" book, the Book of Life, contains the names of a second class, consisting of those who are redeemed (20:12, 15; see also 3:5; 13:8; 17:8; 21:27). The third class, consisting of presumably the vast majority of humankind, rise, face judgment, and are cast into the lake of fire (20:15).

The lake of fire is a particularly fearsome prospect. It represents the "second death" (21:8). Apparently, those who are consigned to the lake would far prefer simple death or annihilation. However, the Beast and the Other Beast (or false prophet) face eternal torment there along with the devil (20:10). Revelation nowhere suggests that those who enter this lake face anything other than tor-

---

30. See J. Davies 2023, 111.

31. Some commentators and indeed some early Christians regarded Rev 7:1–17 and 14:1–5 to indicate martyrs (see Boxall 2006, 125–26, interacting with Caird 1993, 94–98). Although this identification constitutes a minority opinion, I regard 14:4, which describes the 144,000 as having been "redeemed from the earth," to identify at least the 144,000 as martyrs (see Bauckham 1993, 76–80).

32. Sumney 2009, 24–26.

33. Hill 2001, 30–31, 220–21; see Boxall 2006, 113.

ment. As we shall see, it is possible to read Revelation differently, but we must begin by acknowledging what the lake of fire imagery entails.

Those whose names are recorded in the Book of Life may anticipate a blessed eternal fate. Only they may enter the New Jerusalem (21:27). Revelation offers mixed signals concerning this group: their names are recorded from the foundation of the world (13:8; 17:8), but the risen Jesus also threatens to erase those who do not conquer (3:5; see also 22:19). This blending of assurance with threat is characteristic of Revelation. The New Jerusalem is glorious. There the saints will worship and reign with God and the Lamb forever, join the risen Jesus on his throne (3:21), and no longer deal with sadness, death, pain, and evil.

In some respects, the New Jerusalem may seem less than compelling. The absence of evil and suffering, of course, has much to commend it. One might describe the river flowing through the city as a greenway, noting that fresh water was quite scarce in ancient cities, as were delicious fruits.[34] I do not wish to minimize these realities. But the city's gold and precious stones are hard and shiny, not comforting. It offers water to drink and a new fruit to eat every month, but it lacks wine, bread, and savory food. One might dismiss these observations as frivolous, far removed from Revelation's range of concerns. But Revelation attributes wine, fine fabrics, and savory spices to the unholy Babylon, so the contrast is more than accidental. We might say Revelation advances an ascetic aesthetic, largely distant from the pleasures of taste, touch, and smell.[35]

Revelation offers a blessed eternal future on its own terms. Although the New Jerusalem seems sterile in some respects, it also features a warm light, the intimate company of God and the Lamb (22:3-5). Its reality is social and embodied. In the letters to the seven assemblies, Jesus extends rewards that acknowledge the saints' accomplishments, giving meaning to their earlier lives. Although many modern people associate worship with quiet formal settings (and many do not), ancient audiences would have imagined the city's worship as full of sights, sounds, and smells. The absence of evil and suffering opens space for freedom. Great theologians have argued that a world without moral choices is not truly free, a position I find compelling.[36] However, Revelation imagines a future in which those choices have found their blessed resolution in freedom from evil and suffering in a world largely defined by those realities.

I do not intend to be overly rigid in distinguishing between resurrection hope and the idea that humans have immortal souls. We are in the realm of

34. Huber 2023, 341-42.
35. Carey 2009.
36. See Hick 1966, 217-21, 234-41.

poetry, image, and symbol. Revelation's portrait of the martyrs all but implies that their souls survive their deaths. Revelation even uses the noun *psychē* to describe their existence before the second resurrection (6:9; 20:4). I am, however, committed to resurrection as a key metaphor that is often neglected in both theology and piety.

Resurrection offends both our modern secular mindset, in which humans die just as other animals do and remain dead, and the spiritual mindset that attributes to us an immortal soul. It also defies logic. Modern people understand that when we die, our bodies decompose and their components eventually nourish other organisms.[37] Resurrection insists that our bodies and what we do while we inhabit them matter, even beyond death. The theologian J. Richard Middleton reminds us that resurrection hope emerged in contexts of political repression and imagines God's people coming to rule over their world, precisely the scenario Revelation advances (5:10; 20:4, 6; 22:5).[38] Resurrection also reminds us of our mortality and dependence upon God. For these reasons, I elevate the language of resurrection without staking some claim about human essence or the precise nature of an afterlife. The symbolism of resurrection provides the language by which Revelation envisions a social and active afterlife.

Many readers, myself among them, find the lake of fire repulsive for moral and theological reasons. How many people, if any, perform so much wickedness in one lifetime to merit eternal torment? Moreover, Revelation comes across as extremely exclusive; only those recorded in the Lamb's book escape the lake of fire. Revelation labels the rest of humankind as "the Inhabitants of the Earth" who are cast into the lake (20:15; see also 21:8). So we have two problems: the moral offense of eternal suffering inflicted upon human beings, which is compounded by assigning that fate to the overwhelming majority of persons.

I choose to emphasize Revelation's more hopeful passages, recognizing that they appear outnumbered and outweighed in the book as a whole. This is a theological and hermeneutical choice, its value lying in calling attention to aspects of Revelation that are often neglected. Two passages related to the New Jerusalem open the path to this optimistic reading. First, one of Revelation's most prominent allusions to Isaiah depicts "the nations" walking by the holy city's light and the "kings of the earth" bringing their glory (tribute, perhaps) into it. If the city is meant to include only those designated as saints at a partic-

---

37. Allison 2016, 19–43.
38. J. R. Middleton 2014, 131–54.

ular point in time, there would be no purpose in maintaining open gates that allow former outsiders to come in (21:24–25; see also Isa 66:17–23). Second, the leaves on the tree of life provide "healing for the nations" (22:2), extending hope for their inclusion. Revelation does not abandon its exclusive language. Sinners and unclean persons are not permitted (21:8, 27; 22:11). One might argue that Revelation holds both views in tension without attempting to resolve the question, which is a fair appraisal.[39] Alternatively, Revelation opens a path for a far more inclusive reading than is generally assumed, one that anticipates healing and reconciliation with those the book currently regards as hostile.

Ultimate Things

This chapter asks whether Revelation has an eschatology. Revelation attempts nothing like a discursive or systematic treatment of topics like cosmology, the number and nature of supernatural beings, death and the afterlife, and the end times. Then again, neither does any biblical book. If contemporary readers desire to pursue those topics in Revelation, we also confront complications. Revelation challenges readers to discern the language of poetry and symbol. It confronts us with a cosmology few modern people share: a heaven "up there" somewhere in the sky, a supernatural realm populated with angels and demons, and the scientifically impossible notion of resurrection. Moreover, Revelation presents its story not in a linear sequence but with echoes of the sacred past, images that dramatize realities present in its own day, and judgments that sometimes intensify and sometimes repeat one another. For all these reasons, readers who desire to think eschatologically with Revelation must be clear that most of what we discern is the product of our own choices, if we are unaware of our own biases.

Revelation presents us with a heaven (or sky) that interacts with earth. Human beings can influence heavenly events with our behavior, and heavenly beings (including Satan and the demons) affect conditions on earth. I do not personally attribute the world's evil to demonic activity, but Revelation does remind me that human evil on the grand scale does not boil down to straightforward moral choices, or at least that such vexing realities are subject to easy solutions. At the same time, Revelation's outlook confronted its first reader/hearers with a potential hope that their own faithful witness would contribute to the ultimate downfall of Satan, the Beast, and their accomplices—and soon. Two thousand years down the road, we recognize that John was wrong

---

39. J. Davies 2023, 239.

in expecting Rome's imminent demise. We may conclude, therefore, that Revelation is irrelevant. Or we may choose to believe that our faithful behavior contributes to good's ultimate triumph over evil, in large part by uniting our collective witness with divine agency. Revelation challenges us to believe precisely that.

Revelation dares to imagine that God will intervene and rectify history. With its constant allusions to Hebrew Scripture and to Jesus's faithful witness, Revelation grounds this hope in what we already believe about God. The book opens by reminding its reader/hearers of Christ's living presence in their midst (1:4–7). Much as the presence of the Holy Spirit unites us with the power of the resurrection, Revelation echoes the testimonies of creation, exodus, prophetic hope, and Jesus's ministry.[40] It recalls Israel's twelve tribes and the twelve apostles (21:12–14). All these reminders of God's past and present doings fuel the hope that God still works for the world's redemption.

As far as the saints are concerned, Revelation resolves all things with three images: resurrection, judgment, and the New Jerusalem. If we are scientifically inclined, resurrection is literally impossible to imagine. Bodies, which begin dissolving immediately upon death, do not and cannot reconstitute. Revelation scandalizes the imagination by depicting a judgment that consigns the vast majority of humankind to eternal torment. And the New Jerusalem, a realm of light and beauty that comes down from heaven to earth, is more than we can take in, likely because that is John's desired rhetorical effect. If we choose to elevate some aspects of Revelation above its desire for vengeance (6:9–11), we can read it optimistically: the city gates remain open (21:25), and the city's fruit can heal all people (22:2). Although the resurrection, judgment, and the New Jerusalem may not make literal sense to us, their symbols present us with significant gifts. All three symbols value our socially connected and embodied lives, a future that wonderfully transcends our present yet maintains a fundamental continuity with it.

Revelation asks a great deal of its readers. This applies to imaginative reading as well as to faithful behavior. In receiving its challenges, those seven assemblies faced daunting circumstances. Withdrawal from imperial worship and commerce evoked the possibility of repression and deprivation. Moreover, Roman power and glory dominated their visual and social landscape: "Who is like the beast, and who can fight against it?" (13:4). They also had the ability to opt out of Revelation's demands. So do readers today. We can name good ethical and theological objections to John's vision, as we assume some of John's

---

40. Carey 2023, 213–15.

first reader/hearers did. Unlike optimism, which we largely experience as a disposition of personality, hope requires a measure of choice.

Lisa Marie Bowens argues that Black Americans have drawn from biblical eschatology to critique present circumstances in the light of an impending judgment and to join as partners with God in effecting social change.[41] Without appealing to Revelation directly, she declares that with apocalyptic eschatology "hope and justice are futuristic and occur outside of human history but are deeply affected by what happens inside human history."[42] And she demonstrates that Martin Luther King Jr. held fiercely to hope—not empty pie in the sky hope, but hope that inspires "the tireless efforts and persistent work of men willing to be co-workers with God."[43]

Revelation testifies to us that hope is both possible and necessary (1:2). Hope provides a framework for analyzing evil when it seems far too insidious and complicated for us to assess and resist. Revelation's hope in particular presents us with the possibility that our own faithful testimony makes us partners with the risen Jesus in overcoming idolatry, violence, and exploitation. And resurrection hope reminds us that God—and only God—is the source of life who can redeem the whole of our embodied lives.

41. Bowens 2019, 213.
42. Bowens 2019, 217.
43. Bowens 2019, 220; quoting King's 1963 "Letter from Birmingham City Jail," 290.

Pathos, Emotion, and Affect in Revelation

R EADERS OFTEN REPORT EMOTIONAL REACTIONS to Revelation.[1] In my experience, they attribute these responses to Revelation's nature as visionary literature complete with sensational imagery. At least in popular circles—I am thinking of a conversation I experienced just two days before writing this paragraph—we tend to dissociate the visionary from the literary, as if John is simply describing an overwhelming experience.

But Revelation is thoroughly rhetorical. John aims to influence his audience's beliefs, dispositions, and behaviors. He wants his reader/hearers to abandon every entanglement with imperial worship, commerce, and power. He aggressively foregrounds what's at stake: people who follow his program will expose themselves to economic and social risk, even to the possibility of death.

We should appreciate that many would have regarded John's message as extreme. The Christian teachers he labels as the Nicolaitans, Balaam, and Jezebel likely regarded his teaching as too extreme. Biblical interpretation often assumes that scriptural authors succeeded in winning over their audiences and then explains "how" an author's literary strategies accomplished just that. But we have no evidence, apart from the fact that people kept distributing copies of their works, that they actually succeeded in their aims. This "success of the author" interpretation shortcuts the critical appreciation that John may have faced an enormous uphill climb, rhetorically speaking.

The ancients understood that persuasion involved more than simply advancing a compelling logical case, that is, the mode of persuasion the ancients identified as *logos*. Revelation's interpreters have tended to emphasize this logical dimension of Revelation by explaining how its language and symbols would

---

1. I previously published a study on *pathos* in Revelation (Carey 2008). This chapter builds on that work but largely moves in different directions.

have made sense. But speakers also needed to connect with their audiences at a deeper level. They sought to win over an audience's trust by demonstrating their personal character (*ēthos*) in terms of their expertise, trustworthiness, and positive intentions (Aristotle, *Rhet.* 2.1.5 [1378a]). Aristotle identified *ēthos* as "the most lordly proof" (*Rhet.* 1.2.4 [1356a], my translation), an opinion basically shared by the Roman rhetoricians Cicero (*De or.* 2.184) and Quintilian (*Inst.* 5.14.29–31). Chapter 2 identifies Revelation's construction of authority, or *ēthos*, as authoritarian.

But the ancients also recognized the role of emotion (*pathos*) in persuasion. Aristotle considered *pathos* so important that his *Rhetoric* develops an entire psychology of the emotions (2.1.5–11.7 [1378a–1388b]).[2] Cicero agreed that speakers will benefit from studying psychology, since "the orator's virtue is pre-eminently manifested either in rousing men's hearts to anger, hatred, or indignation, or in recalling them from these passions to mildness and mercy" (*De or.* 1.53 [Sutton and Rackham, LCL]; see also 2.186).[3] And Quintilian distinguished public rhetoric from scholarly discourse, advising that "unless we attract them by the charm of our discourse or drag them by its force, and occasionally throw them off their balance by an appeal to their emotions, we shall be unable to vindicate the claims of truth and justice" (*Inst.* 5.14.29 [Butler, LCL]). Quintilian also regarded the emotional appeal as "the most powerful means of obtaining what we desire" but cautioned about the difficulty of executing it well (6.2.1).[4] Generally speaking, ancient speakers and most authors took serious account of the need to move reader/hearers into new ways of perceiving and interacting with the world. To paraphrase Harry O. Maier, sometimes we need to ask not so much what one of Revelation's passages or symbols means but rather "What does it do?"[5]

Slippery Data

Assessing the presence of an emotional appeal in any text, particularly an ancient one, comes with complications. Although Revelation is not a speech, it likely was delivered aloud among the seven (or more) assemblies. Perhaps we should say it was "performed" for them. A significant aspect of rhetorical performance involved strategic use of both body and voice, a reality that likely

2. See Olbricht 2001; deSilva 2009, 175–92.
3. Kastely 2004, 221.
4. Vickers 1988, 77.
5. Meier 2002, 97.

applies to the public "reading" of texts. With Revelation, however, we are left to analyze only a written text.[6] Thus, we cannot know how Revelation affected its first reader/hearers. Some interpreters discuss how Revelation would have instilled fear or achieved other emotional effects, but we have all tried to evoke emotions from others and failed. Why assume that is not the case with John and Revelation? Therefore, we are left to infer John's design and intent from the text alone and to acknowledge the limits of what we can know.

A second problem involves applying ancient rhetorical standards to Revelation. John may not have received formal training in Greco-Roman rhetoric, yet our discussion has opened with the formal categories taught to elite young men in Greek and Roman cities. To that objection, we may reply that Aristotle's *Rhetoric* not only develops the philosopher's own philosophical perspective but also includes a great deal of what he had observed in practice. John may have possessed some rhetorical education given his skill and scholarship as a writer; however, even if he lacked formal training, John would have observed both formal and informal public speech and intuited rhetorical skills simply by being an observant person. So long as we apply ancient and even contemporary rhetorical conventions with care, they can provide insight into Revelation's emotional appeal.

Third, one might object that analysis of the emotions, such as we observe in authors like Aristotle, Cicero, and Quintilian, does not account for factors that run deeper than named emotion. Modern theorists have developed a field called affect theory to assess this level of human response that we do not name aloud and of which we may not even be conscious. As contemporary readers, we may look at our fellow citizens and wonder, "How could they hold *that* viewpoint when it is riddled with contradictions and flies in the face of all evidence?" The answer to that sort of question often involves how such commitments make people feel rather than how it satisfies reason. Some of those feelings can be named, while others perhaps cannot, or at least do not, work at a conscious level. Diverse models of affect theory exist, some emphasizing emotions we can easily name, and others more attuned to visceral responses that may indicate "precognitive" phenomena we do not necessarily identify as emotions, the "shapes and textures that inform and structure our embodied experience at or beneath the threshold of cognition."[7] This dimension of experience likely applies to nonhuman species as well as to us.[8] For example,

6. Kennedy 1998, 224.
7. Schaefer 2015, 24, 27; see also Koosed and Moore 2014, 385–85; Bray and Moore 2020, 2–6.
8. Schaefer 2015, 179–82.

consider what psychologists call "elevation," which can be defined as the feeling of being "lifted up," often with "an open, warm, or glowing feeling" in parts of the body such as the heart. Elevation seems to produce certain behaviors. For example, when people observe charity or gratitude, they are more likely to emulate those behaviors.[9] It is admittedly difficult to pin down how these subconscious, transconscious, and nonlinguistic dimensions of experience are accessible to interpreters of texts.[10] Biblical scholars are prone to interpret as if they stand apart from the experience of reading. But "how does one read for affect without themselves being affected?"[11] Affect theory does not provide rules for assessing Revelation's emotional or nonlinguistic impact. Rather, it reminds us of the subjectivity that attends our task.[12]

As we move ahead, we will survey several examples of Revelation's appeal to the emotions. This is only a small selection of possible case studies, but they help us appreciate Revelation's literary and rhetorical design—and its potential power for ancient audiences as well as for later readers. Many of these examples have received sophisticated scholarly attention. This chapter attempts to be distinctive in bringing together what look to be direct appeals to the emotions with the more sublime aspects of experience we might label as affect without distinguishing neatly between the two.[13]

Rhetorical Technique

As with all facets of rhetoric, the ancients developed and practiced techniques for achieving emotional effect. John employs a few. Having informed his reader/hearers that he will relate "all that he saw" (1:2), John continually points to what he has seen (forty-five times) and heard (twenty-six times), apparently in an attempt to provoke the imaginations of his reader/hearers. He and other speakers within the narrative also direct the audience to "look!" (twenty-five times).

Ancient rhetoricians had multiple categories for this sort of rhetorical technique. *Prosōpopoeia* involves the personification of abstract concepts. We see this in how Revelation uses the Beast and the Prostitute to represent personified dimensions of Roman imperial power and the Bride to embody the New

9. Haidt 2006, 93–95.
10. Schaefer 2019.
11. Kotrosits 2016, 34.
12. Kotrosits 2016, 35.
13. For an instance of a scholar recognizing the distinction and framing their approach in terms of "parting ways," see Moore 2014, 157 n. 3.

Jerusalem. *Ekphrasis* is the technique of providing vivid description.[14] Students just beyond the elementary level of Greco-Roman education practiced *ekphrasis* along with *synkrisis*, the latter being the art of building comparison and contrast.[15] In deploying these techniques, ancient speakers sought to achieve vividness, clarity, and stylistic propriety with respect to their subject matter.[16] Paul appeals to these techniques directly on one occasion: "It was before your eyes that Jesus Christ was publicly exhibited as crucified!" (Gal 3:1), a reference to his preaching and (obviously) not to the Galatians being physically present at Jesus's crucifixion.[17]

Paul's above appeal to placing an image "before the eyes" of his audience reflects widespread advice given to orators in Greek and Latin rhetorical traditions. A lesson book attributed to Aelius Theon describes *ekphrasis* as "descriptive language, as they say, bringing what is portrayed clearly before the eyes" (*Prog.* 118).[18] Aelius Theon then sets out examples of effective *ekphrasis* and classifies various usages of the technique. Likewise, the Rhetorica ad Herennium instructs speakers to develop word pictures so striking they will stick in an audience's memory (3.37). The Latin rhetorician Quintilian provides a sample instance of *ekphrasis*: should an accuser dramatize a murder, provoking an emotional response to the deed? Quintilian answers in the affirmative: "Shall I not see one make striking the blow and the other man falling? Will not the blood, the pallor, the groans, the last gasp of the dying be imprinted on my mind?" (*Inst.* 6.2.31–32).[19] Quintilian wants the audience to *see* the murder in detail. Compare his example with Revelation's description of mortals facing divine plagues:

> Then the kings of the earth and the magnates and the generals and the rich and the powerful and everyone, slave and free, hid in the caves and among the rocks of the mountains, calling to the mountains and rocks, "Fall on us and hide us from the face of the one seated on the throne and from the wrath of the Lamb, for the great day of their wrath has come, and who is able to stand?" (6:15–17)

14. *Ekphrasis* has gained increasing levels of attention among Revelation's interpreters and in biblical interpretation more generally. See A. Yarbro Collins 1999; Huber 2013; Henning 2014; Whitaker 2015, 2024; Robbins 2016; Barnhill 2017; Stewart 2017; and Luther 2024. The 2024 essays by Luther and Whitaker appear in Henning and Neumann 2024a.

15. Pernot 2005, 147–49.

16. Whitaker 2015, 39, 45–53.

17. Henning and Neumann, 2024b, 4.

18. Translation from Kennedy 2003, 47.

19. Quoted in Henning 2014, 64; Henning and Neumann 2024b, 1.

If John did not receive formal rhetorical training, he certainly knew how to draw a vivid picture. But unlike the Greek and Latin theoreticians (so far as I know), he also adopted the prophetic and apocalyptic convention of constructing bizarre symbols. Hildegard of Bingen's illuminations, Albrecht Dürer's woodcuts, and William Blake's watercolors suggest how challenging it must be to depict a New Jerusalem made of precious materials, a Son of Man with a sword protruding from his mouth, and multiheaded winged monsters.[20] Vivid as they are, these images can be too much to take in. In that respect, they do not reflect standard rhetorical advice.

At some level, John is conveying information with these word pictures. But he also works at the level of feeling. Those of us who have experienced drama through audio recognize the power of spoken imagery. John sometimes describes his own response, as if he is guiding his audience to experience what he "felt," including fear (1:17–18), sadness and perhaps suspense (5:4–5), amazement (17:6–7), and awe (22:8–9). This is only speculation on my part, but I believe images like the Son of Man and the New Jerusalem aim to communicate a sense of the numinous reality that transcends the human imagination and defies ordinary description.[21]

We discussed earlier how Revelation blends other voices with John's to reinforce his message (chapter 2). John's choruses speak to an affective level. For example, the martyrs in 6:9–11 cry out for vengeance: "Sovereign Lord, holy and true, how long will it be before you judge and avenge our blood on the inhabitants of the earth?" (6:10). John has already introduced them as having been "slaughtered for the word of God and for the testimony they had given," an image well suited to evoke a measure of tension or fear within the assemblies. If ancient reader/hearers of Revelation heard John in the manner I suggest here, what sorts of physical sensations would have attended this desire for retribution? What emotional word would cover it? Modern readers might reflect upon moments when we also desired revenge: how did that desire affect our bodies? Another example of this involves how the heavenly choirs affirm the justice of the plagues that ravage the earth. Consider the emotional appeal here: "because they shed the blood of saints and prophets, you have given them blood to drink. It is what they deserve!" (16:6). We might attribute similar affects at work when we encounter the Two Witnesses, their corpses left to rot while the Inhabitants of the Earth gloat over them (11:9–10). Violence against the saints promotes fear, indignation, and perhaps determination—emotions all useful in motivating people to action.

20. Regarding Hildegard in particular, see Huber 2013, 89–126.
21. See García Ureña 2021, 498.

John also allows his negative characters to convey emotion to his reader/hearers. I will offer just three examples. First, Revelation provides vivid description when the Inhabitants of the Earth suffer from various plagues. "They will long to die, but death will flee from them" (9:6). An audience might feel a measure of identification with the Inhabitants of the Earth, but their refusal to repent suggests that John seeks to evoke righteous indignation (9:20–21). Again, when they suffer scorching heat among other plagues, they intensify their unworthiness by cursing God and refusing to repent, even as they gnaw their own tongues (16:9–11). Rather than pity, it appears John is promoting revulsion. As we saw in Chapter 2, disgust features prominently in authoritarian discourse.

Second, John brings the world's adulation of Rome "before the eyes" in the reaction to the Beast:

> In amazement the whole earth followed the beast. They worshiped the dragon, for he had given his authority to the beast, and they worshiped the beast, saying, "Who is like the beast, and who can fight against it?" (13:3b–4)

For inhabitants of the seven cities, this scene would recall moments from their own experience: scripted and rehearsed outbursts of praise for Rome, the emperor, or local elites.[22] We cannot claim access to John's literary intent, much less its actual effect on his first audiences, so we must use disciplined imagination. A moment like this could evoke dread, awe, or even a resentment that nourishes courage.

The third and final example spotlights a passage we will discuss later in this chapter. The depiction of the earth's rulers, merchants, and seafarers lamenting Babylon's destruction (18:9–19) may have invited some members of John's audience to share their sadness. Others may have experienced these scenes as comical, voicing fantasies of Rome's downfall. Within the narrative, however, the laments of Rev 18 inspire no sympathy toward Babylon or to her associates.[23] As the story moves on, these laments evoke rejoicing, another instance in which a heavenly chorus underscores the righteousness of God's judgments (19:1–4). Revelation apparently envisions not a monolithic audience but one in which some reader/hearers enjoyed the benefits of imperial commerce while others did not. Babylon's judgment scene admonishes those who are entangled with the imperial system (18:4), but (as we discuss below) it promotes aversion and contempt among those who resent Rome (19:1–4). These categories of persons likely overlap. Almost everyone is implicated in Roman culture and commerce, but resentment runs deeper for some than for others.

22. Jenkins 2023.
23. Huber with O'Day 2023, 272; A. Yarbro Collins 1980; 1984, 121.

Revelation's strategy toward Babylon resembles the one it applies to the Beast: an acknowledgment of Rome's grandeur accompanies recognition of its murderous and monstrous qualities. This approach appeals to emotion at a complex level. Within the seven assemblies, perhaps everyone *felt* the weight of Roman glory. Some may have heard warning and admonition concerning their relationship to beastly power, while others may have already feared the consequences of opting out. In my judgment, Revelation's primary affective work requires instilling aversion toward imperial networks of military might, propaganda, and commerce. A measure of fear—whether of God's judgment, of Roman suppression, or both—also serves this end.

Direct Address

One prominent feature of ancient apocalypses is the participatory role played by the visionary narrator.[24] Not only does John report what he sees and hears, but he also receives direct commands and explanations from heavenly beings, responds to questions, makes mistakes, relates his feelings, and explains things that are not made explicit in the vision itself. All these factors contribute to both *ēthos* and *pathos*. By drawing reader/hearers into John's perspective and presenting him as a relatable figure, they enhance his status as a reliable guide and build a relationship of trust. John invites his reader/hearers to regard him as a fellow sibling who shares their hardships and blessings (1:5–9). Revelation complements John's prominent role by speaking directly to the seven assemblies in multiple ways. Although John is unlikely to be present with them when they hear the book, they will hear themselves as part of the experience.

Revelation opens and closes with John addressing the assemblies. After presenting the book as an apocalypse received from God through Jesus, John promises to share his entire experience and blesses those who obey the prophecy he shares. He then frames the entire book as a letter addressed to all seven assemblies (1:1–4; see also 22:21). As discussed in chapter 1, scholars frequently reflect on these mixed generic clues: apocalypse, prophecy, and letter. Nevertheless, John addresses each mode to his audience. He closes Revelation with another blessing combined with a curse directed against anyone who alters the book (22:18–19). Ancient reader/hearers would have found themselves directly addressed in these opening and closing movements.

Revelation purports to describe John's personal visional experience. However, John occasionally speaks directly to the assemblies within the body of

24. Carey 1998.

Revelation's narrative (4:1–22:6). After introducing the Dragon and the Beast, John echoes the challenge that appears in each of the seven letters to the assemblies: "If someone has an ear, let them hear" (13:9), followed by these words of exhortation:

> If you are to be taken captive,
>   into captivity you go;
> if you kill with the sword,
>   with the sword you must be killed.
> Here is a call for the resistance and faith of the saints. (13:10–11)[25]

If John could film his vision, the camera would turn away from the action and point directly at his own face. He warns the assemblies that the Dragon and the Beast constitute a grave danger, and the only appropriate response is to muster resistance and faith.

When John describes the torment that awaits those who worship the Beast, John addresses his audience directly with similar words: "Here is a call for the resistance of the saints, those who keep the commandments of God and hold fast to the faith of Jesus" (14:12).[26] These two "looking straight into the camera" moments frame the challenge that confronts aspiring saints: they can suffer at the hands of Satan and the Beast, or they can endure the more fearsome judgment of God. Resistance is the only viable path forward.

Twice John invites his reader/hearers to exercise wisdom in discerning the Beast's identity. The first example calls them to count the Beast's number 666, a riddle that continues to challenge interpreters (13:18). The most common resolution to this riddle identifies the Beast with the emperor Nero; in Hebrew, the numerical value of his name adds up to 666 or 616, depending on spelling variations. However, this would have required an exceptionally keen audience to work out the riddle from Greek when the calculation works only in Hebrew. Yet, no other resolution has won as many adherents.

The second riddle is closely related, but John handles it differently. "This calls for a mind that has wisdom," he challenges, but then he immediately explains the riddle (sort of). The Beast's seven heads have two meanings. They "are" seven mountains, but "also" they "are" seven kings. The Beast itself constitutes an eighth head (17:9–11). Commentators roundly agree that the seven

---

25. Translation modified from the NRSVue. In particular, I have translated *hypomonē* "endurance" as "resistance."

26. Translation modified from the NRSVue.

mountains allude to Rome as the "city on seven hills," but they wrangle over which heads to pin on which Roman emperors. It is reasonably likely that both riddles point to Nero in some way: the Beast's first appearance features a head that "seemed to have received a death blow, but its fatal wound had been healed" (13:3), while the eighth head in chapter 17 "belongs to the seven" (17:11) yet still goes to destruction.[27] It appears that John anticipates future distress for the saints that evokes the specter of Nero's violence in the past.

We must hold our interpretations of the two riddles lightly. But they do point to an affective dimension of their appeal. John invites his audience into the riddle-solving process, making them part of the story. Whether the difficulty of the two riddles alienates some persons among the assemblies poses another question.

John may also speak directly to his audience when he bids them to rejoice over Babylon's destruction: "Rejoice over her, O heaven, you saints and apostles and prophets! For God has condemned her condemnation of you" (18:20). He has already identified his reader/hearers as saints on several occasions, including the two direct addresses of 13:10 and 14:12. And while he has not identified them as prophets explicitly, he does exhort them to bear Jesus's testimony. Later an angel establishes a link between saints who testify and the status of prophets: "I am a fellow servant with you and your brothers and sisters who hold the testimony of Jesus. Worship God! For the testimony of Jesus is the spirit of prophecy" (19:10). John does not identify the saints as apostles, but he does assign them the title of prophet, if they testify faithfully.

I have already argued that John marshals heavenly voices, including the voice of Jesus, to lend authority to his message (chapter 2). Jesus also speaks directly to the assemblies in Revelation's opening and closing sequences. His most prominent speaking parts are the letters to the seven assemblies. Here Jesus speaks as the fearsome Son of Man, whose appearance inspired John to collapse and who stands among the churches in their vulnerable circumstances. This combination of fearsomeness and assurance suits the seven messages well, as they contain words of threat and of comfort. The combination would also be familiar to researchers in authoritarian parenting and governance. Authoritarian fathers protect children from a dangerous world by providing protection and punishing disobedience.[28] In authoritarianism, a strong *man*

---

27. Craig R. Koester does about as well as one can in sorting through the interpretive options and their complications (Koester 2014, 71–78, 570–71, 678–79). On Nero as a key symbol after his death, see Klauck 2001.

28. O'Brien 2008, 77–100; Lakoff 2004; and L. T. Johnson 2018.

purportedly defends the people from outside threats but also imposes fear upon the populace. These two principles, authoritarian parenting and rule, are closely related, as the Libyan dictator Muammar Gaddafi clearly articulated: "In a Bedouin society, with its lack of government, who can prevent a father from punishing one of his children? It is true that they love him but they fear him at the same time."[29] In the seven letters, the risen Jesus addresses the churches in authoritarian terms: he loves them, he expects them to love him, he assures them of blessings in return for their obedience, and he pronounces threats in case they do not comply. Jesus's appearance in Rev 1:13–20 prepares reader/hearers by combining a fearsome appearance with signs of his care. As Revelation closes, Jesus declares, "Surely I am coming soon," a promise that simultaneously voices threat and reassurance (22:20; see also 22:12–13).

By speaking directly to the audience, John and Jesus invite Revelation's reader/hearers to participate in the story. John generally does so to focus their attention and engage their involvement, while Jesus offers both comfort and admonition.

ANTICIPATION AND SURPRISE

In chapter 2, we examined Revelation's egalitarian mode of address to its audience. John assures the saints that he participates in their common distress, invites them to partake in Jesus's identity as faithful witness, and calls them to share in Jesus's ultimate conquest. Earlier in this chapter, I argued that John's accounts of his own experience of and response to his vision may promote a secondhand measure of those affective states among his audience. John also employs another rhetorical device that has the potential to pull its reader/hearers along with his vision: the building of anticipation and surprise.

Revelation 5 carries heavy weight in Revelation. It reveals the book's most prominent symbol, the Lamb. We have already discussed this scene and will do so again later. For now, I would like to call attention to how Revelation builds anticipation within the scene, turning suspense into surprise.

The first step involves building anticipation. Inside the heavenly throne room, John observes the sealed scroll. The question, "Who is worthy to open the scroll and break its seals?" promotes anticipation, as John invites his reader/hearers to await a revelation: Who, if anyone, can open the scroll? This anticipation grows into suspense in two more steps. First, John learns that no one is worthy to open the scroll, and his weeping amplifies the suspense. The

29. Gaddafi 1998, 64; quoted in Ben-Ghiat 2020, 42.

announcement that the Lion has conquered and acquired authority to open the scroll then returns John and his audience to anticipation.

The second step is the surprise. Instead of the Lion, John sees instead the standing-slaughtered Lamb. The Lamb takes the scroll and will soon open it, but John faces the rhetorical challenge of reinforcing the sense of surprise. To this end, he does what countless screenwriters do: he brings in dramatic music to celebrate the moment. This is not Revelation's first choral moment (see 4:8–11), and there will be others, but it does elevate the Lamb to divine status.

We encounter another moment of surprise in chapter 11. The chapter starts with the Two Witnesses, whom commentators cannot identify with confidence, raining judgment upon their foes. But once they finish their testimony, the Beast makes its first appearance. The Beast fights the Witnesses, conquers them, and kills them, leaving their corpses to rot in the streets. This is the moment in the movie when sad music swells while the screen depicts unfocused images of crowds rejoicing in the presence of evil.

"But" (*kai*; 11:11) Revelation turns to a surprise. After three and a half days of exposure, God infuses the Two Witnesses with a life breath, and they stand on their feet. Their enemies watch in fear as they ascend into heaven and further plagues strike the city (11:11–13). At the moment of deep sadness, God suddenly intervenes to vindicate and glorify the Two Witnesses.

Following the surprise of chapter 11, Rev 12 quickly sets up another conflict and anticipation. The passage features a menacing Dragon, two threats, then two miraculous escapes. John observes two portents in the sky: While a Woman Clothed with the Sun is suffering the pains of labor, the great red Dragon waits to devour her child. The Woman's escape is not particularly dramatic. Having given birth, she flees into a divinely prepared wilderness refuge. (We are never told directly what happens to the infant; most likely, we are to infer the Woman takes the child with her.) While she remains hidden, a heavenly war erupts and the defeated Dragon is cast down to earth. Suspense rises a second time, as the exiled Dragon pursues the Woman again. This time, however, the earth rescues her.

On a couple of other occasions, John claims that he *cannot* share what he has heard. In chapter 10, for example, seven thunders speak words that are intelligible for John to record. Previously in the book, John had already promised to relate everything he sees (1:2). But after the seven thunders speak, a heavenly voice orders John not to write what he has heard. The information remains his, but his audience is not privy to it (10:4). Things are a little more complicated in chapter 14, where John hears the 144,000 sing a new song that only they can learn (14:3). John apparently hears the song and cannot learn it, and thus he cannot share it. Several interpreters have argued that these scenes enhance John's authority with relationship to his reader/hearers; he knows things they cannot hear.[30] We might also consider the emotional and affective dimensions of mentioning something but then withholding it from the audience. Whatever John's design or its actual effect, he raises anticipation by mentioning these sounds, but the surprise he offers is negative. He cannot or will not share what he has encountered. Such a move could arouse curiosity—or it could disappoint the audience and push them away from John's point of view.

CRISIS, FEAR, AND ASSURANCE

Appeals to crisis and fear provide common features in political rhetoric, especially authoritarian discourse. The assurance that the crisis will find a happy resolution appears nearly as frequently. John portrays the seven assemblies as living in a time of crisis, an experience he shares. As his vision opens, John claims to share with them in persecution (*thlipsis*), kingdom, and resistance (*hypomonē*; 1:9).[31] He attributes his presence on Patmos to "the word of God and the testimony of Jesus." In Revelation, testimony (*martyria*) accompanies persecution and martyrdom (e.g., 1:5–6; 2:13; 12:11). Therefore, many interpreters accept the traditional account that John has been exiled to the island for his preaching or prophesying.[32] Jesus the faithful witness has given his life. Now John and his colleagues face similar danger.

Persecution motifs abound in Revelation. The letter to Smyrna alludes to persecution and the possibility of imprisonment (2:9–10). The same letter mentions the "faithful witness" (my translation) Antipas, who has been killed (2:13). And the letter to Philadelphia implies faithfulness in the face of an unspecified pressure (3:8). Meanwhile, the martyrs in Rev 6:9–11 suggest that John has heard of other (perhaps many) such persons. Revelation's clearest call to its hearers notes the possibility of martyrdom (12:10–12). The Beast makes war on the saints and conquers them (13:7), people who refuse to receive the Beast's mark cannot participate in commerce (13:16–17), and the Prostitute intoxicates herself with the saints' blood (17:6; see also 18:24; 19:2). John seems determined that this audience understands that they face trying times.

Until about forty years ago, scholars assumed that Revelation was composed in response to Roman persecution.[33] Yet despite the New Testament's many references to persecution, historians do not believe that Rome perse-

---

30. Ruiz 1994; Carey 1999, 201; deSilva 2009, 133.

31. On *thlipsis* as "persecution," among other possible meanings, see Huber with O'Day 2023, 16. For *hypomonē* as resistance, see chapter 9 of this book.

32. See deSilva 2009, 33–34.

33. Moss 2013.

cuted Christians as a matter of policy in the first century. In 1984, Adela Yarbro Collins assessed Revelation as a response to "perceived crisis." And in 1990, Leonard L. Thompson undermined the arguments for official persecution as a context for Revelation, helpfully pointing out that literary apocalypses, including Revelation, are a type of crisis literature. As I indicated in chapter 1, I believe Revelation is in part responding to known instances of repression and even violence. These episodes may have come not from Roman authorities but rather from neighbors and local elites. After all, it is the Beast from the Land, presumably a reference to local elites who promote imperial cults and festivals, who enforces worship of the Beast from the Sea. Even when such hardships are scattered or infrequent, they nevertheless provoke a sense of persecution in vulnerable communities. Although I doubt that official imperial persecution stands in Revelation's immediate context, I imagine that Revelation reflects actual alarm. And I agree with Adela Yarbro Collins that John means to instill that alarm among the assemblies, a fear that suffering may be imminent. As far as John is concerned, the Beast and the Prostitute enact violence against the saints (13:7; 17:6; 18:24).

Crisis rhetoric plays a critical role in ancient Jewish and Christian apocalyptic discourse, especially texts like Revelation that speak to politics and the course of history. These frameworks require condemnation of the present age as evil along with an assessment of time that asks how long God's people must wait for deliverance.[34] We might note that crisis rhetoric performs similar functions among contemporary end-times preachers. Premillennialists believe world conditions will, and therefore must, decline to a desperate state before Jesus returns to set things right. They call the final period of conflict the "Great Tribulation." Postmillennialists maintain that the reign of God will advance until Jesus returns to bring all things to fulfillment. The premillennialists continually turn to the news for signs of crisis, which confirm their end-times timetables. But my own study of postmillennialist Christian nationalist preachers reveals that they, too, describe the present moment as a turning point in history. In the meantime, they argue, Christians must wage spiritual warfare against the demonic powers that work evil in the government and society.

From Revelation's point of view, there's more to fear than persecution. Among the seven assemblies, only the Smyrneans avoid receiving threats from the risen Jesus. If the Ephesians do not repent, they will lose their lampstand (2:5). If the assembly in Pergamum does not repent, Jesus will make war on them with the same sword he uses against his enemies (2:16; 19:15). Those who

34. O'Leary 1994, 44–51.

consort with Jezebel in Thyatira face "great distress" (2:22). The assembly in Sardis had better shape up, or else Jesus will come like a thief (3:3). Even the Philadelphians, who receive strong praise, are commanded to hold onto what they have, lest someone take their crown (3:11). And the Laodiceans get a double dose: Jesus threatens to spit them out of his mouth (3:16) and to "teach" them (3:19). All this occurs in addition to the combination of blessings and curses that open and close the book, the warning to "come out" from Babylon in order to avoid her plagues (18:4), and other indications of the audience's precarious status. Having just pronounced "the wine of God's wrath" against those who worship the Beast, Revelation then offers a word of exhortation:

> Here is a call for the endurance [resistance] of the saints, those who keep the commandments of God and hold fast to the faith of Jesus. (14:12; modified from the NRSVue)

Revelation's fearsome admonitions apparently aim to inspire faithfulness. After all, "Blessed are the dead who from now on die in the Lord" (14:13).

Revelation envisions a period of great suffering or tribulation before the final conflicts that lead to Jesus's reign in the New Jerusalem, all of these occurring within the framework that "the time is near" (1:3). A series of severe plagues devastates the earth and its creatures. It appears that the saints will live through these horrors along with the rest of humankind, but this is a difficult matter to resolve.[35] We hear that the number of martyrs has yet to be fulfilled (6:11). Although the saints are spared from the plague of locusts, the text also implies their presence during that period (9:4). The warning that persons who do not receive the Beast's brand will be excluded from commerce also suggests the possibility that the saints may face hardship (13:16–17; see also 12:17; 13:7). However, the risen Jesus promises the assembly in Philadelphia that he will spare them from the "hour of trial" that will soon test the Inhabitants of the Earth (3:10). Commentators generally agree that Revelation does not follow a linear timeline, making it difficult to know whether the saints should expect to endure this final period of crisis. In fact, it is hard to determine whether Revelation suggests any such timeline before the final battle.

Revelation's crisis rhetoric works in complex ways. The present moment is frightening. It features persecution, animosity from the Inhabitants of the Earth, imperial hostility personified in the Beast and the Prostitute, and even assaults from Satan the Dragon (12:17). In the immediate future, things will

---

35. See Koester 2014, 324, 331.

grow even worse, with the high likelihood that the saints will endure still greater trials. As forbidding as these prospects are, Revelation reminds the assemblies that God's judgment is more fearsome still. Nothing unclean enters the holy city (21:27). As David A. deSilva puts it, the great crisis "before all else is the forthcoming visitation of God and God's Messiah."[36]

Revelation tempers its appeal to fear with comfort and assurance. Readers must assess how effectively this technique works. As someone who experienced Southern football coaches throughout my youth, I can attest that fear can be remarkably effective, but it also leaves behind wounds. John's first vision of the risen Jesus prompts the prophet to fall to the ground as if he had died, but it also foregrounds a strong dose of assurance. John has already reminded the audience that despite their common struggles (1:9), they share an exalted status as they await Jesus's return (1:5–7). Here the fearsome Son of Man stands among seven golden lampstands, which represent the seven assemblies, and he holds seven stars, which represent the seven angels or messengers of these assemblies.[37] The image communicates assurance that Jesus stands with and attends to the welfare of these believers.

Revelation is filled with such comfort and assurance. The letters to the assemblies indicate that Jesus "knows" their circumstances and is concerned for their welfare. Each assembly receives the promise that they can "conquer," a verb pointing directly at Roman invincibility, and thereby receive eternal blessing. Conquest, we know, can entail hardship to the point of martyrdom (12:11). But the assurance of Jesus's victory over his opponents reinforces this promise. Visions of heavenly worship, especially worship scenes involving the saints, promote the reader/hearers' aspirations and enhance them with a sense of awe. And, of course, the vision of the New Jerusalem aims to evoke a sense that an unimaginably glorious future awaits those who endure.

The Democratic politician Rahm Emanuel famously claimed, "You never want a serious crisis to go to waste. And what I mean by that, it's an opportunity to do things that you think you could not do before."[38] His principle also explains the suspicion aroused when a political leader invokes the rhetoric of crisis. Crisis rhetoric is ubiquitous among authoritarians, so much so that good-faith attempts to name a crisis such as a pandemic or climate change are met with cynicism. Thus, some of Revelation's interpreters have questioned the book's reliance on crisis.[39]

36. DeSilva 2009, 109.
37. I cannot offer a resolution of the "angel/messenger" translation problem in Rev 1:20.
38. Wall Street Journal 2008.
39. See Duff 2001, 129.

While I do not perceive John as having cooked up an imaginary crisis, I do affirm that crisis rhetoric is a dangerous tool. Nevertheless, I read John as part of a movement defined by Jewish apocalypticism that perceives the world order as hostile to God's purposes and God's people. I suggest that John has experienced or heard of enough hardship endured by followers of Jesus that he interprets the present moment as especially portentous. Likely the crisis of the First Jewish Revolt, which brought about the destruction of Jerusalem along with the slaughter and enslavement of thousands of Jews, contributed to this outlook. But John also fears that his reader/hearers may not perceive the crisis as he does and may not share his response to it. His appeal to fear is designed to activate those who may share his alarm and to persuade those who do not. The appeal to comfort proposes to strengthen them in their resistance.

AVERSION, JEZEBEL, AND THE PROSTITUTE

In chapter 2 we discussed Revelation's appeal to disgust, particularly by means of dehumanizing John's opponents. Other scholars have rightly framed this sort of technique as a form of humor relating to the grotesque. Humor engages us at an affective level; we often laugh without choosing to do so. Humor with a biting edge also alienates audiences from the butt of the joke. In other words, humor can promote an audience's aversion toward a person, a group, or even a concept. Sarah Emanuel convincingly demonstrates how such humor contributes to Revelation's function as Jewish resistance literature. Emanuel also provides a contextual understanding of what may have amused ancient audiences. But humor, especially mockery, can also serve authoritarian ends. Emanuel does not make this point explicitly, but she does observe that Revelation appears "to simultaneously detest and desire the imperial throne," evidence of a tension between anti-imperial and pro-imperial impulses.[40]

My interest in aversion does not necessarily account for or exclude humor. It relates both to debasement and dehumanization, the grotesque as a means of both claiming attention and building revulsion toward those John would attack.[41]

Revelation's misogyny (see chapter 7 below) controls its invective against Jezebel and the Prostitute. The former represents an insider among the seven assemblies (a competing prophet), while the latter provides a cipher for Roman imperial networks of diplomacy and commerce. Revelation does not necessarily "choose" female symbols here. Although it is not her real name, "Jezebel" likely refers to an actual female prophet. Moreover, it was common

---

40. Emanuel 2020, 6.
41. Emanuel 2020.

in the ancient world to refer to cities and nations with female iconography, so it comes as no surprise that John figures Babylon/Rome as a woman. Misogyny comes into view when John promotes aversion to Jezebel and the Prostitute with sexualized language—language he does not apply to male-coded symbols.[42]

The risen Jesus accuses Balaam (and presumably the Nicolaitans) of promoting the eating of idol-meat and of practicing *porneia*. I have argued that these twin accusations boil down to one thing: participating in Roman idolatry, particularly in eating meat that has been offered to various deities. Jesus accuses Jezebel of the same paired crimes, but he intensifies the accusations and the consequences that apply to her (2:20–24). *Porneia* precedes idol-meat only in her indictment, to which Jesus adds her need to repent of *porneia* herself. Jezebel has apparently forfeited her opportunity to repent, which still extends to "those who commit adultery with her." Now Jesus will throw her on a bed and kill her children (the Greek emphatically reads: "I shall kill her children in death"). Given the intensity of the language surrounding *porneia* and adultery, and the ways that language is addressed to her specifically, I agree with those who read all this imagery in terms of sexual debasement.

Jezebel provides an instance in which we may feel fairly confident in assessing the rhetorical aims of this emotional and affective appeal. Sexual debasement as a means of promoting aversion, particularly involving charges of prostitution, was a common feature of Roman polemic.[43] Admittedly, Revelation also uses Jezebel to promote fear; whoever aligns with Jezebel is about to suffer (2:22). But the project also depends upon debasing Jezebel so that John's reader/hearers will disassociate from her.

We learn from the beginning of Revelation that Babylon is a prostitute. As noted in chapter 1, John's word choice (*pornē*) connotes a common, likely enslaved, prostitute, but his imagery suggests that the Prostitute has access to wealth.[44] The text mentions her opulence, which is tainted with foulness, including her intoxication of the Inhabitants of the Earth, her golden cup filled with abominations, and her own intoxication from drinking the blood of the saints (17:1–6).

John's sexualized imagery may give away a suppressed attraction. David Spurr identifies "hidden and uncontrollable energies" in literature that erot-

---

42. Again, I would refer to Emanuel's sophisticated reading of "why" John treats Jezebel differently than his other opponents (2020, 104–15).

43. Moore 2014, 123.

44. Glancy and Moore, 2011.

icizes colonized peoples.[45] Feminist readers have detected precisely this suppressed desire in John's depiction of Jezebel and the Prostitute. John's attempt to break their allure for his reader/hearers betrays his recognition of their attraction (17:6). John's attempt to create aversion may or may not have been effective, but it seems compromised.

John's condemnation of his enemies is absolute, but his sense of self-assurance sometimes seems shaky. Harry O. Meier assesses this complex effect with special acuity. John mocks his enemies for their violence, their idolatry, and especially their hubris. But he too falls to worship an angel "not once (19:10; 22:9) but twice."[46] John's "blunder" reminds readers that they are also subject to admonition.

> Enjoying the full awareness of what they [the Inhabitants] fail to see, we look down and smile at the arrogant blindness of their enduring wickedness. Perhaps we even grin with bemused incredulity. Thus we might remain smug in our heaven, smiling that all is so unwell in the world below, were it not for John's sudden plummet into this mess of idolatry. For now, at the Apocalypse's end, we are less certain of ourselves, not wholly immune from our own laughter.[47]

I find Meier's reading helpful. John does dehumanize Rome and those who collaborate with it. He even dehumanizes persons who follow Jesus but whom he regards as accommodating idolatry. He imagines sexualized violence inflicted upon Jezebel and Babylon. The rhetoric of aversion aims to enhance resistance to imperial culture with its idolatry, violence, and exploitation. Like its cousin disgust, aversion is an especially powerful rhetorical motivator.

EMULATION, JESUS, AND THE SAINTS

Emulation constitutes the obverse of aversion in Revelation's literary universe.[48] All of us can recall persons we emulated as children. My Uncle Norman played low-level professional baseball in the 1930s, one of many reasons I admired him. When he told me he played with no padding in his glove, I went home, took a knife, and pulled the padding from mine. Only eight years old,

45. Spurr 1993, 177.
46. Meier 2002, 169.
47. Meier 2002, 170.
48. Aristotle contrasted emulation with contempt (*Rhet.* 2.11.7 [1388b]).

I thereby learned not to copy everything about someone I admired. As adults, we are scarcely less prone to identify a person we admire and adopt their example. We never outgrow emulation.

Classical rhetoric regarded emulation as an emotion that could motivate behavior. Aristotle defined emulation (*zēlos*) as the desire for goods possessed by others that one lacks in oneself to a degree. It is, he argues, the virtuous counterpart of envy, which seeks to diminish those who possess something we desire for ourselves. Emulation applies not only to status and possessions but also to virtues (*Rhet.* 2.11.1–3 [1388a–b]). The ancients perceived an intimate relationship between emulation and imitation, as do we modern folk. Imitation involves copying an attribute of another person's behavior, personality, or work, a primary means by which ancient students learned writing and rhetoric, while emulation involves free adaptation.[49] My focus here rests upon emulation, a desire to identify with someone else.

Revelation encourages its reader/hearers to emulate Jesus, of course, as well as other figures within the narrative, including John himself. David A. deSilva reads Jesus's address to Laodicea as including the phrase, "Be emulous" (3:19).[50] But Revelation's Jesus is a forbidding figure. Revelation reminds aspiring saints that Jesus loves them (1:5; 3:9), but it does not portray Jesus in inviting ways. Although the risen Jesus stands among the seven assemblies, John's initial response to his encounter with Jesus is to collapse in fear (1:17–20), and Jesus's addresses to the assemblies mix promise with threat. Jesus resides in the heavenly throne room, a setting at once both glorious and distant. Jesus's revelation as the Lamb resembles no petting zoo ovine anyone has ever seen, with his seven horns, seven eyes, and evident wounds (5:6). When Revelation issues an invitation to attend the Lamb's wedding feast, the Lamb is strange and fierce in appearance, and the supper involves human flesh (19:17–21).

For all these reasons, and because following Jesus exposes the saints to repression, Revelation's burden is to foster a desire to join Jesus. To this end, John adopts three notable strategies. First, Revelation figures emulation of Jesus as attainable by extending promise. Jesus has conquered through his death and resurrection (5:5). With that authority he assures all seven assemblies that they have the capacity to conquer and thereby receive the blessings Revelation extends. A key passage defines what conquest means for Revelation:

49. Schippers 2019.
50. DeSilva 2009, 222. DeSilva addresses Aristotle's treatment of emulation in some ways parallel to my own discussion.

Then I heard a loud voice in heaven, proclaiming,
"Now have come the salvation and the power
    and the kingdom of our God
    and the authority of his Messiah,
for the accuser of our brothers and sisters has been thrown down,
    who accuses them day and night before our God.
But they have conquered him by the blood of the Lamb
    and by the word of their testimony,
for they did not cling to life even in the face of death.
Rejoice then, you heavens
    and those who dwell in them!
But woe to the earth and the sea,
    for the devil has come down to you with great wrath
    because he knows that his time is short!" (12:10–12)

This heavenly proclamation offers multiple arguments that promote emulation. Aspiring saints participate in the devil's defeat by holding firm to their testimony despite the threat of death. One imagines, much as the Roman governor Pliny reported to the emperor Trajan decades after the composition of Revelation (*Ep.* 10.96), that most early Christians would have chosen survival over persistence. But Revelation repeatedly appeals to the example of faithful witnesses, that is, martyrs. People know they can fulfill this requirement because others have done so. Consider Antipas the "faithful witness" (2:13) or the crowds of martyrs alluded to in 6:9–11; 7:1–17; 14:1–5; 15:2; and 20:4–6. These martyrs contribute to the Lamb's victory, a potentially strong motivation. The challenge is tempered by the assurances that the devil's defeat is already accomplished and that the time for courageous witness is "short."

A second strategy, an appeal to awe, reinforces emulation. Revelation assigns a glorious status to martyrs. Martyrs apparently reside in heaven immediately upon their deaths, while most mortals must await the second resurrection. Revelation 6:9–11 describes the martyrs' presence in heaven, and it distinguishes between the martyrs' participation in the first resurrection and the second resurrection that applies to humankind in general (20:5–6, 11–15). Revelation 14:4 describes the martyrs as the "firstfruits" redeemed from humankind. Paul apparently shared this view of martyrs' exalted reward (Phil 1:20–26; 3:10–11).[51] The martyrs appear in scenes of awe.[52] We first encounter him

---

51. See Carey 2023, 224–26.
52. Again, deSilva (2009, 194–98) discusses awe in a different context. I consider him

them under the heavenly altar (6:9–11). Later, they stand and worship directly before God and the Lamb (7:1–17), learn the Lamb's secret song (14:1–5), sing in heaven (15:1–4), and eventually receive thrones of their own and judge the world (20:4). Revelation does not call these Lamb followers to seek martyrdom, but it does require that they expose themselves to it. It buttresses this fearsome calling by appealing to glory.

A third means by which Revelation promotes emulation is identification. John creates a virtual cloud of witnesses. Other believers, notably Antipas (2:13), have passed the martyrdom test. They now reside in glory, and aspiring saints fulfill their calling in the present. The mysterious Two Witnesses of Revelation 11:1–13 also persist in their testimony until the Beast conquers and kills them, leaving them dead until God restores their lives and brings them to heaven. Not only may John's reader/hearers share status as faithful witnesses with all these above figures, but they also join with John himself, who writes from Patmos precisely because of "the word of God and the testimony of Jesus" (1:9). John likewise claims to witness faithfully in another way: by testifying to the entire contents of his vision (1:2). Beyond the many martyrs and identification with John himself, faithful witnesses also share an exalted identity with Jesus. He is, after all, the first "faithful witness" (1:5). Revelation attends intensively to these faithful witnesses, who reside in heaven (6:9–11) and worship God (7:1–12; 14:1–5; 15:1–4). Revelation assigns the same duty to would-be saints that Jesus, Antipas, John, the Two Witnesses, and the glorious martyrs have fulfilled: faithful testimony, the very spirit of prophecy (12:11; 19:10). The story shows that they are capable of fulfilling this assignment. They may not endure torture and execution; thus, they may not receive the most glorious status. Nevertheless, their testimony unites them with all these figures and contributes to the Lamb's ultimate victory.

Revelation asks a great deal of its reader/hearers. Emulating Jesus as a faithful witness is a calling most will reject or abandon. Therefore, John encourages the assemblies through Jesus's promises that they can endure, opens them to moments of awe that enhance their identification with Jesus, and invites

---

a dear friend, and we have corresponded closely over more than two decades. We also published on Revelation's appeal to *pathos* nearly simultaneously (Carey 2008). I find it remarkable that, looking back on his earlier work, we were discussing similar dimensions of Revelation nearly simultaneously, and that later my own approach to Revelation and the emotions would run so close to what he published fifteen years ago. Having thought I structured this chapter independently, I frankly do not know how to assess my own level of dependence on his work here.

them to identify with Jesus and a host of other faithful witnesses, all of whom contribute to Jesus's ultimate victory.

Feeling Revelation

Readers routinely share their emotional assessments of Revelation. But interpreting a text's affective appeal is a notoriously slippery task. The ancients developed strategies, with some rhetoricians even developing psychological theories, to help orators win over their audiences at emotional levels. Those insights and techniques provide some guidance for identifying how John may have crafted his message. As other scholars have demonstrated, Revelation's appeals to fear, indignation, and emulation, for example, comport with this ancient advice, as does the book's use of vivid imagery. Contemporary scholarship recognizes that affective appeal often works at levels we do not necessarily associate with named emotions. For example, humor works at physiological as well as psychological levels. This research opens new categories for exploring Revelation's capacity for deep persuasion, but it does not prescribe a discrete set of methodologies. Our assessment of Revelation's emotional and affective appeal requires that we read psychology back into an ancient text.

This chapter also sought to add some insights to the valuable contributions of other scholars. We began by sketching some of John's literary techniques, especially the use of vivid description to manipulate emotion by dramatizing the emotional states of negatively valued characters such as the Inhabitants of the Earth and the rulers, merchants, and seafarers who lament Babylon's destruction. Second, we examined how Revelation uses direct address to guide and challenge its reader/hearers. Third, we pursued Revelation's use of anticipation and surprise, presumably to raise engagement with the audience. Fourth, we dug into Revelation's reliance on crisis rhetoric, a common feature in apocalyptic discourse, especially as John evokes fear and offers assurance to strategic ends. Our fifth and sixth topics represent two sides of the same coin: how Revelation promotes aversion toward some values but emulation with respect to others.

Revelation asks the assemblies to make significant sacrifices and to assume mortal risks. Those challenges involve loyalty, solidarity, and danger. Simple logical argumentation is insufficient for moving an audience to adopt extreme attitudes and behaviors. Thus, Revelation appeals heavily to affective levels of response.

Along with chapter 2, this discussion foregrounded elements of authoritarianism in Revelation's rhetoric. That chapter and the present one emerged from two of the three fundamental "proofs" in ancient rhetorical theory, that is, the speaker's person (*ēthos*) and the hearers' emotional response (*pathos*). Quite a few interpreters, myself included, have analyzed how Revelation appeals to *ēthos* and *pathos* over the past three decades, generally drawing upon those ancient rhetorical frameworks. With respect to Revelation's affective dimension, I also drew in this chapter upon others' research concerning *ekphrasis*, the rhetorical deployment of vivid description, as well as upon contemporary affect theory. Ancient categories are essential for placing Revelation in a meaningful generative context, but they do not exhaust our resources for analyzing how Revelation builds authority and engages its reader/hearers.

Revelation indeed participates in authoritarian discourse. I do not foreground this concern as a criticism of the book, at least not directly. Instead, I believe Revelation's authoritarian dimensions raise fundamental challenges for responsible interpreters. As I write, political authoritarianism poses direct threats to democracy all over the world. Freedom House, a widely respected nonprofit that measures global democracy, declared 2023 the seventeenth consecutive year of "global deterioration" in democratic governance while also noting signs that the decline may be reversing.[53] Persistent church sexual abuse scandals demonstrate how dangerous the intersection is where religion and authority meet. Authoritarianism is dangerous indeed.

Yet, there are also moments when faithful people must distinguish good from evil, establish boundaries and norms for their communities, and claim moral conviction. In moments of crisis, we need apocalypticists, those who will expose wickedness and speak with sharp, double-edged tongues. Revelation cannot tell us when those moments arrive or what stances require the posture of moral authority, but it does remind us such moments exist. We can use Revelation as a case study for communal reflection. What kind of authority can we claim? What beastly principles need unveiling and resisting? And what dangers lurk when we align ourselves and our understandings with God's truth?

---

53. Freedom House 2023.

Wealth and Poverty in Revelation

REVELATION CONTAINS MANY REFERENCES to wealth, poverty, money, commerce, and precious materials. These interests tend to cluster in the letters to the seven churches in chapters 2 and 3 as well as later in the book with the comparison of the Prostitute and the Bride. Concerns around commerce do feature elsewhere, notably in the reference to scarcity in 6:5–6 and the requirement in 13:16–17 that one must bear the mark of the Beast in order to buy or sell goods. Interpreters have generally concluded that Revelation addresses paired concerns: (1) a conflict involving wealth and commerce among the seven churches, and (2) a critique of Roman commercial exploitation. These readings assume that Revelation provides a window, albeit an unclear one, to actual conditions at the time of its composition. This is likely the case, but I am more interested in the story level of the book and how exactly Revelation speaks to wealth, poverty, trade, and the desire for nice things.

The interest in wealth displayed in the book has led some researchers to investigate the material conditions in the seven cities that Revelation addresses. This type of work is important for our reading of any text from the ancient Mediterranean world. Particularly, scholars have debated one issue that is highly relevant for reading Revelation: the distribution of wealth within the general population. Some argue that the proportion of persons who enjoyed above subsistence-level income was very low, with a fabulously wealthy elite comprising less than 2 percent of the population alongside another 1 or 2 percent who were also quite wealthy and perhaps a "middling group" of 6 to 12 percent who enjoyed surplus resources.[1] Others perceive that middling group as being significantly larger, perhaps comprising 15 percent of the population with twice that ratio present in significant cities.[2] Based in prominent

1. Scheidel and Friesen 2009.
2. Longenecker 2010, 44–59.

commercial centers, Revelation's seven Asian assemblies likely involved small groups of individuals related to one another through household or trade but with some economic diversity.[3] Most Jesus followers would have lived at or below subsistence-level poverty.[4] Our present aim is not to map out the distribution of resources in ancient Thyatira, for example, but to provide a plausible and relevant context for understanding Revelation.[5] Just as we encounter economic disparities in literature such as 1 Corinthians and James, we should imagine diverse viewpoints regarding wealth, poverty, commerce, and empire within the seven assemblies.

Critiques of economic exploitation and of the wealthy are not rare in ancient Jewish and especially Christian apocalyptic literature.[6] Many readers will be familiar with apocalyptic literature as a vehicle for counterimperial critique and resistance. Revelation does not directly indict people for being wealthy, but parts of 1 Enoch do. In the Similitudes of Enoch (1 En. 37–71), rulers and other powerful people lament that wealth is corrupt and will not save them from death (63:10).[7] The most intense condemnation of wealth appears in the Epistle of Enoch (1 En. 92–105).

> Woe to those who build their houses with sin;
>> for from all their foundations they will be overthrown,
>>> and by the sword they will fall.
>> And those who acquire gold and silver in judgment will quickly
>>> perish.
> Woe to you, rich, for in your riches you have trusted;
>> from your riches you will depart,
>>> because you have not remembered the Most High in the days
>>> of your riches. (1 En. 94:7–9)[8]

The epistle goes on to indict sinners whose riches help them pass as righteous persons, enjoying luxury while they oppress the poor (96:4–8). The assumption is that people accumulate wealth precisely because of their own corruption (97:7–10; see also 99:13; 103:5). Whereas Revelation suggests a critique of slavery (Rev 18:3), the Epistle of Enoch attributes slavery to oppression (1 En. 98:4).

---

3. Oakes 2020, 28.
4. Downs 2013, 160.
5. See Oakes 2020, 72–87.
6. On Second Temple Jewish literature generally, Mathews 2013, 42–139.
7. Cited in Mathews 2013, 128.
8. Translations of 1 Enoch are taken from Nickelsburg and VanderKam, 2004.

The third Sibylline Oracle is not a literary apocalypse, but it shares some features of apocalyptic discourse. Like Rev 18:12–13, it includes an indictment of Rome for expropriating gold and silver from territories it has conquered (Sib. Or. 3.175–184).[9] For that matter, even Greek and Roman authors castigated Roman rapacity and consumption.[10] We shall consider one specific example later in the chapter.

Other Christian apocalypses also speak to wealth, poverty, and exploitation. These concerns stand among the primary themes of the Shepherd of Hermas, perhaps written around the same time as Revelation.[11] In Hermas clinging to wealth divides the rich from the poor in the church (Herm. 17.1–10; 75.1). According to Hermas, the poor need the rich to tend to their material needs, while the poor pray on behalf of the rich (51.5–9). The Ascension of Isaiah condemns "elders and shepherds" who corrupt true doctrine and exploit their positions in pursuit of wealth (Ascen. Isa. 3:21–26). Revelation focuses primarily upon exploitation from beyond the assemblies and the responses of Jesus followers to economic necessity, while Hermas and the Ascension of Isaiah focus upon conflicts within their respective groups. Although wealth and poverty may not be prominent among ancient Jewish and Christian apocalypticists, the concerns are not unique to Revelation.

Roman elites were fully aware of their own rapacity. They understood domination and exploitation as the way of the world and were glad to be the beneficiaries. The historian Tacitus attributes the following speech to Calgacus, a resistance leader in what is now Scotland: "Harriers of the world, now that earth fails their all devastating hands they probe even the sea: if their enemy has wealth, they have greed; if he is poor, they are ambitious; East and West have glutted them; alone of mankind they behold with the same passion of concupiscence waste alike and want. To plunder, butcher, steal, these things they misname empire; they make a desolation and call it peace."[12] As in Rev 18, Calgacus goes on to name the expropriation of persons, slavery and conscription, as evidence of Roman predation. Almost surely, Tacitus composed this speech himself, though he may have had access to some report of it. In either case, the speech demonstrates that Tacitus understood the reasons other peoples resented the Romans.

9. Cited in Mathews 2013, 133–34; see also Bauckham 1993, 378–83.
10. See Royalty 1998, 208–09.
11. Osiek 1983.
12. Tacitus, *Agr.* 30.3–31.2, quoted in Wengst 1987, 52; and Elliott 2008, 184 n. 58.

REVELATION'S REFERENCES TO WEALTH, POVERTY, AND EXPLOITATION

Robert M. Royalty summarizes Revelation this way: "The Apocalypse of John describes a wealthy God, a golden-clad Messiah, and their angelic forces destroying an opulent trading city and rewarding their true and loyal followers with a city of gold and jewels."[13] As he points out, "Gold is the first and most prominent aspect" of Jesus's initial appearance in Rev 1:12–20. The one like a Son of Man stands among seven golden lampstands and wears a golden belt around his breasts (1:12–13).[14] These features precede the description of his white woolly hair, flaming eyes, and other features. Later, the one like a Son of Man wears a golden crown (14:14), and the seven angels who pour out seven plagues from the seven golden bowls also wear gold belts across their breasts (15:6).[15] Commentators generally do not pursue the question whether Jesus's belt or sash consists of gold as a fabric or simply gold-colored fabric. There are good reasons, however, to identify the material as consisting of gold (see Dan 10:5).[16]

Two of the seven letters to the Asian assemblies directly assess the matter of prosperity. The assembly in Smyrna experiences persecution and poverty, although Jesus describes it as rich (2:9), while Jesus castigates the church in Laodicea for thinking it is rich but being "wretched, pitiable, poor, blind, and naked" in terms of fidelity (2:17). Each instance elevates spiritual over material affluence or poverty. Readers attending to Revelation's rhetoric of wealth and poverty regard the two messages as opposite sides of the same coin: the Smyrneans receive spiritual wealth despite their material deprivation, while the Laodiceans' material wealth cannot disguise their spiritual poverty.[17] The letters' two references to eating idol-food may also indicate economic disparity within individual assemblies (2:14, 20). Many ancient people could not have afforded meat as a staple of their diets but would have enjoyed meat in civic and cultic celebrations, which almost always included religious observances. Moreover, meat offered in the public markets often came as excess from temple offerings.[18] These letters reflect a rhetorical agenda and may not reflect how many within the assemblies understood their circumstances. Our goal is not to reconstruct the situation but to situate the text in its broad cultural context.

13. Royalty 1998, 39.

14. Royalty 1998, 42.

15. Revelation 1:13 uses *mastos*, while 15:6 uses *stēthos*. These terms are commonly translated as "chest," but both usages are plural, suggesting breasts.

16. Aune 1998, 1:94; Beale 1999, 210.

17. Royalty 1998, 161–62; Mathews 2013, 157–66.

18. Duff 2001, 51–58.

The heavenly throne room in chapters 4–6 includes a deity who "looks like jasper and cornelian," a rainbow that somehow resembles an emerald, a sea of glass that looks like crystal, and twenty-four elders who wear golden crowns and will cast them before the throne.[19] God's altar, we later learn, consists of gold as well (9:13). The elders also bear golden bowls full of incense (see 8:3). Thousands of angels sing praise to the Lamb, proclaiming him worthy of receiving wealth along with power, wisdom, might, honor, glory, and blessing.

The seal, trumpet, and bowl judgments include matters related to wealth, poverty, and commerce. The third seal portrays soaring price inflation related to staples like wheat and barley, with prices holding steady for olive oil and wine (6:5–6). The fourth evokes war along with the famine and disease that accompany it (6:8).[20] A judgment like inflation in grain prices would affect the poor more severely than the rich, but Revelation envisions calamities that unite all persons, "the rich and the powerful, and everyone, slave and free" (6:15; see also 13:16–17; 19:18; 20:12) in their suffering. But the saints identified in chapter 7 survive the ordeal to dwell with God free from hunger and thirst (7:16).

The trumpet judgments also cause harm to the sea, including sea creatures and ships (8:9; 16:3). Some readers consider these judgments to reflect the harm that powerful humans actually brought upon the earth, such as a depletion of sea life caused by the Roman fishing industry.[21] Micah D. Kiel notes that Revelation offers no replacement for the sea in the new heavens and the new earth, judging the sea's displacement in the context of Rome's claim to dominate the Mediterranean. Its destruction removes the medium from which Rome could conduct war and extract resources.[22]

Revelation does not ascribe wealth only to God, the Lamb, and the Lamb's followers. Idols are crafted from gold, silver, and less expensive resources, reflecting the diverse economic statuses of those who worship them (9:20). The Beast has power over commerce. The Other Beast requires all persons, "both rich and poor, both free and slave" to receive the mark of the Beast in order to buy and sell (13:16–17). When Revelation reveals Rome as the Prostitute, she wears luxurious garments and fine jewelry and drinks from a golden cup. After depicting merchants and sailors lamenting her destruction because of the wealth the Prostitute has generated (18:4, 11–19), Revelation pauses to indicate

19. It appears that 4:11 may envision the singing and crown casting as a future event (Moloney 2020, 94).
20. See Howard-Brook and Gwyther 1999, 142.
21. Kiel 2017, 38.
22. Kiel 2017, 78–88.

the goods in which she trafficked, emphasizing luxury items by placing them first in the list:

> cargo of gold, silver, jewels and pearls, fine linen, purple, silk and scarlet, all kinds of scented wood, all articles of ivory, all articles of costly wood, bronze, iron, and marble, cinnamon, spice, incense, myrrh, frankincense, wine, olive oil, choice flour and wheat, cattle and sheep, horses and chariots, slaves—and human lives. (18:12–13)

The list is rhetorically powerful in several respects. By beginning with items very few people could afford and then concluding with the blunt phrase "slaves—and human lives," it dramatizes the true cost of imperial wealth. The list also suggests the reach of Roman imperial power. Scholars have tracked down the sources for various items from Spanish gold and silver to Indian precious stones, from Chinese silk to Moroccan wood.[23] The list makes clear that Roman luxury resulted from violent expropriation. In the words of Pablo Richard, "The satisfaction of the vices of the rich and the luxury of Rome is what determines the ethics and scale of values of the great city."[24]

The real wealth appears when the Bride descends. The language of jasper and crystal appears again (21:11), and John's language turns poetic. A city constructed entirely out of gold cannot be clear as glass, but this one is (21:18). Jewels adorn the foundations of the city walls (21:19–20). The proverbial pearly gates and golden (yet transparent) streets appear (21:21). The open gates receive "the glory and the honor of the nations" (21:26), language that suggests tribute. The scene alludes to Isa 60:11, where the nations bring their wealth into Zion's perpetually open gates. However, Revelation uses the terms "glory" and "honor" several times, never drawing an explicit association to wealth (4:9, 11; 5:12–13; 7:12).[25] Although I believe the allusion to Isaiah indicates tribute, I am not confident in that judgment. The New Jerusalem is opulent enough in any case.

Hunger and famine may be present elsewhere in Revelation, but they have no place in the New Jerusalem, where fresh water and fruit abound (22:2). If Revelation addresses anything like a reasonably representative cross section of the population, we may assume that many who first heard it performed or read aloud knew hunger and thirst. The imagery of abundant fresh fruit and water would have appealed to many ancient reader/hearers. They would have

23. Bauckham 1993, 350–71.
24. Richard 1995, 137.
25. Koester 2014, 822.

known that fresh fruit was a luxury, and that fresh water was hard to come by in an ancient city. Although the goods shipped by Babylon (i.e., Rome) offer more texture and diversity than simple water and a monthly piece of fruit, we should also imagine the delight promises of fresh water and fruit could inspire in the imaginations of an ancient urban audience.[26]

Although the Bride's opulence exceeds that of the Prostitute, she also displays a peculiar simplicity. In contrast to the Prostitute's clothing, the Bride's fine linen consists of the saints' righteous deeds (19:8). And whereas the Prostitute offers cinnamon, spice, wine, oil, choice flour along with wheat, and even meat, the Bride provides one piece of fruit per month with water to drink (22:2).

Coming to Terms

Revelation's imagery of wealth, poverty, famine, and commerce involves contrast, reversal, replacement, and critique. It also functions to pit some among John's reader/hearers against others.

The most obvious contrast involves the Prostitute and the Bride. Both represent cities: the Prostitute represents Babylon/Rome, whereas the Bride represents the New Jerusalem. The Prostitute drinks the saints' blood; the Bride's linen is identified with the saints' righteous deeds. Each of these figures also has a male consort. The Prostitute rides the Beast, who will turn against her, and all the nations participate in her *porneia*; the Bride marries the Lamb and welcomes persons of every social status within her gates. The Freudian phrasing here is relevant. The Bride has walls and open gates; the Prostitute has neither walls nor gates. One is adorned in luxurious garments; the other is elegantly clothed but in the modest way appropriate to brides in John's culture. The Prostitute expropriates great wealth for her allies until it is all destroyed. Some scholars suggest that Babylon's extravagant wealth would have connoted moral depravity to ancient audiences.[27] Even greater wealth decorates the New Jerusalem. Revelation calls the saints to "come out" from Babylon (18:4), whereas entry into the New Jerusalem constitutes the greatest imaginable blessing (21:7).

Revelation also contrasts two kinds of persons: those who worship the Beast, and those who follow the Lamb. Each class receives marks: those who receive the mark of the Beast receive access to buy and sell, while those who follow the Lamb undergo persecution (13:7, 16–17). The Beast worshipers, re-

---

26. Underestimated in Carey 2009.
27. Royalty 1998, 102–11; Frilingos 2004, 105–6.

ferred to as the Inhabitants of the Earth, are associated with Babylon and its destruction (17:8), while the Lamb followers inherit the New Jerusalem.

John's program advances both reversal and replacement. Revelation acknowledges the Beast's power and dramatizes the Prostitute's opulence. Both figures evoke wonder (13:4; 17:6–8). In the end, however, the Lamb conquers the Beast, while Babylon falls to destruction. One might add that the Beast and the Prostitute experience the most debasing of fates: the Prostitute is devoured by the Beast and its ten horns (17:16), the Beast thrown into the lake of fire along with the false prophet, and, we might add, the Beast's worshipers eaten by birds (19:20–21). The Beast's power cannot withstand that of the Lamb, and the Prostitute's splendor is exceeded by that of the Bride.

Reversal is a primary characteristic of resistance literature, which was composed to counter and critique imperial domination. The Beast's conquests yield to those of the Lamb, and the Prostitute's wealth gives way to the Bride's splendor. These reversals indicate the liberatory posture of resistance literature. But studies of postcolonial and resistance literature reveal that reversal generally (or perhaps even always) bears the traces of that which it critiques. I have called this pattern "symptoms of resistance." Rather than imagine a holy community that relegates opulence to irrelevance, Revelation adopts Rome's insistence upon wealth and appropriates it for the saints.[28] In an optimistic reading, Revelation rejects Roman avarice by replacing Roman wealth with the wealth of the New Jerusalem. The rulers of the nations bring tribute into the holy city, much like how Rome extracted tribute from other peoples (21:24). One might ask whether the rhetoric of reversal and replacement are sufficient means for imagining God's inbreaking world.

This question raises the matter of critique. Revelation's critique of Rome is reasonably clear. The empire generates violence. It ties commercial access to idolatry, specifically worship of the Beast. It represents Roman wealth as the product of corrupt (*porneic*, to coin a phrase) arrangements among rulers, merchants, and logisticians. Most tellingly, Revelation points out how Rome's expropriation of goods depletes lands and exploits people. Once we articulate these critiques, perhaps we can arrive at a chastened yet hopeful reading.

We should contemplate what a completely hopeful appreciation of Revelation sounds like. Scot McKnight offers one: "This is what New Jerusalem means to John, the churches, and to us today: *God's presence with God's people in unending intimacy and splendor.* God provides water and food and a city and

---

28. Royalty 1998 makes this argument without appealing to postcolonial or resistance theory. For my earlier work, see Carey 2006.

shelter and safety, and all the jewels and materialism of Babylon are turned toward God, flooding the New Jerusalem with gifts stacked on gifts like a cosmic Christmas tree."[29] McKnight makes several interpretive moves in apparent anticipation of the concerns we have already articulated. He combines intimacy with splendor, rendering the New Jerusalem's gleaming gold and jewels a sign of divine glory rather than evidence of materialism. He emphasizes the city's livability, including access to water, food, shelter, and safety. He also draws out Revelation's material critique of Babylon. Perhaps most important, rather than directing the city's wealth toward the Lamb's followers, he imagines them "turned toward God" in worship. Expressing a related sentiment, Robyn J. Whitaker argues that "God's dwelling place deserves every decoration, because all the ornate jewels point to God's glory and power."[30] So far as it goes, McKnight's is a compelling reading.[31]

Revelation flips the Roman script by ascribing wealth to the Bride and her citizens, who apparently receive wealth from other peoples. Yet, in the heavenly throne room golden crowns are to be vehicles for worship and thrown before the throne (4:10). In this New Jerusalem, no one is wearing jewelry, eating beef or mutton, or guzzling wine (18:12–13). The only sign of exploitation is that these rulers bring their "glory" into it. One could read their action as voluntary worship rather than extracted tribute.

REVELATION'S DEMAND

Revelation sits before us as a literary text. Many readers approach it as if it floated free from any originating context, leaving it at liberty to speak directly to any time and place with no need for nuance or qualification. But Revelation did address seven assemblies of Jesus followers with a pressing challenge. We ought not respond to its wealth imagery apart from what we can reasonably imagine about the lives of those people. In their context, how should we understand what Revelation is asking of them?

Most scholars interpret Revelation as reflecting the circumstances of actual assemblies to a degree. However, some interpreters regard the letters as complete fiction. Although I don't know whether we can move beyond speculation, I believe we can be sure that Revelation does not provide a neutral perspective

---

29. McKnight with Matchett 2023, 152–53.
30. Whitaker 2023, 114.
31. One might read supersessionism in McKnight's following comments, which discuss the absence of a temple in the holy city (McKnight with Matchett 2023, 153).

on these assemblies. The letters to the churches reflect diversity and conflict, and economic issues also appear to be in the picture. We should also admit our historical inferences are based on small amounts of evidence. Although some scholars show high levels of confidence in their conclusions, we're left to follow the clues in these letters as best we can.

We have already observed some disparity among the risen Jesus's assessments of the seven assemblies. They convey the impression that Smyrna is poor, while Laodicea is rich (3:17). The letters also indicate direct conflict within the churches (and conflict outside of them as well). As we saw earlier, the risen Jesus condemns movements he associates with the Nicolaitans (2:6, 15), Balaam (2:14), and Jezebel (2:20–25) along with a group he labels as false apostles (2:2). John accuses them of promoting *porneia* and eating idol-food. The term Nicolaitans apparently refers to a group, the only opponents John associates with two different assemblies. Although scholars tend to link the Nicolaitans with Balaam due to their appearance together in the letter to Pergamum (2:14–15), we know little else about them. We cannot identify their teachings or the origin of their name with confidence. Nor do we know anything about the would-be apostles to whom John refers.

We are also left with contention involving the so-called idol-food and *porneia*. Although we could engage them as concerning purely matters of "religious" practice, these issues likely bear upon economics as well. It is entirely possible these phrases involve separate accusations, specifically that *porneia* refers to actual "non-halakic sex acts."[32] But most interpreters understand them as two ways of indicating the same thing: participation in meals that involve meat that has been previously offered to a deity. John, being deeply engaged with the Hebrew prophets, knows the scriptural convention of representing idolatry through the metaphor cluster of prostitution, adultery, and promiscuity.

So we have a conflict. John insists that Jesus followers must avoid entanglement with idolatry in any form, specifically eating meat that may have been associated with sacrifice. To be clear, ancient Roman cities featured religion everywhere, from personal, household, and association gods to great festivals and temples as well as the worship of Rome and its rulers. Apparently Balaam, Jezebel, and likely the Nicolaitans tolerate or promote participation in the larger society and its religious trappings. We can only imagine what their arguments may have been, perhaps something in line with language from 1 Cor 8. There, Paul discusses the question of eating meat that has been offered to idols. As Paul observes, some might argue that the deities who receive such sacrificial worship have no power, no existence even, and therefore pose no

32. Emanuel 2020, 100.

threat (8:4–6). They might even argue that Christians are free to make such choices, since such sacrificial food has no spiritual power (8:8–9). Or they might even take a more pragmatic approach, noting that the costs of isolating from civic culture, trade guilds and other necessary associations, and even family rituals are simply too high. However, John says God condemns these prophets and their works.

Many Christian readers readily follow John's invective. He thinks believers in the assemblies participate in idolatry when they participate in meals that bear associations with idolatry. Thus, John is faithful, while his opponents are compromisers. This assessment is all the more attractive when we add our awareness that meat eating in the ancient world reflected economic and social status: meat was expensive, and access to great banquets discriminated the haves from the have-nots. Not only is John's point of view more faithful, it may be more inclusive. This reading pattern construes Revelation as an inspirational witness to purity and faithfulness toward Jesus.

This above set of assumptions requires more reflection. For years, I've led students in the following thought experiment: "Imagine you were a stone mason in Ephesus or one of the other assemblies. The stone mason guild provides you access to work, a social network, and even burial insurance. But you follow Jesus, and every stone mason gathering involves sacrifice to a patron deity. What happens if you avoid those meetings?" Students immediately grasp the point. If John requires absolute purity from any and every taint of idolatry—"you do have a few people in Sardis who haven't stained their clothing" (3:4)—he is demanding a profound sacrifice.

A recent study by Anna M. V. Bowden gives flesh to precisely that scenario by investigating the material lives of marble workers in ancient Ephesus. Other scholars have pointed out that withdrawing from the economy in the way John suggests would have exposed Jesus followers to destitution, she observes, but their readings remain abstract rather than grounded in choices that ancient people could reasonably have been expected to make.[33] She argues that Revelation's interpreters "read John's imperative in Rev 18:4 as addressed to males with space to act and something to lose," as if ordinary laborers could leave their trades for other opportunities.[34] On the contrary, she maintains that marble workers who abandoned their trade would have struggled to survive. "John's head is in the clouds, completely out of touch with the 'on the ground' realities of the working poor."[35]

---

33. Bowden 2021, 22.
34. Bowden 2021, 41.
35. Bowden 2021, 163.

J. Nelson Kraybill has proposed that we investigate a more prosperous group of Christians: those "with ready access to the ships, docks, and guild halls that serviced Rome's enormous appetite" and who "used commercial networks of the empire to advance their own social and economic status."[36] He recognizes that John's program would have caused economic difficulty for these Christians as well.[37] But Kraybill wrote before New Testament scholars had absorbed the analyses of economic stratification available to Bowden and contemporary scholars. The letters to the assemblies support the notion that some Jesus followers in the assemblies likely achieved prosperity, as Kraybill suggests, but we should also follow Bowden by accounting for the broad population base that led precarious lives.

John is an extremist. Competing prophets like the so-called Jezebel, Balaam, and possibly the Nicolaitans advise Jesus adherents to continue their work, social relationships, and family lives, rendering them moderates in comparison to John. John's call to "come out" (18:4) and maintain clean garments (3:4) would have exposed many among his audience to isolation, deprivation, sickness, and death.

By acknowledging John's extremism, we open the path to imagine his opponents as Christian prophets, not simply false prophets, who held an opinion that readers today can understand. I do not use the term "extremism" to marginalize John but rather to clarify the case he is making. A great deal is at stake. On the one hand, John correctly understands that one cannot separate imperial commerce from imperial worship.[38] On the other hand, Revelation argues that refusal to participate in the trappings of imperial worship can bring persecution and possibly death. Without saying it directly, John calls his reader/hearers to do precisely that—to avoid contact with pagan worship in every context. He further requires withdrawal from entanglement with a corrupt commercial system. That too could be deadly.

Hearing the Challenge

Some commentators embrace John's point of view. Others reject John as ethically defective. But few weigh the issue in the way Bowden does by taking full account of the precarious lives endured by John's reader/hearers. Bowden also passes a negative judgment on Revelation, one I share to a point, and she has advanced the conversation significantly.

36. Kraybill 1996, 16; see also Mathews 2013, 11.
37. Kraybill 1996, 197.
38. Kraybill 1996.

Let us accept that John was a radical, one who condemned other prophets who recommended less extreme ways of engaging a thoroughly religious and thoroughly imperial context. Having chosen to engage Revelation theologically, I seek to neither amplify John's call nor reject it outright. Instead, I recommend interrogating it dialogically.

Let us recall White Southern preachers of the early 1960s, especially the "moderate" ones. The moderates likely accepted that segregation was immoral. At a minimum, they regarded the hatred and mistreatment of Black people as un-Christian. They also believed, and with good reason, that speaking out directly against segregation would have bitter consequences. Speaking out could cause them to lose their careers. Their families could face harassment and even violence. They themselves might lose their lives for speaking out. To my knowledge, no White Southern preacher was murdered for supporting civil rights, mostly because so few of them did so directly. But termination of employment, harassment, and violence did occur. Had they confronted segregation explicitly, their communities would have labeled them as extremists. Today, we would say that they all failed.[39] But how many of those among us who are White would have counseled them to be more assertive back in 1964?

These are the challenges I have in mind by labeling John an extremist. However imperfect they may have been, many of the historical figures we now consider heroes were extremists in their own day, including prominent abolitionists, women's suffrage activists, civil rights workers, and Stonewall fighters. I write, however, in an era marred by other kinds of Christian extremists, persons working to undermine democracy in several nations all in the name of religion. Recent polling indicates that Americans who agree with the prompt "God intended America to be a new promised land where European Christians could create a society that would be an example to the rest of the world" comprise about 30 percent of the general population, and they are far more likely than others to endorse political violence as a viable path forward (26 percent to 9 percent among those who reject that prompt).[40] By specifying *European* Christians, the first prompt indicates racism in addition to (or as an element within) Christian nationalism. Extremism is not necessarily evil, but we have good reasons for regarding it with caution.

Hearing Scripture requires discernment. If we take it seriously, we will attempt to allow Revelation a chance to speak from its own context, assess its message critically and constructively, and bring it into conversation with our own con-

39. See Marsh 1997 and 2001.
40. Jones 2023, 301–2.

texts. In the abstract, I sympathize with John's assessment of Rome. Rome used force to extract wealth from other societies, directing that wealth only to a few. It relied upon violence and slavery to pursue those ends. And, with help from local elites, Rome sanctified its practices through ritual and sacrifice. Alongside other ancient Jewish texts, especially apocalypses, Revelation condemns Roman imperialism and idolatry, and it does so with a particular emphasis on commerce.

Commentators sometimes debate whether John's primary preoccupation involved Rome or the churches featured in the seven letters. Although the seven letters open John's message, a great deal of the book involves the Dragon, the Beast and the Other Beast, the Prostitute, and the Inhabitants of the Earth. I suggest we could frame John's concerns this way: his primary agenda speaks to the seven assemblies, but Roman domination provides the context for that agenda. I find it unhelpful to weigh which factor is more important.

Revelation's challenges to those assemblies largely amount to loyalty, participation, and witness. Contemporary readers may frame our engagement with Revelation in those same categories, acknowledging context as an essential factor in our response. This chapter has focused on economic factors, where John's primary demand is that the Lamb's followers must withdraw entirely from participation in an exploitative commercial system.

I doubt we could identify a society in recorded history in which commercial activity did not involve exploitation and oppression. Certainly no modern society can avoid implication in economic harm. John depicts the Prostitute riding the Beast, a reminder that violence always undergirds such relationships. It makes sense that Revelation would ask Lamb followers, including ourselves, to undertake serious examination of their economic participation as workers, managers, logisticians, and consumers—and to make sacrificial decisions as necessary.

Bowden's project reminds us that the burden of doing justice does not fall evenly. Poor and working people are most vulnerable to economic injustice and other inequities that attend it. They are also likely to suffer more severely if they make radical changes to their employment and other lifestyle circumstances. If Revelation's demands pressed hardest upon the poorest of its ancient audiences, contemporary readers may draw a counterinference: in contemplating public action, we must take account of people's need for security and survival. I am no political economist and have no business pressing my analysis beyond this point. However, I will say that religious leaders bear an obligation to raise such questions in their faith communities.

Revelation's message concerning wealth and commerce is inadequate. It apparently fails to consider the most vulnerable among the seven assemblies.

If John does account for them, he is willing to expose them to suffering, as he is for all of the Lamb's followers. He condemns those who disagree with him, and in Jezebel's case he does so in the most debasing terms. But suppose that at a fundamental level John's extreme position was an appropriate response to his circumstances. Even then, Revelation would prove inadequate to address every time and place because it, like Paul's letters and like every other document that exists, is grounded in a particular context.

Yet, Christians still need to hear Revelation. Far too few Christians take account of economics and commerce in the light of the gospel. We could discuss the global plague of the prosperity gospel here, but I am just as interested in our unquestioning deference to wealth and success without analysis. The Bible is filled with concern for the poor and objection to exploitation. Revelation stands apart for its unveiling (*apokalypsis*) of how economic exploitation relates to imperial practices and to ideology: "no one can buy or sell who does not have the brand, that is, the name of the beast or the number for its name" (13:17). The work of the Other Beast is to promote and enforce imperial ideology (13:11–15). Faithfulness to Jesus ought not be aligned with a partisan political agenda, but it does require critical analysis of this relationship between ideology and economics. People are doing this work, but contemporary Christians need to pay attention.[41]

41. By no means am I deeply read in this area. My own aspirational reading list includes Meeks 1989; Long 2000; Tanner 2005; Agamben 2011; Oslington 2014; Schwarzkopf 2019; and Dorrien 2021.

A Queer Book

REVELATION IS A QUEER BOOK. This poor attempt at humor needs defending, and we all know a joke's not funny if you have to explain it. The attempt operates at two levels. First, books about Revelation routinely open by telling us how hard it is to understand. I have saved that comment for this chapter. Second, Revelation performs gender queerly, provoking complex webs of debate concerning how it imagines and presents gender (for men and women and beyond) and sexuality.

These matters need attention in a pressing way as we are truly entering a queer world. Although LGBTQ+ persons have long been subject to repression, legal efforts to suppress them have intensified in the United States and other nations where political authoritarianism is on the rise. Controversies have included the content of school libraries, gender-affirming care for minors, representation of LGBTQ+ persons in classroom conversations, and access to public goods and opportunities for transgender students. Mike Johnson, Speaker of the US House of Representatives, has raised panic in fundraising pitches. In asking "patriots" to support the National Republican Campaign Committee, Johnson has argued that "America is hanging by a thread," in part because "1 in 4 high school students identifies as something other than straight—what are they being taught in school?"[1] In fairness, Johnson is alarmed by actual changes in American society. Whether they have less to fear than previous cohorts did or for other reasons, more and more people are identifying as queer. The US Centers for Disease Control conducts regular studies of adolescent health. Between 2015 and 2021, the share of adolescents self-identifying as LGBTQ+ or questioning rose from 11 to 26 percent.[2] Because Johnson and many of his allies appeal to the Bible as a definitive moral standard, might it be useful to engage Revelation's queerness?

1. Metzger 2023.
2. Lonas 2023.

Feminist, Womanist, and Queer Interpretation

Before engaging Revelation directly, we should briefly scan how conversations concerning Revelation and gender have developed since about 1990, when the first wave of feminist biblical scholarship was achieving broad influence. Indeed, it was in 1987 that Elisabeth Schüssler Fiorenza, a leading interpreter of Revelation, presented the first Society of Biblical Literature Presidential Address by a woman.[3] This chapter provides a brief survey of feminist, womanist, and queer approaches to Scripture, with special attention to the interpretation of Revelation.

As I intend the term, feminist interpretation begins from a commitment to the welfare of women. In the editor's introduction to the premier series of feminist biblical commentaries, Barbara E. Reid characterizes the movement as "Women interpreting the Bible through the lenses of their own experience."[4] Feminist interpreters employ diverse reading strategies. Some readers recover women's lost histories or neglected female characters. Some critique the patriarchal assumptions cooked into common interpretations. Some assess the value of texts for women. Within all this diversity lies one baseline criterion: what is good (and bad) for women? Feminists have not always agreed regarding the answers to this question, one that is present before investigating the biblical text.

The first and second waves of feminist scholarship debated whether and how Revelation is good and bad for women. Brief comments on Revelation in Elizabeth Cady Stanton's *The Woman's Bible* foreshadow debates that would occur nearly a century later. Matilda Joslyn Gage regarded the Woman Clothed with the Sun of chapter 12 as representing "the Divinity of the feminine," while Stanton regarded her as "representing the church" in a way that indicated respect for women. But Stanton also addresses Babylon the Prostitute: "The writers of the Bible are prone to make woman the standard for all kinds of abominations."[5] Likewise, whereas second-wave feminist scholars Elisabeth Schüssler Fiorenza and Adela Yarbro Collins regarded Revelation as problematic for women but more liberatory than harmful, Tina Pippin and others responded by rejecting Revelation as "not a tale for women."[6] Pippin argued that "in the Apocalypse women are disempowered in every way, especially in the erotic dimension," and that the New Jerusalem excludes women en-

---

3. Schüssler Fiorenza 1988.
4. Reid 2023, xxvi.
5. Quotations from Stanton et al. 1988 [1898], 182–84.
6. For particularly focused discussions, see Schüssler Fiorenza 1991, 122–24; Pippin 1992, 103–5; and A. Yarbro Collins 1993, 32–33.

tirely.[7] These conflicting perspectives set the stage for feminist conversations about Revelation for more than a decade and still receive discussion among feminist scholars.[8]

Feminist biblical scholarship opened paths for broader considerations regarding gender. Gender applies not only to self-identified women, a point that would seem obvious apart from the long-standing tendency among scholars to discuss gender only with respect to women. Womanist interpretation began with the perception that feminist thought attended to the lives of White women, often with a bias toward class privilege, while Black theology tended to neglect gender as an analytical category. Although it remains a majority Black movement, Womanist interpretation has come to include the work of other women of color as well. Womanist interpretation foregrounds and values the needs and experiences of Black women and other women of color. It stands apart for its embrace of intersectionality. In addition to race and gender, womanist criticism accounts for economic class, social status, and sexual and gendered expression, among other factors. Introducing an authoritative collection of essays, Gay L. Byron and Vanessa Lovelace describe womanist interpretation as, first, placing a keen focus on "the multilayered and interlocking systems of oppression and microaggressions" that harm women of color in all contexts; second, as drawing upon black cultural traditions as resources for interpretation; and third, as exercising a commitment to end the "multidimensional oppression faced by women of color."[9]

Clarice J. Martin published perhaps the first womanist reading of Revelation, arguing that in condemning slavery (18:13) Revelation at once speaks to and reflects the histories and concerns of Black women. Black women's experience informs our reading of Revelation, while Revelation mirrors the lives and histories of Black women. Martin's reading is straightforwardly liberationist and does not address the gender problems identified by many feminist readers.[10] However, more recent womanist interpretations of Revelation have appropriated postcolonial theory, reading Revelation as an example of resistance literature directed toward Rome. Both Shanell T. Smith and Lynne St. Clair Darden have drawn upon the theorist Homi Bhabha, whose concept of hybridity maintains that even anti-colonial literature necessarily draws upon the conventions of the empires it opposes.[11] With particular attention to the presentation of Babylon as the Prostitute in Rev 17–18, Smith adopts what she

---

7. Pippin 1992, 70–71.
8. As in Hylen 2020, 469–72; Huber with O'Day 2023, xlix–lii.
9. Byron and Lovelace 2016, 8–9.
10. Martin 2005.
11. S. Smith 2014; Darden 2015. See also Maier 2020, 508–11.

calls an ambi*veil*ent posture: John resists Rome by depicting it with the same misogynistic imagery Rome deploys against its subjects. Smith emphasizes her own compromised status as someone at once both victimized by and dependent upon exploitative economic structures. Darden focuses on the worship in the heavenly throne room (Rev 4–7), noting how John glorifies the Lamb by adopting patterns from imperial worship. In the end, both Smith and Darden use Revelation to read themselves and their own social settings, a mark of womanist interpretation. Neither embraces Revelation in an unqualified manner.[12]

Finally, queer interpretation emphasizes the distinctive perspectives of LGBTQ+ people, whose lives transgress dominant cultural assumptions regarding gender and sexuality. According to one landmark essay, queer interpretation emerged as a response to the AIDS crisis, which revealed the high stakes in the language societies use and avoid.[13] From a location both marginal and subject to violence, and thus sometimes pejoratively labeled as "queer," it pursues "vigorous and unmethodological dislocations of identity."[14] That is, queer readings challenge neat categories, distinctions, and assumptions by attending to the inconsistencies and strangenesses of texts. It understands queerness as "less an identity and more a disposition, a mode of examining the processes that cast certain people and practices into categories of normal and abnormal."[15] To read queerly can involve reading the Bible in ways that affirm the lives of sexual and gender minorities. But queer reading has come to embrace the queerness often imposed on LGBTQ+ persons as an analytical category in its own right, often engaging postmodern or deconstructionist cultural theory. As for Revelation, Lynn R. Huber describes her approach as "exploring how readers on the LGBTQIA+ spectrum experience and engage the text and . . . using the insights of queer theory, a critical and activist perspective, to engage the text."[16] Arguing that John "works within" conventional ancient gender norms, Huber and O'Day also point out how "his vision often pushes at and plays with traditional gender expectations."[17]

This chapter adopts all these concerns. Several ancient Jewish and Christian apocalypses resist the empires of their times. In so doing, they often employ conventional female symbols from biblical or other ancient antecedents. How should readers respond when Revelation relies upon misogynistic tropes? But

---

12. I have not foregrounded readings with postcolonial sensitivities by women who are not Black. See Kim 1999; Jacob and Kaalund 2016.

13. Berlant and Warner 1995, 344.

14. Edelman 1994, 114, quoted in Moxnes 2003, 5.

15. Marchal 2012, 210.

16. Huber with O'Day 2023, lvii.

17. Huber with O'Day 2023, lxxiii.

Revelation's engagement with gender does not end there. Symbols that readers have long assumed to be male may demonstrate conventional female qualities, and we find queerness within the story itself. As Pippin pointed out, Revelation deals in desire: a desire for dignity, a desire for freedom, a desire for vengeance, and desires related to sexuality. When it comes to sexuality, Revelation's symbols play surprising roles.

It is no longer in fashion for scholars to present their demographics. In this case, however, it seems self-evident that this straight, White, cisgender, physically able man should avoid prescribing what readers should make of Revelation and gender. My more modest goals are to point out the potentials other readers have identified and perhaps add a layer or two of additional insight, framing the questions that arise in theological perspective.

REVELATION'S FEMALE SYMBOLS

Revelation advances four female characters or symbols: Jezebel, the Woman Clothed with the Sun, Babylon the Prostitute, and the Bride representing the New Jerusalem. Three of these characters play prominent roles in the drama. Revelation presents Jezebel and the Prostitute as wholly negative figures, while the Woman Clothed with the Sun and the Bride are entirely positive. Each one is largely defined through her sexuality. A great deal of feminist interpretation has involved assessing and debating Revelation's value in light of how it represents women through these characters.[18]

Jezebel (2:20–23)

John applies the moniker Jezebel to an otherwise unknown prophet in Thyatira whom he condemns. He accuses her of the same offense committed by other competing prophets: eating idol-food and practicing *porneia*. But whereas John does not hurl sexualized invective against the so-called Balaam or the Nicolaitans, he accuses Jezebel's followers of committing adultery with her and envisions Jesus casting her on a bed and killing her children. In other words, John explicitly sexualizes her behavior.[19]

---

18. See the discussion in Hylen 2020, 467–75.

19. Jamie Davies argues that scholars who read the bed as a sick bed abandon the sexualized context of John's invective against Jezebel, therefore mixing the metaphor at work. "Though the image is deeply disturbing, it is the appropriate judgement for the fornication of false worship" (2023, 69–70). I find this moral assessment "deeply disturbing" as well.

The passage poses a few unresolvable interpretive questions and requires a bit of explication. First, Jezebel is not this prophet's real name. When John refers to Balaam and to Jezebel, he is appealing to biblical characters notorious for leading Israel into idolatry. The biblical Jezebel and Balaam die violent deaths.[20] Second, most interpreters understand the charges of promoting idol-food and *porneia* as pointing to the same thing: participation in worship of deities besides Israel's God and Jesus (see Num 31:16).[21] The Hebrew prophets commonly used sexual sin as a metaphor for idolatry. Third, scholars debate the meaning of Jezebel's bed. Most see it as a sickbed or deathbed, though others perceive the passage's language of *porneia* and adultery as a context that suggests sexual violence.[22] And fourth, although most readers understand Jezebel's children to be her followers, we cannot ignore the possibility that John is threatening Jezebel's biological children. This would be a minority reading, but it is possible that John envisions Jesus executing rape and murder against Jezebel and her children. If John's rhetoric were directed at an American politician, the FBI would be on the alert.

We lack sufficient information to resolve these questions, leaving us to deal with the language we have. John applies highly sexualized language to Jezebel in ways he does not to Balaam and the Nicolaitans. And the language is violent. It appears that Jezebel's sexualized degradation has to do as much with her gender as with the teaching she promotes. This is all the more evident when we read her in Revelation's broader context.

The Woman Clothed with the Sun (12:1–17)

The Woman Clothed with the Sun is an entirely positive character. She appears in the sky clothed with the sun, with the moon under her feet and a crown of twelve stars on her head. Many interpreters have turned to ancient astronomy and astrology to make sense of her. Indeed, the ancients paid great attention to the sky, building myths around its features and scanning it for portents. Some Jewish apocalyptic literature explores the sky, the seasons, and the sources of weather. The Woman Clothed with the Sun is experiencing birth pangs when the great red Dragon confronts her, waiting to devour the child as soon as she gives birth. The child is "snatched away and taken to God and to his throne," while the Woman flees to a refuge in the wilderness that God has provided.

---

20. Sarah Emanuel raises the possibility that the name Jezebel aims to emasculate a male prophet (2020, 116; see also Huber with O'Day 2023, 49).
21. But see Huber with O'Day 2023, 47–48.
22. See the discussion by Graybill 2023, 52–53.

The story of the Woman Clothed with the Sun pauses while a great conflict erupts in the sky. The great angel Michael and his angelic army defeat the Dragon and his angels, throwing them down to earth. During this conflict we learn that the Dragon represents Satan.

Cast to earth, the Dragon and his minions are free to do mischief. The Dragon again pursues the Woman, but again she is miraculously delivered and escapes to the wilderness. Even the earth (perhaps itself a female character) comes to the Woman's aid.[23] Having failed to destroy the Woman and her child, the Dragon becomes angry and makes war against "the rest of her children," who happen to be Jesus's followers.

This passage poses significant interpretive problems. Through the centuries, readers have proposed specific identities for the Woman. The Dragon first wants not the Woman but her child, leading readers to identify the child as the Messiah, Jesus. But the Woman gets most of the attention. Church tradition has tended to identify her as Mary or sometimes as the church. Critical scholars have likewise explored other associations, tending to gravitate toward Israel and its exile. Since a classic study by Adela Yarbro Collins, we cannot ignore resonances between this passage and other ancient myths that involve female deities being pursued by serpent-like adversaries, most notably the legend of Leto and Python. Just as Leto's child Apollo grows up to kill Python, so too Israel's Messiah ultimately defeats the Dragon.[24] We do not need to resolve the Woman's identity in order to discuss the presentation of gender here. And we may not need to choose one particular option in order to understand the story.[25] In the language of myth and poetry, we have "not so much alternatives as aspects."[26]

What can we say about the Woman? She is glorious, a heavenly figure crowned with stars. She is strong enough to flee after giving birth, but only after God rescues her child. God protects her and cares for her in the wilderness. The conflict initially revolves around her child, yet the Woman is the positive figure who holds our attention. Her importance—both to the Dragon as well as to the story—rests with the child she bears. God delivers the child and her, but they are separated at least for three and a half years (12:6, 14). This traumatic experience receives no attention.[27] What matters is that the Woman bears this particular child and receives miraculous deliverance.

23. See Barr 2009, 57; Huber with O'Day 2023, 179.

24. A. Yarbro Collins 1976; see also the lucid discussion of the myth in Whitaker 2023, 70–73.

25. See McKnight with Matchett 2023, 84–87.

26. Barr 2009, 60.

27. See Jacob and Kaalund 2016, 230.

Babylon the Prostitute (16:17–19:4)

Babylon the Prostitute is Revelation's most compelling female character. Not that I am defensive, but if you won't take this man's word for it, consider John's reaction: "When I saw her, I was greatly amazed" (17:6). Robyn J. Whitaker wonders whether "John might be a little *too* struck by what he sees," while Tina Pippin describes her as "seductive" and John's reaction to her as "erotic."[28]

But John should know better. Revelation twice announces Babylon's destruction prior to her appearance (14:8; 16:19). Just before John sees her, an angel prepares him to witness the Prostitute's judgment, sharing her corruption and the harm she inflicts on the Inhabitants of the Earth (17:1–2). Although she rides the Beast with its blasphemous names, that does not deter John from describing her luxurious clothes, glistening jewelry, and golden cup (17:4). To some degree, John's wonder is aroused because such opulence accompanies sexual sin, idolatry, and murder.

The Prostitute faces abject debasement and destruction. Revelation justifies her fate by dramatizing her many sins. She rides the Beast, reflecting their intimate relationship. I regard the Beast as a cipher for Rome's imperial authority and the Prostitute as the great city itself with its ties to diplomacy and commerce. After Rome's destruction of Jerusalem, Jewish authors begin to use the title "Babylon," the first empire to decimate the holy city, to denote Rome (see 1 Pet 5:13; 4 Ezra 3:1–2). Babylon the Prostitute drinks the saints' blood, sharing in the Beast's persecution of them (17:6; 18:24; see also 13:7). She corrupts everyone, engaging in *porneia* with the kings of the earth and intoxicating the Inhabitants of the Earth. Those who lament her destruction tell the story: rulers who benefit from her power; merchants who trade in luxuries, war goods, and human beings; and those who grow wealthy from sea trade. If Rome is enticing, it is because of her opulence. John wants readers to focus on her idolatry, corruption, exploitation, and violence.

For all these reasons, Babylon faces destruction just as the Dragon, the Beast, and the Other Beast do. But once again, only the Prostitute's demise is sexualized. Even the Beast hates the Prostitute, or at least its ten horns do: "they will make her desolate and naked; they will devour her flesh and burn her up with fire" (17:16). She suffers in proportion to her promiscuity (18:7).

Modern readers benefit from pondering the Prostitute's likely status because Revelation gives mixed signals. Although she relates to kings and merchants, and although she lives in luxury, John identifies her as a *pornē*, that is, not an elite

28. Whitaker 2023, 88; Pippin 1992, 65–66.

courtesan but a debased sex worker. By "dress[ing] her in imperial garb," John uses her to implicate Rome and its imperial system as a "Whore-Empress."[29] Most ancient *pornai* were enslaved, and the name tattooed on Babylon's forehead suggests an enslaved status. John trades in the stereotype that she is nasty.[30] As Lynn R. Huber (with Gail R. O'Day) points out, her violent and sexualized death was then, and still is now, an all too common fate for sex workers.[31]

In addition to the Beast, Revelation's symbolic system links Babylon the Prostitute to Jezebel and to the Bride. Jezebel and Babylon are both implicated in *porneia*, and both face violent, exposed deaths. Whereas Babylon rides the Beast, a sexually suggestive image, the Bride marries the Lamb. Both figures represent cities. Both are associated with precious metals and jewels. And while Babylon wears scarlet and purple with her jewels, a level of immodesty that would have been frowned upon in Roman society, the Bride is "adorned for her husband" (21:2), presumably in a modest white gown (albeit shining in this case) with little ornamentation. Her fine linen composed of the saints' righteousness (19:7–8) contrasts sharply with the Prostitute's cup filled with abominations and the saints' blood (17:4, 6). In contrast to the Prostitute, the Bride is pure.[32]

The Bride (19:5–21:5)

Revelation juxtaposes the Bride against the Prostitute even more directly than it does the Lamb against the Beast. Comparisons and contrasts of two value systems represented as two women amount to a standard literary and rhetorical motif both in the ancient Mediterranean generally and in biblical traditions and apocalyptic literature specifically.[33] Both of these female characters own a double identity by being paired with a city: the Prostitute is Babylon (i.e., Rome), and the Bride is the New Jerusalem. We first hear of Babylon's judgment before the Prostitute makes an appearance (16:19); we first learn of the Lamb's marriage to the Bride not long before she makes an entrance (19:7). We also first hear of the New Jerusalem far earlier in the book (3:12). As we have seen, the Prostitute and the Bride contrast one another in terms of their clothing, but they are also both associated with precious stones and metals. (We will say more about this comparison.) Obviously, the Prostitute faces judgment and destruction, while the Bride endures forever. John calls his reader/hearers

29. Huber 2013, 61, 67.
30. Huber with O'Day, 2023, 248–49; see also Glancy and Moore 2014.
31. Huber with O'Day, 2023, 259.
32. Huber with O'Day 2023, 249, 288–90, 326–37.
33. Rossing 1999, 17–59; Humphrey 1995.

to "come out" from Babylon, language that assumes their implication with it. But Revelation values the ultimate good as entering the New Jerusalem.

The Bride is an entirely positive character, but that does not exempt the symbol from critique. For although the Bride is glorious (21:23), she does not act, and she speaks only one word throughout the entire book: "Come" (22:17). This is the only instance of direct speech from a female character in Revelation. We also overhear Babylon's hubristic inner thoughts (18:7). Like the Woman Clothed with the Sun, the Bride is important because of her relationship to masculine characters; the former bears a child, while the latter marries the child after he has grown. All four female characters in Revelation are determined by their sexual status: promiscuous woman, mother, prostitute, and bride.

Even the Bride's glory is subject to examination. The Bride features pearly gates, golden streets, and bejeweled foundations. She bears fresh water and fruit. And her wedding is a cause for rejoicing. Light illumines her every moment. But if I may write tongue in cheek, is she really all that captivating? John does not express amazement at her appearance. Her wedding feast is disgusting, as it involves birds devouring the flesh of those who fight against the Lamb (19:17–21). As Huber points out, the imagery is gruesome. John uses the word *sarx* (flesh) five times in 19:18 alone.[34] Some commentators refuse to identify the wedding feast with this grim scene, even treating the two as inhabiting different scenes or representing separate meals.[35] We might describe that treatment as optimistic at best.

Taste is subjective, but I find the Bride to be less attention grabbing than the Prostitute.[36] Both women are identified with precious metals and stones, things that are cold and hard. According to Roman convention, the Bride wears a garment of fine linen that she has woven herself. Revelation identifies this gleaming fabric as "the righteous deeds of the saints" (19:8).[37] The Bride, after all, dwells in perpetual light. But whereas the Prostitute trades in fine linen, she does not wear white, choosing colorful garments instead. The Bride offers fresh water and fruit, a new variety once a month (22:1–2), while the Prostitute drinks wine and blood (18:6) and trades in a rich array of spices, staples, and meats: "cinnamon, spice, incense, myrrh, frankincense, wine, olive oil, choice flour and wheat, cattle and sheep" (18:13). At the risk of overgeneralization, the Prostitute offers a richer variety of textures and tastes than does the Bride. This is probably John's point. While the Prostitute is portrayed as disgusting in many respects, John acknowledges her appeal. After all, the Beast has its own temporary ad-

34. Huber 2023, 300.
35. As separate meals, see Reddish 2001, 369–70.
36. Carey 2009; see also Pippin 1992, 82.
37. Huber 2013, 77–78.

vantages—"Who is like the beast, and who can fight against it?" (13:4)—and no one can buy or sell without bearing the mark of the Beast (13:17). In elevating the Bride and debasing the Prostitute, Revelation adopts an ascetic aesthetic.

Checking In

Feminist debates concerning Revelation's female characters have tended to revolve around a cluster of topoi: liberation, misogyny, and literary convention. Interpreters have pitted Revelation's perceived liberative or counterimperial potential over against the rhetorical deployment of reductionist and misogynist symbols or metaphors. According to Pippin, "The roles of women in the male myth of the Apocalypse are virgin, whore, and mother—beloved and hated—but always under male control and domination."[38] The complicating factor involves weighing the moral value of a literary trope common to biblical and other ancient cultures: women and their sexuality as metaphors for nations, cities, and values. Readers of Isaiah (1:21), Jeremiah (2:20; 3:1–9; 13:27), Ezekiel (16:1–58; 23:1–49), and Hosea (4:12–18) recognize the convention of representing Israel's unfaithfulness as female prostitution and then framing divine judgment as sexual violence.[39] Following Athalya Brenner, we might label this convention "pornoprophetics."[40] For that matter, although Victory (*Nikē*) was a female deity, Roman iconography routinely depicted military conquest as the sexual capture of women.[41] Thus, contrasting ideal women over against debased women was a stock rhetorical technique.[42]

Some feminist commentators acknowledge the dangers of this literary pattern, but they weigh other factors just as heavily or even more so. Schüssler Fiorenza, the classic debate and conversation partner among Revelation's feminist interpreters, advances her weighting system explicitly: "Such a liberationist reading of Revelation's rhetoric subordinates the book's depiction of cosmic destruction and holy war to its desire for justice, which is repeated throughout the book. It puts in the foreground those rhetorical features of the text that aim at moving the audience to practical engagement in this struggle for God's qualitatively new world of salvation."[43] This framing leaves open lines for rebuttal. Can a book be liberationist for women when it trades in misogyny? And

38. Pippin 1992, 83.
39. A. Yarbro Collins 1984, 121.
40. Emanuel 2020, 116, citing Brenner 1997, 153–74.
41. Lopez 2008.
42. Again, Rossing 1999, 17–59; Humphrey 1995.
43. Schüssler Fiorenza 1991, 122.

is Revelation all that liberationist to begin with, considering its depictions of decimation for the world and most of its inhabitants?

In my view, these debates have largely resolved into one affirmation and one area of ambiguity. Revelation's symbolic women "function as metaphors and signs rather than any attempt on John's behalf at depicting real women."[44] But as Hanna Stenström argues, "When it comes to gendered symbols, none of them is 'only a symbol.'"[45] Symbols do important cultural work and should not be minimized. This affirmation effectively cancels the argument that Revelation's symbols are necessarily less potent for good or harm than its other dimensions. This general perspective lends itself to an ambiguity that marks many feminist and womanist interpretations, often inflected through postcolonial theory. Revelation may inspire resistance to oppressive systems, but it also carries the baggage of imperial misogyny.[46]

Gender beyond Women

As with the rest of society, biblical scholarship has taken its time in recognizing that gender does not apply only to women. Moreover, having opened the door to ambiguity regarding Revelation's presentation of female characters, we might be ready to query ambiguity regarding gender beyond simple masculine/feminine categories.[47]

To my knowledge, Tina Pippin has offered the first published interrogation of masculinity in Revelation. Interpreters have long struggled with Rev 14:1–5, which presents the Lamb's 144,000 followers singing a new and exclusive song. These followers "have not defiled themselves with women, for they are virgins" (14:4). Commentators have long struggled to make sense of the identity and chastity of the 144,000. Pippin acknowledges that Adela Yarbro Collins had already attributed to John "possibly hatred and fear both of women and of one's own body."[48] Over a century ago, R. H. Charles opened the possibility, which seems likely to me, that this group represented an "elite" assembly among the countless saints. Charles also reported a consensus view that the group *"must embrace both men and women."* But he then acknowledges that the group's refusal to "defile themselves with women" requires that women

---

44. Huber 2013, 57.
45. Stenström 2009, 52; quoted in Hylen 2020, 476; see also Paul 2001.
46. See Marshall 2009; Stenström 2009; S. Smith 2014; Darden 2015; Carey 2006.
47. Huber 2003, liii. For a brief summary of this work, see Hylen 2020, 478–80.
48. Pippin 1992, 50, citing A. Yarbro Collins 1987, 89.

must be excluded, an apparent contradiction within his own commentary.[49] Pippin agrees, describing the New Jerusalem as a male-only establishment.[50] In her later work with J. Michael Clark, Pippin characterizes the singing in 14:2–3 as a "virtual gay men's chorus."[51] Pippin also recognizes the element of male desire in the command to "Come out of her, my people" (18:4) and the recurrence of the verb "come" in 22:17.[52] It seems Revelation's elite force is all male, and they do not "come" with women.

Things get pretty queer once Revelation's masculinity is no longer taken for granted. The one like a Son of Man is coded as masculine and a warrior. His appearance is so intense that John crumbles in fear (1:17–18). What symbol is more masculine than a sword that vanquishes one's enemies? Yet, some commentators note that this intimidating Son of Man figure also has breasts, not simply a chest, that are bound like those of a woman.[53] Sarah Emanuel writes that "Revelation's Christ has boobs," and after assessing Jesus as "Christ in drag" she observes "the Son of Man's resemblance to the well-dressed, well-breasted Whore."[54]

Revelation's Jesus is vulnerable in ways Roman men conventionally should not be; he is a lamb and not a lion, a wounded one that has been slaughtered. This is hardly an image for a victorious warrior. When Revelation describes Jesus as the one who was "pierced" (1:7), it again runs afoul of ancient (and current) ideals that a man's body should be firm and impermeable; he should be the agent and not the object of penetration.[55] Christians faced no choice but to account for Jesus's crucifixion and the stigma that attended it. Revelation interprets Jesus's vulnerability as his faithful witness (1:5), the weapon with which he vanquishes evil.

The 144,000 inherit the New Jerusalem. But do women inherit it as well? I am inclined to think so, but that interpretation requires distinguishing between the 144,000 and the great multitude in chapter 7. In any case, the 144,000 are all men. In one sense, they *enter* the Lamb's Bride; in another, they themselves *constitute* the Bride. We should note that although many interpreters assume an identification between the Bride and the church, Revelation does

---

49. Charles 1920, 2:8.

50. Pippin 1992, 50.

51. Pippin and Clark 2006, 759.

52. Pippin 1992, 82.

53. Huber with O'Day 2023, 21–22; citing Rainbow 2007. Huber also cites Stephen D. Moore's fascinating observation concerning "bitch tits" in steroid-enhanced bodybuilders (Moore 1995, 52–53).

54. Emanuel 2020, 183–85.

55. Emanuel 2020, 180–81.

not make this identity explicit. The book speaks to seven churches but never mentions a church in the larger, more universal capital-C sense. In any case, because biblical authors identify Israel, named after a patriarch, as God's bride, and because the ancients commonly personified male-dominated cities and dominions as women, Revelation's reader/hearers would readily have understood the Prostitute/Bride contrast. Just as the prophetic Israel-as-wife convention to some degree feminizes Israelite men, the Prostitute-Bride motif suggests a feminization of those who inhabit these cities.

These suggestions are more than mere play. They open conversations about how Revelation communicates divine agency (or perhaps power), what models followers of Jesus should emulate, and how we want to imagine these things ourselves. Revelation presents God and the one like a Son of Man as fearsome warriors. But when Revelation promises to reveal a fierce lion, the mortally wounded but risen Lamb appears in its stead (5:5–6). The Lamb's wounds indicate penetration, a feature distinctively unmasculine in the Greco-Roman world.[56] (The same likely applies to the Beast in 13:3, 8.) The Lamb's followers imitate the Lamb with their testimony or martyrdom (1:5; 2:10; 3:14; 12:11; 17:6) and their prophecy (1:3; 19:10). Yet, John and his male colleagues apparently prefer one another's company (14:4–5), struggle to control their own desire (18:4), and bear the ambivalent relationship of at once *being* the Lamb's Bride and *entering* her. For all the intensity, blood, and glory ascribed to them, the Lamb and its followers demonstrate a great deal of vulnerability. As in 4 Maccabees, suffering is the path to victory.[57]

WHAT READERS DO

This chapter does not prescribe how readers should respond to Revelation's gender dynamics. Nor does it break much ground in the interpretation of these issues. Instead, it relies heavily on the work of other scholars, offering judgments here and there. I am including this chapter because Revelation's gender troubles and possibilities remain among the weightiest objections to the book. I have no intention of explaining away such problems.

In my view, scholarship has moved beyond binary "good and bad" ethical and theological assessments of Revelation's female characters. Once we accept that Revelation appropriates some of the most damaging and perduring scripts concerning women, we free ourselves from any compulsion to explain them away. Revelation can envision male and female agents, but its female agents

56. Frilingos 2003, 261–65.
57. Harris 2019, 63–64.

function in ways determined exclusively in relation to sexuality—promiscuity and prostitution versus motherhood and bridehood. These roles split the imagination into dualistic oppositions, a reality that pervades Revelation in every respect but is particularly dangerous for women. Feminist and feminist-identified interpreters largely integrate this perspective into their readings. Yet they generally continue to engage the book in ambi*veilent* ways, often drawing upon feminist and postcolonial perspectives.[58]

None of this is to suggest that scholars have "arrived" at a unified or fixed perspective. However, more recent scholarship moves us beyond the kind of conversation that plagues biblical interpretation in popular discourse: some people must have a "pure" Bible at any cost, while others reject the Bible or parts of it out of hand. With few exceptions, we treat other texts with nuance, not only teasing out their gifts and limitations but also seeking to account for them.

Interpretations that query masculinity in particular and gender and sexuality in general also hold promise, particularly at our fraught cultural moment. A great deal remains to be explored concerning the biology and psychology of gender and sexuality. At the same time, queer-baiting activists deploy the Bible to insist that there are only two genders and that only particular behavior patterns are appropriate to each.[59] To date, biblical scholars have contributed manifold queer interpretations, but while pro-gay biblical apologetics have achieved cultural salience, publications oriented toward queer interpretation have not achieved similar impact. Yet one readily understands the potential benefits that would occur when many readers appreciate the queerness of biblical characters and tropes. The Bible, whatever we mean when we use the term, does not present gender in the neat packages some people assert. Certainly Revelation does not.

There is value in demonstrating Revelation's queerness. Attending to Revelation's gendered complexity, perhaps especially its presentation of Jesus, provides an imaginative resource for persons who live beyond prevailing gender norms. It holds promise for us cishet (cisgender, heterosexual) folks too. None of us fulfills others' gendered expectations (or our own) perfectly; to greater and lesser degrees, many of us choose not to. Queer interpretation extends the possibility of imagining and cherishing these dimensions of ourselves and for undermining rigid codes that serve us so poorly.

58. S. Smith 2014.
59. Schearing and Ziegler 2014; Du Mez 2021.

Violence and the Bloody Lamb

S OME TIME AGO, A GRASSROOTS THEOLOGIAN invited me to lunch. His question: what's the matter with Revelation? As a pacifist, this person regarded Revelation as somehow different from the rest of the New Testament because of its violent imagery.[1] Could I, as a biblical scholar, offer some perspective that could help him sort through his problem?

For scholars and laypeople alike, the question of violence dominates our reflections on Revelation. People criticize Revelation for several reasons. It's too otherworldly and world denying, some say.[2] It offers "pie in the sky" salvation rather than a vision for living in the world, others suggest. Over the past thirty years, as noted in the previous chapter, feminist interpreters have provided conflicting responses to Revelation's female symbols. Some have assessed Revelation as irredeemably misogynistic.[3] Others have noted that Revelation shows no interest in transforming the world, only a program for destroying God's enemies.[4] Among theologically inclined interpreters and many others, the problem of violence is hard to avoid. "Most scholarly interpreters," notes Susan E. Hylen, "treat the violence of Revelation as a problem to be addressed."[5] John E. Phelan Jr. claims that "any appreciation for Revela-

---

1. Despite the other virtues of his argument, I shudder when Richard A. Spencer speaks of "the introduction of a concept of God that is remarkably like the Yahweh Sebaoth of the ancient Hebrew faith into New Covenant Scriptures" (2001, 72). My lunch companion shared this impression that somehow the Old Testament (Jewish?) God is more violent than the (Christian?) God of Jesus, and that Revelation's failure involves not being "Christian" enough.

2. For a counterargument, see Rossing 2005, 165–82.

3. Especially influential have been Pippin 1992; Schüssler Fiorenza 1991, esp. 117–39; and A. Yarbro Collins, 1993. See also the essays collected in Levine 2009. Observe the very different inflection that occurs when a womanist interpreter like Clarice J. Martin adds race and class to gender (2005). I find particularly compelling the treatment of Hylen 2003 (see also Hylen 2020).

4. Keller 2005, 36.

5. Hylen 2011.

tion must be tempered by reflections on what some might call the 'dark side' of Revelation."[6]

In my experience, Revelation's interpreters tend to divide into two opposing camps: they either call out the violence in Revelation as problematic, or they justify why Revelation's violence makes theological and ethical sense.[7] One commentator even asks "why this divine violence goes hand in hand with the nonviolence of the earthly Jesus and his followers."[8] While many interpreters have addressed the question, few actually pause to articulate precisely what we mean when we call Revelation violent. At one obvious level, Revelation is a text and specifically a story. It cannot "perform" violence in any literal sense. Revelation does depict and refer to violence, however. Not only does Revelation describe violence by evil agents, but most interpreters believe it attributes violence to God and to Jesus. Some would say the book even fosters the desire for violence within its audience. More debatable is the question whether a literary text can actually *cause* violence. Surely some people have used Revelation to justify their own violent behavior. Then again, most of Revelation's readers have not done so.

If few have taken the time to spell out what we mean by calling Revelation violent, still fewer have sketched the diverse dimensions of the question. If Revelation describes violence, portrays God (or Jesus) as violent, encourages believers to pursue violence, or bends our imaginations toward violence, these issues require our attention. This chapter models one response to the problem by teasing out multiple dimensions of the question.

JUSTIFIABLE VIOLENCE?

Ancient readers were not especially concerned about violence in Revelation. They worried more about the book's authorship, its impenetrability, and, especially after Constantine, its subversive political potential. But modern readers frequently condemn Revelation on account of its violent outlook. Friedrich Nietzsche regarded Revelation as "the most rabid outburst of vindictiveness in all recorded history," while D. H. Lawrence could not abide its "grandiose scheme for wiping out and annihilating everybody who wasn't of the elect."[9] The psychologist Carl

6. Phelan 2004, 66.

7. Hylen 2011, 777; see also Skaggs and Doyle 2007. Exceptions to this pattern would include those who acknowledge Revelation's violence as problematic without condemning the book outright. For one classic case, see A. Yarbro Collins 1984, 161.

8. Decock 2012, 185. I find Decock's posing of the question limited in that it assumes Jesus's own rhetoric was nonviolent.

9. Nietzsche 1956 [1887], 185; Lawrence 1980 [1931], 63.

Gustav Jung believed that John of Patmos suffered from powerful internal conflicts and thus attributed Revelation's violence less to "a metaphysical mystery than to the outburst of long pent-up feelings such as can be frequently observed in people who strive for perfection."[10] Some New Testament scholars share this view. W. D. Davies has rejected Revelation's "abortive hatred that can only lead, not to [the Roman authorities'] redemption, but to their destruction."[11] John Dominic Crossan has put it this way: "The peace donkey of the historical Jesus in the Gospels trumps the warhorse of the apocalyptic Jesus in Revelation."[12]

Some readers argue that Revelation's violence is justified. We might recall from chapter 2, for example, Allan A. Boesak, who offers a straightforward and credible defense. Having endured persecution, imprisonment, and torture at the hands of South Africa's apartheid regime, Boesak wrote, "If [Christ's] cloak is spattered with blood, it is the blood of his enemies, the destroyers of the earth and of his children."[13] Boesak does not deny that Revelation attributes violence to the Lamb, but he regards that violence as just. The elimination of injustice may require divine violence.

Also influenced by Boesak, Brian K. Blount considers Miroslav Volf's take on the question. Having observed the horrific conflict that engulfed the Balkan states in the 1990s, Volf asserts that the idea of "God's refusal to judge will invariably die . . . in a scorched land, soaked in the blood of the innocent."[14] For his part, Blount holds out for nonviolence. Despite the testimonies of Boesak and Volf, Blount stresses that in Revelation neither believers nor the Lamb himself deploys violence. Rather, both "conquer" through their testimony.[15] Boesak and Volf argue that divine justice may require the violent overthrow of oppressors, a position Blount acknowledges but ultimately cannot accept. If we commit ourselves to belief in God's passion for justice, might not that very conviction tie us to the possibility of divine violence?[16]

VIOLENT AGENTS, VIOLENT DESIRE

Most readers acknowledge the presence of violence in Revelation, particularly violence attributed to God, with some condemning it and others defending it.

---

10. Jung 1954, 125, quoted in Klassen, 1966, 301.
11. W. D. Davies 1962, 2:176, cited in Klassen 1966.
12. Crossan 2015, 37.
13. Boesak 1987, 124.
14. Volf 1993, 304; quoted in Blount 2009, 5.
15. Blount 2009, 5.
16. O'Brien 2008, 117–24. See also Mangina 2010, 96–97.

Others, however, have acknowledged that Revelation depicts violence but have denied that it attributes that violence to God, Jesus, or Jesus's followers.

Revelation does clearly narrate violent actions on the part of evil supernatural powers. The Dragon, who is Satan (12:9), pursues the Woman Clothed with the Sun in order to devour her child (see 12:4). The Beast makes war against the Lamb (17:14) and his followers (11:7; 13:7–8), while the Prostitute who rides the Beast drinks the blood of the saints and of Jesus's witnesses (17:6). In an image that suggests something profound about the relationship between evil and violence, the Beast even turns its violence against its ally the Prostitute (17:16).

Revelation also attributes violence to ordinary people, those it calls "the Inhabitants of the Earth." They shed the blood of saints and prophets (16:6), and the martyred saints cry out for vengeance against them (6:9–10). The Inhabitants of the Earth also rejoice when the Two Witnesses are killed (11:10). While Revelation primarily attributes violence to the Dragon, the Beast, and the Prostitute, the Inhabitants of the Earth make willing accomplices.

But what about violence on the part of God and God's people? Central to a nonviolent interpretation is the figure of the Lamb, Revelation's most prominent way of depicting the risen Jesus. According to Loren L. Johns, Revelation does not call believers to pursue violence in any way, but it does include "messianic war motifs." Those images, including the double-edged sword protruding from the Lamb's mouth (1:16; 2:12; 19:15, 21), must be understood in the context of Revelation's Lamb Christology. The Lamb's initial appearance is particularly telling: John is told to expect the Lion, but instead there appears the Lamb "standing as if it had been slaughtered" (5:5–6). The double-edged sword symbolizes the Lamb's faithful testimony, not an actual weapon (1:5).[17] According to this line of interpretation with the Lamb as Revelation's "controlling metaphor" for Jesus, the book can hardly be accused of promoting violence. Instead, the Lamb's nonviolent testimony trumps the imagery of destruction and chaos. This view seems especially congenial for pacifist interpreters but also for many others who share it as well.[18] As Barbara R. Rossing argues, in Revelation war is waged against God's people and not practiced by the Lamb or his followers; even when Jesus does "make war" (2:16; 19:11), he does so nonviolently.[19]

One problem for the nonviolent Lamb argument involves how the Lamb uses the double-edged sword. The risen Jesus threatens to "make war" with

---

17. Johns 2005, 204–5. For Johns's fully developed argument, see Johns 2003.

18. Kraybill 2010, 135–36. In addition to Johns (2003 and 2005) and Kraybill, see Anabaptist interpreters Swartley 2006, 332–39; and Yeatts 2003, esp. 115–19.

19. Rossing 2004, 121; see also Blount 2009, 5.

the sword against the Nicolaitans, a group John vehemently opposes (2:16). Later in the great final battle, the Lamb strikes down his enemies with the sword (19:15, 21). Indeed, the Lamb's robe is dipped—or better, dyed—in blood (19:13).[20] Given such imagery, it is far from obvious that the Lamb is entirely nonviolent. Further emphasizing this is the one like the Son of Man, another symbol for Jesus, who previously in chapter 14 deployed a sickle to harvest the grapes of the earth, threw the grapes into "the great winepress of the wrath of God," and produced a quantity of blood that pooled up to the height of a horse's bridle for two hundred miles (14:17–20).[21] The scene in Rev 19 repeats this winepress imagery (19:15). Moreover, the martyrs receive assurance that their desire for vengeance will be fulfilled (6:9–11).

Some interpreters regard the blood on the Lamb's garment as his own, a reminder of his faithful sacrifice.[22] Ted Grimsrud argues that Revelation's references to blood always indicate the blood of Jesus or his followers, never that of God's enemies.[23] (He does not address the blood that pollutes the earth and the waters in Rev 8:7, 9; 11:6.) It is through their own blood that these actors overcome evil (1:5; 5:9; 12:11).[24] According to Grimsrud, the enormous amount of blood indicated in 14:20 communicates "that the self-sacrificial love of Jesus and his followers is abundant enough to heal the countless multitudes!"[25]

To be sure, those who follow the Lamb do not pursue violence within Revelation, nor does the book encourage them to do so. Instead, they "conquer" the Dragon through the blood of the Lamb and through their testimony, risking death for the sake of their witness (12:11; see also 2:13; 13:7). In a violent world where people are slaughtered and taken captive, the saints are called simply to resist (13:10), a matter we will explore in chapter 9. The letters to the assemblies in chapters 2–3 show that the saints must reject those "Christian" teachers who conflict with John, but the letters do not call them to use violence to do so. Instead, their call is to remain faithful and loving, to resist (e.g., 2:19), and to keep their garments clean from the contaminations of idolatry (3:4).[26] As

---

20. On this translation issue, see the discussion in Koester 2014, 755.

21. P. Middleton argues that Revelation's Jesus is both the Lamb and the Lion, executing God's violent judgment in these scenes (2018, esp. 121–31).

22. Nicklas 2012, 243.

23. Grimsrud 2022, 161. If Christ's robe is "dyed" in blood, it is more likely to be his own blood than if we understand the robe as "dipped" in blood. See the discussion in Koester 2014, 755–56.

24. Grimsrud 2022, 162.

25. Grimsrud 2022, 167.

26. The term "Christian," though perhaps helpful in indicating persons devoted to Jesus,

Phelan puts it, Revelation "insists that we [contemporary readers] follow the lamb in suffering and witness and leave ultimate judgment to God."[27]

BLOODTHIRSTY?

Although Revelation calls believers to faithful witness rather than violent resistance, it does give voice to the desire for violence on the part of its audience. Often underappreciated, this may be the aspect of Revelation that motivates many of its critics. One could well argue that the revealing of the Lamb in place of the promised Lion "trains" Revelation's readers to abandon force and the desire for violence (5:1–14). However, Revelation soon gives direct voice to the desire for vengeance with John seeing the heavenly altar in chapter 6, under which reside the souls of the martyrs. These martyrs cry out for vengeance in 6:10: "Sovereign Lord, holy and true, how long will it be before you judge and avenge our blood on the inhabitants of the earth?" The martyrs do not receive direct assurance that vengeance is coming, but they are told to wait as one plague after another strikes the earth and it inhabitants. This cry for vengeance provides the first example of a fascinating literary and rhetorical technique. Rather than express the desire for violence and vengeance directly, Revelation displaces those desires to heavenly voices. Moreover, the calls for vengeance and celebrations of violence occur precisely at the book's most disturbing moments, and they attribute the infliction of suffering to God's justice.

The martyrs' plea for vengeance does not occur in a literary vacuum. It follows immediately upon the devastation that accompanies Revelation's notorious four riders (6:1–7). A quarter of the earth has been given over to violence, famine, and disease, yet the martyrs want more. On several occasions, Revelation follows moments of devastation with songs of praise. For example, after the ascension of the Two Witnesses, an earthquake kills seven thousand people, who wind up giving glory to God. Immediately after this catastrophe, heavenly voices break out in song, including the lines:

> The nations raged,
>> but your wrath has come,
>> and the time for judging the dead,

---

is anachronistic. John never uses the term and in fact may not have conceived of a distinctive movement, such as the one that we would later call Christianity. As John W. Marshall puts it, "I don't see any Christians" in Revelation (2005, 35). On the other hand, John distinguishes assemblies from synagogues and identifies "followers of the Lamb." Thus, Revelation may reflect an emerging "Christian" identity. For more on the question, see Marshall 2005.

27. Phelan 2004, 82.

> for rewarding your servants, the prophets and saints and all who
>   fear your name,
>   both small and great,
>   and for destroying those who destroy the earth. (11:18)

Likewise, when blood flows as high as a horse's bridle for two hundred miles and we hear that seven angels are prepared to pour out the final round of plagues, those who have conquered the Beast offer praise: "Just and true are your ways, King of the nations!" (15:3). After the first three plagues, which include the annihilation of every sea creature and the transformation of the earth's waters into blood, an angel declares God's justice, an acclamation echoed by another heavenly voice (16:5–7). Similar praise accompanies the destruction of Babylon the great city (18:1–8; 19:1–5). After all, God's "judgments are true and just" (19:2).

In Revelation, this literary technique of displacement uses heavenly voices, including glorified saints, to interpret divine violence as a justified response to human injustice (see 6:9–11). There is no denying that the songs of praise name divine violence, as many explicitly attribute human and cosmic suffering to divine judgment. Moreover, they tend to accompany some of the most intense portrayals of devastation within the book. One such song introduces the bowl judgments, what David L. Barr calls "a successive bombardment upon the earth" (15:3–4).[28] Another is inserted between the third and the fourth bowl (16:5–7). The seventh bowl opens the destruction of Babylon the great city, an event that leads to two cycles of praise (18:1–8; 19:1–5). These songs of praise may be designed to mitigate potential revulsion within Revelation's audience. But what if John accurately anticipates that some readers will find the book's violence objectionable?[29] By removing the cries for vengeance and commendations of divine violence from John's own voice to those of the martyrs and the heavenly beings, Revelation invites the audience to sing along.

Realistic Violence

Revelation's violence may be part of a larger story, it may be fictional, and it may represent a mere desire for vengeance rather than a call to violent action. Nevertheless, we have seen that some interpreters regard violence as a reasonable and justifiable response to injustice. Others acknowledge the presence of violence in Revelation and *do not* endorse the concept of divine violence, yet

---

28. Barr 1998, 131.
29. Carey 1999, 128–32.

these same interpreters defend Revelation as emphasizing the violence that was characteristic of Roman imperial domination. In this perspective, Revelation does not promote violence but rather depicts imperial violence realistically.

David A. deSilva offers a particularly sophisticated example of this approach. He acknowledges that Revelation has been charged with "reinscribing" the dominant culture's violence in depicting the demise of the evil forces and their followers, and he does not deny the charge. However, he relegates Revelation's violence to "a secondary position, almost as a cleanup operation," Instead, it is "self-giving love and self-sacrificing witness" that amount to Revelation's "ultimate argument."[30] Revelation's nonviolent witness occurs "in the face of" the inherently violent practices of society. Revelation counters the violent and exploitative nature of Roman culture with a nonviolent witness.[31]

Revelation unsparingly reveals the violence of Roman imperial culture. Rome promised peace, but Roman peace implied the exploitation of native populations through the threat of military force. In the Roman province of Asia, the location of Revelation's seven assemblies in modern-day Turkey, local elites would go to great lengths to glorify the Roman emperor. Having petitioned the Roman Senate for permission, cities would put on festivals and build statues and temples in honor of one emperor or another. Revelation acknowledges this reality by describing the "whole earth" following the Beast (13:3). The Beast receives worship: "Who is like the beast, and who can fight against it?" (13:4). But of course, the Beast, however admired it may be, is hideous. From its first introduction, readers encounter the blasphemous names on its head (13:1). Soon they hear its "haughty and blasphemous words" (13:5–6; see also Dan 7:8, 11, 20) and learn of its murderous campaign against the saints (13:7). How, some readers would argue, can we imagine God's judgment of such a bloody regime without violent outcomes? If "the coming of God and the Lamb must spell the end of the world in its present constitution," what would that look like?[32] Surely a world simultaneously held together and ripped apart by violence will not go away quietly.

According to this reasoning, Revelation does what other literary apocalypses do: it "uncovers" (the literal meaning of the verb *apokalyptō*) the truth about the world its audience inhabits. Rome asserted the rhetoric of glory, claiming the moon and the stars, literally, for itself and its emperor. In apocalyptic literature, cosmic imagery often bears political connotations. Ancient

30. DeSilva 2009, 342.
31. DeSilva 2009, 342–43.
32. Mangina 2010, 107.

people saw astral events as portents of political change, just as Matthew interprets the star of Bethlehem as the sign of a king's birth (Matt 2:1–11). Revelation itself identifies Jesus as "the root and the descendant of David, the bright morning star" (Rev 22:16). A star appears in Roman coinage as a symbol of the deification of Julius Caesar.[33] Revelation appropriates the symbols of Roman imperial rhetoric by writing the story of Jesus in the stars.

Revelation acknowledges Roman glory, but it does so in a subversive way. We see this most clearly as John introduces the Prostitute. Many interpreters have noted that Revelation's violence takes on a misogynist cast, particularly in the sexualized violence against Jezebel (2:22–23) and the Prostitute (17:16).[34] As was the case with the not-Lion-but-Lamb, we must pay attention to the sequence in which the Prostitute is introduced. Revelation 17:1–6 begins by presenting her identity, her judgment, and her association with the Beast. The passage concludes by reinforcing her identity and portraying her as drunk with the blood of martyrs. Within this framework, John also writes of her luxurious clothing and jewelry. The strategy is hardly subtle, and the effect is clear: what looks glorious is actually murderous and profane. When the Beast and its allies strip the Prostitute naked, devour her, and burn her (17:16), some would argue that this only shows "the self-destructive nature of evil."[35] In doing so, these readers may overlook the next verse, which attributes all these things to God's will. Revelation, in this interpretation, uncovers the inherent violence in the Roman imperial system, whatever its glorious pretensions.

Rhetorical Violence and the Work of Resistance

Perhaps the most popular way to defend Revelation against the charge that it is a violent book involves pointing out the obvious: Revelation is a book, not a sword, and the violence it depicts is rhetorical or symbolic rather than actual. Moreover, Revelation's violent imagery often draws upon conventional biblical language. Therefore, some argue, readers should read *through* the violence to the deeper meaning of Revelation's call for its audience to avoid injustice and idolatry.

This argument takes several forms, but it has been most classically articulated by Elisabeth Schüssler Fiorenza. Schüssler Fiorenza reads Revelation in terms of power and justice, with a judgment that includes destruction for "all those

---

33. Koester 2014, 843–44.
34. See n. 3.
35. Boxall 2006, 249. To be clear, Boxall acknowledges the offensive nature of this passage.

who 'corrupt the earth'" (quoting 11:18).[36] Following this judgment comes a renewed creation marked by "the glory, life, light, and happiness of God's empire of salvation."[37] Any ethical assessment of Revelation must begin by recognizing the book as a response to oppression, foregrounding its liberating message and allowing the destructive moments to recede. To this point, Schüssler Fiorenza's interpretation resembles those that justify Revelation on the grounds that its violence serves justice, but she is doing something different. She is naming some parts of the book as more essential than others because the "symbolic universe of Revelation" seeks justice.[38] Schüssler Fiorenza further recognizes the potential for Revelation's gendered symbolism to undermine its liberating message, a problem within Revelation's own rhetoric and not simply among its readers.[39] In her later work, however, and in response to Tina Pippin, Schüssler Fiorenza makes a different case.[40] She argues that Revelation's gendered language is indeed dangerous, but readers should recognize that its true purpose was to undermine idolatry. The Prostitute image condemns a city, not a woman, and it does so in conventional (i.e., biblical) language directed against idolatry.[41]

This appeal to rhetoric and symbol takes many other forms. Wes Howard-Brook and Anthony Gwyther argue that Revelation's violent imagery is rhetorically *necessary*, a version of "tough love." They write, "If empire threatened traitors with execution, 'heaven' had to offer the more powerful threat of the lake of fire. If empire offered the wares of global commerce, 'heaven' had to be covered with gold and jewels and choice fruit the year round. These are metaphors, not literal descriptions."[42] Others, however, see metaphor and symbol as strategic choices rather than unavoidable conventions or stylistic necessities. In another reading through an explicitly rhetorical hermeneutic, David A. deSilva tends to defend John's larger aims while also recognizing that John could have done things differently. In appealing to violence, particularly gendered violence, John may challenge the domination systems of his day, but he also reinscribes them.[43]

In my view, appeals to the symbolic or rhetorical function of Revelation's violence often carry a serious deficiency. They fail to appreciate the power of

---

36. Schüssler Fiorenza 1991, 120.
37. Schüssler Fiorenza 1991, 121.
38. Schüssler Fiorenza 1991, 122.
39. Schüssler Fiorenza 1991, 130–31.
40. Pippin 1992.
41. Schüssler Fiorenza 1998, 219–22. See also Rossing 1999; 2004, 132–33.
42. Howard-Brook and Gwyther 1999, 267.
43. DeSilva 2009, 324–31, quotes from 328.

symbol and metaphor. An interpreter who regards Revelation's deployment of violent traditional images "as a kind of *theologia negativa*" has indeed thought seriously and constructively about the problem. Such a reading holds on to the value of God's ultimate victory but leaves the means of that victory a mystery.[44] Unfortunately, authors who make such appeals rarely indicate familiarity with the theory of metaphorical language, even the venerable work of George Lakoff and Mark Johnson.[45] It is not enough to translate Revelation's holy warfare as spiritual warfare, as if this mathematical reduction would leave no remainder.[46] As Pieter G. R. de Villiers observes, "Words like these can kill"—not directly, of course, but more readers have legitimated their violent propensities by appealing to Revelation than to, say, Acts.[47]

Susan E. Hylen's work refuses both sides of a false alternative. According to Hylen, few scholarly interpreters err in taking metaphors literally, but too many attempt to leave metaphor behind by translating it into some other realm of meaning. It *matters* (Hylen's strategically chosen word) what metaphors one chooses, for to greater or lesser degrees metaphors live on beyond providing a simple point of comparison. Language choices shape meaning. Moreover, readers misunderstand metaphor when they choose one metaphor over another when Revelation provides conflicting images. For example, Revelation does offer the slaughtered Lamb, but that Lamb makes war with a sword—albeit a sword of testimony.[48] The Lamb's testimony does not paint over the image of the sword.

Violence as Symptom

Revelation may not call followers of Jesus to enact violence. But it does promote a desire for violence among its readers. It identifies its enemies as despicable characters: not only the Dragon, the two beasts, and the Prostitute, but also the Inhabitants of the Earth who, apparently unable to repent, defy God until their last moments.[49] Having removed its victims from all sympathy, Revelation describes their judgment and torment. Moreover, Revelation employs authoritative voices like martyrs and heavenly beings to both call for and celebrate the violence it describes.

44. Decock 2012, 197.
45. Lakoff and Johnson 2003.
46. M. Thompson 2012, 168.
47. De Villiers 2012, 225.
48. Hylen 2011, 789.
49. Carey 1999, 135–64.

Every attempt to explain away Revelation's violence ultimately falls short at precisely that final point: Revelation celebrates and endorses violence even though it never calls its audience to violent action. More honest than explaining away Revelation's violence problem are those who, like Boesak, find it justifiable. But what about those of us who are neither satisfied with the rationalizations nor persuaded that the violence in Revelation is a good thing? I cannot promise a resolution to the problem, but I would like to propose two considerations.

First, Revelation's violence is symptomatic of the pervasive violence of the imperial reality it resists. Many interpreters have said as much. Fewer are those who follow through to accept the full implications of that view: that we may have much to learn from Revelation without the need to judge it as a "good" or "bad" book, as so many interpreters do.

One might take a psychological approach to the question. Adela Yarbro Collins regards Revelation "as a partial and imperfect vision."[50] Revelation has raised the consciousness of "certain marginal and frustrated early Christians."[51] But it has also provided a measure of therapy by transferring the self-destructive desire for violent action to the internal experience of its audience, allowing the audience an emotional catharsis.[52] Stefan Alkier finds it helpful that Revelation "relocates the desire for revenge to the God who judges and his Christ."[53]

Second, other readers, particularly postcolonial interpreters, gravitate toward more political sensibilities. Postcolonial criticism emphasizes that resistance never attains purity. Those who resist empire remain affected by it, including their adoption of the dominant culture's language and literary tropes. Moreover, the trauma of colonization and resistance necessarily expresses itself among those who resist empire. Even when John addresses his "Christian" opponents, he does so with extreme violence, not so much because of an inherent conflict among prophets in the assemblies, but because the issues at stake directly involved the question of how believers should interact with a culture regarded as imperial, exploitative, and idolatrous. Violence, in this view, might even be assigned to "collateral damage."[54]

In the end, our assessments of Revelation will reflect a prior question: what do we think we need the Bible to do? Scholars' tendency to critique or defend Revelation's violence may reflect deeper issues. Popular interpretation of

50. A. Yarbro Collins 1984, 172.
51. A. Yarbro Collins 1984, 171.
52. A. Yarbro Collins 1984, 163.
53. Alkier 2012, 140.
54. Marshall 2005.

the Bible too often devolves into debates over its "reliability," "inspiration," or "truthfulness." However, theologically inclined readers may find the Bible to be a resource richer than simply a collection of example stories, doctrinal affirmations, and moral prescriptions. We might instead read ourselves and our own contexts into Revelation. Like John, we live in a culture overdetermined by commercial and military power as well as backed by sacred symbols and ideologies. Whatever our assessment of national and global politics, readers in the United States are not uncontaminated by those realities (3:4; 18:4). Contemporary concerns regarding racialized police violence have certainly compromised the sense that political and military power protects US citizens, but on the whole Christian readers in the North American context do not sense that the Beast is out to get them.

In this context, where so many factors complicate our relationship to empire, commerce, militarism, and whatever we call religion, Revelation offers a distinctive witness. It teaches us to imagine faith that resists exploitation, compromise, and false allegiance. But it also models the dangers inherent in a violent militaristic society—a relevant message for citizens of nations that take pride in their military power. The internalized desire for vindication and revenge runs deep, as does the human tendency to divide the world, and even our religious communities, into allies and enemies. One need not follow John's example in order to learn Revelation's lessons.

Mapping "Resistance" in Revelation

N EARLY ALL INTERPRETERS UNDERSTAND Revelation as offering the
New Testament's most pointed criticism of Roman imperialism. Two of
Revelation's most prominent symbols, the Beast and the Prostitute, ridicule
Roman arrogance, idolatry, violence, and exploitation, and Revelation gleefully
depicts the ruin of that "great city." Interpreters disagree sharply regarding how
consistently or thoroughly Revelation resists Roman hegemony. Moreover,
a few scholars regard Rome as a concern secondary to strife among the seven
assemblies to whom John writes.[1] These disagreements scarcely undermine the
general consensus that opposition to Rome constitutes a fundamental concern
within Revelation.

To my knowledge, however, scholars have yet to unpack our options concerning what sort of resistance we should attribute to Revelation, much less
fold and organize them. Biblical scholars deploy the term "resistance" in diverse
ways, often contradicting one another without acknowledging their implicit
disagreements. This chapter assesses diverse ways in which we might imagine
resistance, interprets the cultural context in which Revelation emerged for
hints as to what resistance might or might not have meant, and proposes
several ways in which Revelation does—and does not—embody resistance.

CONCEPTUALIZING RESISTANCE

In 2016, Adam Winn published a collection of essays that presents itself as an
introduction for students and nonspecialists concerning the diverse responses
to empire found within the New Testament.[2] Winn's own programmatic essay
reminds us that although the Roman Empire dominated the New Testament

1. Most compelling among them is Duff 2001.
2. Winn 2016a, x.

world, at that point "few" interpreters had accounted for the "ways in which New Testament texts might be critiquing the *evils* of the Roman Empire."[3] Winn then sketches the diverse options represented within the New Testament. (1) Some authors pronounce doom upon Rome. (2) Others co-opt imperial discourse by appropriating for Jesus titles often granted to the emperor, such as "Lord," "Savior," and "Son of God," and announcing Jesus's triumph and return. (3) Others take a more subtle tack, naming God's justice and thereby suggesting the injustice of Roman rule. Such authors create what the cultural anthropologist James C. Scott named "hidden transcripts," making their critiques apparent to insiders but opaque to those aligned with the authorities.[4] (4) Some resistance occurs more at the level of community formation and sociocultural institutions. For example, when early Christians competed to show honor to one another, they subverted the competition for status that defined Roman social striving. And let's face it, (5) sometimes authors and communities accommodate imperial values and discourses. Finally, (6) Winn notes that several of the volume's contributors appeal to the concept of *hybridity* from postcolonial theory. Resistance literatures may resist or reject the discourses of their oppressors, but both intentionally and unintentionally resistance necessarily draws upon those same cultural resources.[5] Winn does not discuss the literary strategies by which authors debase and mock Rome and its pretensions to glory, an area that has long interested students of Revelation and of apocalyptic literature.[6]

I observe some ambiguity inherent in some of the forms of resistance Winn sets forth. For example, by definition a hidden transcript is difficult for outsiders to detect. Biblical interpreters are "outsiders" to the cultures they study. By what criteria might we observe such subtle patterns of resistance? Likewise, hybridity constitutes a necessary symptom of imperial domination *and* a clever strategy. How do we discern which kind of hybridity is in play for a given case? Perhaps most fundamentally, should we count basic dissatisfaction, a reality present in all societies at all times, as resistance? When a group gripes about the powers of the day or withdraws from social participation, is that group leveraging resistance? Or should we choose another name for their behavior?

Winn's essays overlook one potential form of resistance—outright violence. Many interpreters regard Revelation as a violent book, critiquing it for fos-

---

3. Winn 2016b, 1. Emphasis mine.
4. Scott 1985, 1990.
5. Winn 2016b, 3–13.
6. For example, Laws 1988; Carey 1999; Portier-Young 2011; S. Smith 2014; Darden 2015; and Emanuel 2020.

tering violent impulses. Concepts like war, conquest, and blood figure prominently in Revelation. Although nearly all interpreters concur that Revelation in no way encourages its audience to take up arms, that view has scarcely prevented revolutionaries, whether German peasants or Branch Davidians, from claiming Revelation as their own.[7] We must grapple with the question of how Revelation relates to violence.

Resistance can mean many things. If we wish to describe Revelation as resistance literature, we must determine what dimensions of the book function to resist Roman domination and how those aspects perform resistance.

READING REVELATION IN AN APOCALYPTIC CONTEXT

Revelation is the oldest literary work to call itself an apocalypse (*apokalypsis*), doing so in its very first word (1:1). As discussed in chapter 1, the degree to which ancient authors and audiences recognized apocalyptic literature as an independent literary genre, or perhaps simply as a flavor of prophecy (1:3), is debatable. Nevertheless, Revelation shares a set of literary conventions with other ancient Jewish and Christian literary apocalypses like Daniel, the works that constitute 1 Enoch, 2 and 3 Baruch, 4 Ezra, the Apocalypse of Abraham, the Shepherd of Hermas, the Ascension of Isaiah, and the Apocalypse of Peter. Several of these apocalypses directly address how God's people relate to empire, as do some related works, so that we might regard them as instances of resistance literature. Revelation self-consciously participates within this literary tradition, which may reveal a range of possible responses to empire.

As observed previously in this book, Revelation interacts with the Jewish Scriptures (alluding to but not quoting them) more intensely than any other New Testament work. Daniel (particularly chapters 7–12) figures especially prominently, as it supplies the raw material for Revelation's depiction of Jesus as Son of Man (1:12–20) and of the Beast (13:1–18) along with references to Michael the mighty angel protecting God's people (12:7; see Dan 12:1) and to the mysterious period of "a time, and times, and half a time" (12:14; see Dan 7:25; 12:7).

Recent scholarship regards Daniel as a multifaceted case study in resistance. Interpreters routinely divide the book into two sections. Chapters 1–6 feature a series of "court legends" in which Daniel interprets dreams while he and his companions escape both moral challenges and mortal threats through their faithfulness to God. Chapters 7–12 are thoroughly apocalyptic, narrating a se-

---

7. Often overlooked is Arthur P. Mendel's subtle treatment of violence in the apocalyptic tradition (1992).

ries of Daniel's revelatory experiences. Daniel can also be divided by language: within the Hebrew work a lengthy section appears in Aramaic (2:4b–7:28). This linguistic distinction plays a significant role in contemporary assessments of resistance in Daniel, but we lack space here for a full discussion.[8]

The first half of Daniel imagines faithful Judeans living in exile and subject to capricious rulers, who may reluctantly expose these Judeans to persecution. The rulers are not quite evil, but they can be both foolish and dangerous. In these first six chapters, faithful Judeans observe their traditional diet and offer worship only to the God of Israel. These choices expose them to repression and punishment. God always delivers them from danger. But Daniel's second half takes a more ominous tone. The imperial powers that oppress Israel appear as monstrous beasts, one after the other. They cannot be merely survived; they must be defeated by the "one like a Son of Man" (7:13). Conflict dominates Daniel's several visions, which eventually make clear that the Seleucid ruler Antiochus IV Epiphanes and the Maccabean revolt are in view. Prior to his demise, Antiochus persecutes even the wise, who will receive the gift of resurrection.

Daniel, then, is keenly aware of empire and rebellion. The first half of the book thinks of empire somewhat generically: no matter who is in charge, Daniel and his colleagues survive by maintaining their loyalty to Judea's God and to his customs. Daniel's second half features no dramatic court legends. This apocalyptic section focuses specifically upon one empire, the Seleucid rule of Antiochus IV Epiphanes and its direct, intentional persecution of faithful Judeans.[9] Some Judeans "forsake the holy covenant" (11:30), and others resist militarily (11:32). Daniel's sympathies lie with the rebels, but the book calls its own audience to a different form of resistance. They are the wise (Hebrew: *maśkilim*), who provide instruction to their neighbors and "lead many to righteousness" (11:33; 12:3). Purity defines the conduct of the *maśkilim* (12:10), but Daniel never specifies what that purity looks like. As with the Suffering Servant of Isa 52–53, the suffering of the wise has redemptive value.[10] Instruction, purity, and sacrifice mark the resistance of the wise and distinguish them from Antiochus's Judean collaborators. The act of critiquing Antiochus's arrogance, violence, and illegitimate rule and pronouncing his doom also amounts to a form of resistance.

8. Portier-Young 2010, 98–115.
9. Richard A. Horsley reminds us that Dan 7 interprets Antiochus's empire within "the broader context of the whole sequence of violence by a succession of empires against subject peoples" (2007, 189).
10. Portier-Young, 2011, 272–78.

Revelation leans hard upon Daniel's example. Addressed primarily to the circumstances of *ekklēsiai* (assemblies) rather than to an *ethnos* (people or nation) at war, Revelation shares with Daniel a critique of insiders whose faithfulness is lacking (Rev 2:6, 14, 20–25; 3:15–20). Purity language figures prominently in Revelation, especially the language of white or clean clothes (3:4; 7:13–14; 18:4; conversely 21:8, 27). Like Daniel, Revelation promises its audience eschatological blessing for their persistence, and, like Daniel, Revelation does not call its audience to take up arms.

It is also instructive to compare Daniel with two sections of 1 Enoch that also seem fixated on the Maccabean crisis: the Animal Apocalypse (1 En. 85–90) and the Apocalypse of Weeks (91:12–17; 93:1–10). The Animal Apocalypse depicts Jews as vulnerable white sheep, subject to the predations of faithless leaders and imperial overlords. A ram opens the eyes of the sheep. With divine help, the sheep receive "a great sword" and make war against their oppressors (90:19). For its part, *the Apocalypse of Weeks* envisions a period of apostasy, after which sinners are handed over to the righteous. Both the Animal Apocalypse and the Apocalypse of Weeks share Daniel's understanding of the people being divided between the faithful and the apostate. Like Daniel, these apocalypses promise a blessed future to the righteous. More than does the Apocalypse of Weeks, the Animal Apocalypse also depicts the vulnerability of the faithful to their imperial overlords. Neither vision explicitly recommends the taking up of arms, but both describe it. In this way, they differ from Daniel.[11] As Daniel features the wise instructing their peers, the Animal Apocalypse turns toward hope when the sheep open their eyes. Thus, resistance in the Animal Apocalypse and the Apocalypse of Weeks involves violence, but it also requires fidelity and insight.

Apocalyptic traditions can call the faithful to arms, but Daniel does not. We find a point of contrast in the War Rule from Qumran (1QM), which reached its known form more than a hundred years after the Maccabean crisis. In the War Rule, the "sons of light" march to fight the "sons of darkness." The War Rule associates the enemies with the Kittim, a term generally believed to indicate imperial oppressors. The remarkable thing about the War Rule is that while the sons of light do take up arms and gather in formation, the text does not actually describe their fighting. As in Revelation, Daniel, and the traditions in Enoch, victory belongs to God.[12]

---

11. For both the Animal Apocalypse and the Apocalypse of Weeks, see Portier-Young 2011, 313–81.

12. Bauckham 1993a, 210–37.

The Maccabean crisis spawned the first wave of literary apocalypses. A second followed the disastrous First Jewish Revolt. We might include Revelation along with 2 and 3 Baruch, 4 Ezra, and the Apocalypse of Abraham as apocalyptic responses to that calamity and to Roman hegemony.[13] No longer did violent revolt make sense to these authors. Messianic expectation emerges in a clear way in 2 Baruch and 4 Ezra, especially the hope for a savior to deliver Israel and rectify the world. Both 2 Baruch and 4 Ezra also call for a renewal of Torah obedience. Third Baruch does not embrace messianic hope; instead, it locates salvation in the heavenly realms, which it describes in some detail. Like 3 Baruch, the Apocalypse of Abraham focuses not on the Torah but on proper worship. And like 3 Baruch, the Apocalypse of Abraham also provides a tour of the heavenly realms. In these four apocalypses we see no call to revolutionary activity. Instead, we encounter two basic options for moving forward: an embrace of Torah observance in anticipation of messianic deliverance (2 Baruch; 4 Ezra) and a call to pure worship with a view toward heavenly bliss (3 Baruch; Apocalypse of Abraham). In all cases, resistance involves purity among the faithful and a hope for deliverance in the future or beyond this world.

These apocalypses provide a context for conceptualizing resistance in Revelation. First, the realities of empire and domination feature prominently in these apocalypses; almost all of them demonstrate awareness that the faithful are vulnerable along with some critique of outsiders and of imperial overlords in particular. (We might note that the highly influential Book of the Watchers [1 En. 1–36] addresses empire only suggestively.)[14] Second, calls to violent resistance are rare in the earliest apocalyptic traditions. And third, to greater and lesser degrees most of these texts take an inward turn, calling a righteous few to rigorous fidelity in the face of apostasy. Finally, the Roman-era apocalypses locate salvation beyond the ordinary processes of history, whether through messianic deliverance or in the heavenly realms. Revelation offers *both* kinds of salvation. It depicts a messianic conflict that destroys the forces of evil along with their imperial manifestations. It invites hearers into the heavenly throne room, where glory abounds. And it depicts a New Jerusalem, both heavenly and earthly, which comes down to earth from heaven and in which death is abolished.

Later Christian apocalypses largely turn away from counterimperial resistance.[15] These apocalypses are notoriously difficult to locate chronologically,

---

13. I survey this literature in Carey 2005, 147–78.

14. Portier-Young 2011. See Horsley 2007, 157–63. This interpretation was perhaps first proposed by Nickelsburg 1977.

15. For surveys of these early apocalypses, see Carey 2005, 192–227.

but they all seem to postdate Revelation. The Shepherd of Hermas and the Apocalypse of Peter both reflect concern about persecution, but their primary aim seems to involve righteous behavior within the churches. Salvation resides in the afterlife. The Ascension of Isaiah, which injects Christian material into a Jewish legend, also addresses corruption in the church and the threat of persecution, but it adds two distinct concerns: a condemnation of Israel for failing to recognize Jesus as the Messiah, alongside a christological proposal. Like Revelation, the Ascension of Isaiah sketches an eschatological conflict in which the forces of evil face destruction. The Ascension of Isaiah also promises heavenly glory to the righteous. After Revelation, the earlier Christian apocalypses turn away from a focus upon empire.

The *Hypomonē* Problem

Does Revelation have recourse to language that would conceptualize resistance? A key term in this conversation is the Greek word *hypomonē*, almost always rendered as "endurance," "patient endurance," and "perseverance" in modern English translations of Revelation. Elisabeth Schüssler Fiorenza, however, has promoted the translation "consistent resistance," suggesting that the patterns of behavior to which John calls believers constitute a set of counterimperial practices in which believers are to persevere. Read in this light, *hypomonē* stands in Revelation as "the main Christian virtue."[16]

The vast majority of interpreters recognize Revelation's polemic against Rome, with more recent interpreters even appealing to categories such as "resistance literature," a concept with roots in postcolonial and related literature.[17] But this majority rarely identifies *hypomonē* directly with counterimperial resistance. Craig R. Koester represents this tradition beautifully, linking *hypomonē* with *nikē* (conquest), as I will below, but avoiding the language of empire and resistance:

> "Endurance" is bearing hardship for the sake of a goal, not merely putting up with things to avoid conflict (4 Macc 7:9; 9:8; Rom 5:3–4; Jas 1:3). Jesus both calls for and exemplifies endurance by his faithfulness to God in the face of opposition (Rev 1:5; 3:10, 14; cf. Heb 12:1–2; Ign. *Rom.* 10:3; Ign. *Pol.* 3:2). As athletes and soldiers endure for the sake of victory, Jesus' followers share in his victory over evil and untruth (Rev 2:7, 11, 17; 12:10–11; cf. 4 Macc 1:11; 9:30).[18]

16. Schüssler Fiorenza 1991, 51.
17. Harlow 1987.
18. Koester 2014, 239.

For Koester and others, Jesus and his followers endure for the sake of conquering evil in the abstract, not as a strategy to overthrow Rome. Ian Boxall perhaps presses this further. Likewise avoiding the language of empire and resistance, Boxall does deploy militaristic imagery, characterizing perseverance as "not passive endurance but an active willingness to see the battle through to its bitter end."[19] In a fundamental sense, this line of thinking is correct: Revelation associates Rome, the Beast, and the Prostitute as consorts of Satan, locating Rome within a cosmic network of evil. But the specifically political potential Schüssler Fiorenza assigns to Revelation is occluded by generic appeals to "evil and untruth."[20]

This largely apolitical reading has its advantages. In the New Testament and generally elsewhere, *hypomonē* connotes a kind of determined perseverance. For example, in Rom 5:3–4 it is possible but difficult to imagine that Paul understands suffering to produce resistance among other virtues. Likewise, in Rom 2:7 Paul discusses persevering in good works as a means of seeking glory, honor, and immortality. Classical and Koine Greek lexica alike emphasize this kind of perseverance when discussing *hypomonē* and do not add political or counterimperial considerations.

But 4 Maccabees exemplifies how *hypomonē* can also connote resistance. The book portrays faithfulness to the law as the mark of a true philosophy, one that leads to the torture and death of faithful Judeans under Antiochus IV Epiphanes's rule. One might anticipate that its philosophical bent might overwhelm the political commentary, as when the writer exults that "devout reason is governor of the emotions" (4 Macc 7:16). But that apolitical reading does not hold. On multiple occasions, heroic martyrdom is described as *hypomonē*, often in proximity to the discourse of tyrants and tyranny (7:1–9; 9:1–9). Our modern distinction between religious fidelity and political activism cannot stand up to 4 Macc 9:30, which credits Antiochus's demise to the martyrs' *hypomonē* "for the sake of religion" (9:30). Likewise, 4 Macc 1:11 attributes the courage and *hypomonē* of the martyrs with "the downfall of tyranny."[21]

Perhaps we should consider the plausibility that, when paired with *martyria* (testimony) and *thlipsis* (persecution or tribulation), *hypomonē* constitutes an ongoing practice of resistance in Revelation (see 1:9). Brian Blount steps way out, rendering *hypomonē* as "non-violent resistance."[22] Here we concede an obvious anachronism. Ancient people occasionally did resist their overlords

---

19. Boxall 2006, 39.
20. Koester 2014, 239.
21. Here I am shamelessly tracking the bread crumbs laid out by Koester 2014, 239.
22. Blount 2009, 39.

nonviolently, but they did not articulate the sort of philosophical nonviolence familiar to modern readers. One thinks of the Jews who exposed their necks to the Roman sword in the temple (Josephus, *Ant.* 18.59). In our context, nonviolent resistance conjures memories of Gandhi, King, and Tutu—people who confronted oppression in public ways and with a clear philosophical outlook. If Revelation calls the assemblies to resist, it does not call for organized public demonstration. Nor does it encourage them to take up arms.

Revelation calls its audience to resistance and to testimony. Like 4 Maccabees, it presents faithful testimony as a means to overcome the present empire. It also simultaneously requires and promises conquest. Each of the seven letters to the assemblies in chapters 2–3 extends its blessings "to everyone who conquers" (see also 21:7). Just as Jesus conquers the forces arrayed against him, so do his followers (12:11; 15:2).

Revelation does not place *hypomonē* and *nikē* in direct proximity to one another, although several of the seven letters commend assemblies for their endurance, and all of them feature the command to conquer. Nevertheless, a few key passages demonstrate the relationship between resistance and victory.

Consider Rev 14:1–12, which concludes: "Here is the resistance of the saints, who keep the commandments of God and the faith of Jesus" (my translation). This passage follows immediately upon the horrifying vision of the Beast, who makes war on the saints and *conquers* them (13:7; see also 11:7). Having introduced the Beast, John addresses the audience directly: "Here is the resistance and faith of the saints" (13:10, my translation), a call that anticipates the one in 14:12.

At 14:1, John turns his attention away from the Beast and toward the victorious Lamb and his followers, but this scene resonates with the revelation of the Beast at multiple levels. Many features create direct contrasts between the Lamb and his followers versus the Beast and those who worship him, a set of comparisons too rich for full elaboration here. Both the Lamb and the Beast are characterized by surviving mortal wounds; possessing multiple horns and secret names; speaking through prophets; and receiving worship. The Beast's worshipers receive marks on their right hands or foreheads (13:16), while the Lamb's followers have God's seal on their own foreheads (7:3).[23] The standing Lamb recalls the standing Dragon in 12:17. The Dragon gives its power and authority to the Beast (13:2), just as the Lamb stands in the midst of God's throne. Again, consider how 14:12 echoes 13:10: the Beast's violence cannot withstand the Lamb's ultimate victory. In short, "the resistance of the saints"

---

23. See Laws 1988, 41–42.

occurs in a context dominated by a contrast between the Lamb and the Beast, a context in which John promises ultimate conquest. This we should already know, as the saints have conquered the Dragon through the blood of the Lamb and through their own testimony (12:11). In these ways, Revelation links its call for resistance with its promise of, and demand for, conquest.

PERSECUTION AND CRITIQUE

Until the 1980s, interpreters commonly assumed that Revelation was composed in response to official persecution. The internal evidence seemed clear. Revelation is the earliest extant Greek text to treat *martyria*, or eyewitness testimony, in the sense of martyrdom.[24] Thus, Jesus is the "faithful witness" (1:5), as is a believer named Antipas who has been slaughtered (2:13), while John resides on Patmos because of his own testimony (1:9). Revelation 6:9-11 describes those who have died for the sake of their testimony, and 12:11 links testimony with death. The Beast makes war on the saints and (for a period) conquers them (11:7; 13:7).

This former consensus crumbled under a stubborn reality. Outside the Bible, no solid evidence for a Roman policy of persecuting Christians exists for the period during which Revelation was composed. We have traditions concerning Nero's persecution after the fire of 64 CE, accounts which may be blown out of proportion or even invented.[25] Revelation itself participates in a broader early Christian tradition concerning Nero's return to persecute the church, a fact I regard as evidence of some trauma inflicted upon Christians by the emperor.[26] Even so, Nero's persecution constitutes only one local event. Some scholars also point to a period of persecution attested by the Roman governor Pliny the Younger (*Ep.* 10.96-97). A generation or so after Revelation was composed in a province adjacent to Roman Asia, Pliny received accusations concerning "Christians" in the region. He reluctantly arrested them, interrogated them, and executed those who persisted in declaring allegiance to Jesus. Pliny's narrative again suggests that ancient followers of Jesus might have encountered danger on account of their testimony, but two other factors complicate the picture. First, Pliny is ignorant of any policy to persecute Christians because none existed at that time. Second, his reluctance indicates that he holds no personal or policy-oriented interest in finding them. Again, Pliny is writing after Revelation's composition and in an adjacent province. He

---

24. Trites 1973, 72-80.
25. See the discussion in Moss 2013, 138-39.
26. But see Henten 2000. Defending the role of the Nero myth, see Klauck 2001.

certainly provides no direct evidence of persecution in Roman Asia during the time of Revelation's composition. In short, the idea of systematic persecution of the Christians to whom John is writing is shaky at best.

Yet, I regard the experience of—or the fear of—persecution as fundamental to resistance in Revelation. This is hardly a new perspective, but it does need defending.[27] I accept that we have no external evidence for systemic imperial persecution of Christians during the first century CE. However, four factors lead me to take seriously the probability that some experience of persecution lies behind Revelation, experience that to some degree accounts for the alarm we encounter in the book.

First, Revelation is hardly the only early Christian source preoccupied with the possibility of persecution. All four New Testament Gospels share this concern, as do Acts and the letters of Paul. Beyond Revelation, the earliest Christian apocalypses (the Shepherd of Hermas, the Ascension of Isaiah, and the Apocalypse of Peter) all address the fear of persecution, as do other second-century documents like the Martyrdom of Polycarp and the epistles of Ignatius of Antioch.

Second, Revelation specifically names one victim of persecution, Antipas (2:13), and John locates himself on Patmos as a subject of hardship (*thlipsis*) on account of his witness (*martyria*), language that suggests persecution (1:9). For rhetorical reasons, it is implausible to imagine that John draws these examples out of thin air. If those who heard Revelation read aloud in the assemblies did not recognize their own circumstances, then John would have entirely failed to persuade them. Such disparate understandings are possible but unlikely.

Third, although Pliny's persecution in Bithynia does not directly attest to persecution in John's context, Pliny's concerns do resonate with John's. Pliny threatens Christians who testify to Jesus with execution, and he requires them to worship the imperial gods. Pliny even mentions that the local economy has suffered due to the Christians. Revelation 13 speaks to violence against the saints, describes compulsory worship of the Beast, and claims that no one can buy or sell without first accepting the mark of the Beast.

Finally, one means by which Revelation resists Roman hegemony involves its implicit criticism of empire and emperor. By "implicit," I do not have in mind the sort of "hidden transcript" oppressed persons employ in order to undermine their overlords.[28] Revelation's critique is neither hidden nor subtle; it is simply indirect. Revelation voices this critique through two primary symbols, the Beast and the Prostitute who rides the Beast (17:3). The Beast rises from the sea, as do the

27. Argued classically by A. Yarbro Collins 1984; and Thompson 1990.
28. See n. 4 above.

imperial monsters of Dan 7:2–8; the Prostitute's association with seven mountains alludes to Rome's reputation as the city set on seven hills (17:9). The Beast makes war against the saints and conquers them (13:7; 11:7); the Prostitute is intoxicated from drinking their blood (17:6). The Beast embodies all the evils accounted to the four beasts of Dan 7, transcending them all by receiving worship and by dominating all the inhabitants of the earth; the Prostitute consorts with rulers, tycoons, and sailors, establishing a network of commerce through domination.[29] In describing the Prostitute's demise, John pauses to list the cargo for which her commercial system created a demand: luxury items like precious metals and jewelry but ultimately chariots and slaves (18:12–13). Idolatry, war, commerce, and exploitation define John's portrait of Roman rule. If the members of John's audience openly shared this view of the empire and its gods, they would invite opposition, even local oppression. John apparently has such local repression in mind when he describes the "Beast from the Land," who exercises the first beast's authority and enforces worship of it (13:11–17). Ultimately John's critique of the empire and its emperor extends to a vision of final judgment and utter destruction.

We will never achieve a precise understanding of the historical context that accounts for Revelation's keen interest in persecution. Exactly how and why John anticipated opposition remains unclear. Yet, we have good reason to believe John is responding to some kind of repression, likely occasional and probably local. Antipas's example reminds us of the potential for violent persecution. By adopting and giving voice to John's view, hearers necessarily made public their rejection of Roman legitimacy at the risk of both life and property.

Literary Resistance

Our survey indicates several ways in which we might say that Revelation voices resistance to Roman hegemony. Although it does not call for outright rebellion, Revelation does call followers of Jesus to resist the Beast and its allies by testifying to Jesus in the face of opposition and withdrawing from all the trappings of beastly idolatry. For the Lamb's followers, this is the path of victory. Beyond these behaviors, rigorous and risky as they may be, Revelation offers no program, social ideology, recognizable public movement, or open revolt. Revelation does address communities, but it does not call its audiences to act collectively. To make perhaps too fine a distinction, Revelation calls the Lamb's followers to act communally but not collectively.[30]

29. Bauckham 1993a, 338–83.

30. For an analogous model of resistance, see Brian K. Blount's reading of testimony in Revelation in the light of civil rights initiatives in the Black church (2005, 37–67).

Revelation holds such features in common with other literary apocalypses. Like those apocalypses, Revelation further demonstrates a form of literary resistance through its critique of the emperor and the empire. We have sketched the grounds for this critique: idolatry, oppression, exploitation, and violence as reflected in the symbols of the Beast and the Prostitute. We should also recognize the twin strategies of parody and debasement, common modes of Roman humor.[31]

Roman imperial rhetoric appealed to both glory and debasement. This rhetoric, known to us in statuary, architecture, coinage, and literature, proclaimed the glory of Rome and its emperor and the humiliation of those who attempt resistance. Rome's self-proclaimed glory may seem obvious to many readers.[32] Its rhetoric of debasement may perhaps seem less obvious. Visual rhetoric often depicted Rome's defeated adversaries as women, characterizing them in terms of submission, nakedness, and vulnerability to rape.[33]

Revelation acknowledges Roman glory. Before the fearsome Beast, the world's population cries out, "Who is like the beast, and who can fight against it?" (13:4). Although John reveals Rome as the Prostitute, his description of her still evokes awe: clothed in purple and scarlet; adorned with gold, silver, and pearls; and drinking from a golden cup. In the words of John, "When I saw her, I was greatly amazed" (17:6). No wonder the novelist D. H. Lawrence wrote of her, "The harlot sits magnificent."[34] People expressed devotion and worship to Rome because it brought peace and prosperity to many. John knows this reality, but he is about the work of revelation, unveiling the ugly truth of things. Whatever their apparent glory, the Beast is a monster, and a Prostitute remains, well, a prostitute. John's characterization recognizes Rome's glory and then reveals that glory as superficial. Not for a moment does the Beast possess charm appeal, but it does elicit wonder. Revelation reveals the Beast's ultimate destruction, but it also assigns torment for those who worship the Beast (14:11; 16:2, 10). As for the Prostitute, Revelation acknowledges her splendor but describes her drunkenness (17:6). Her debasement extends to the point that she is stripped naked, devoured, and burned (17:16). As food for cannibals, she shares with the Beast a subhuman status.[35] The misogyny that fuels these images,

31. Emanuel 2020. See also Carey 1999, 135–64; 2008, 157–76; and deSilva 2008, 193–228.

32. Longenecker 2016, 15–46.

33. Lopez 2008.

34. Lawrence 1980 [1931], 121; quoted in A. Yarbro Collins 1984, 169.

35. Tina Pippin has provided the classic critique of misogyny in Revelation (1992). More recently, see S. Smith 2014, 125–74; and Moore 2014, esp. 103–78.

so common in ancient polemic, will disturb modern readers.[36] Nevertheless, by these literary strategies Revelation mocks Rome's pretensions to glory.

COMPROMISED RESISTANCE?

Revelation calls its audience to resist Rome by abstaining from imperial worship and by testifying to Jesus. It reinforces this exhortation through literary critique by parodying Roman glory, setting forth its evils, and conjuring its destruction. In these ways, Revelation both seeks and embodies resistance. Revelation offers eternal blessing to those who conquer.

Yet, interpreters have long assessed Revelation as "a partial and imperfect vision," to quote Adela Yarbro Collins.[37] With her, they have ascribed to Revelation a moral and theological ambiguity—a longing for justice compromised by a desire for destruction. As postcolonial theory found its way into biblical interpretation in the 1990s, "ambivalent" readings of Revelation multiplied. These interpretations called attention to mixed messages in the book, resistance discourse relying upon the rhetoric of empire itself. Revelation critiqued Roman economic exploitation, but it described salvation precisely through images of material opulence.[38] In response to imperial domination, John offers believers status as kings and priests (1:6) and honors them as full partners (1:9), all the while insisting they submit to his unique visionary authority (1:3; 22:18–19).[39] More recently, womanist interpreters have appropriated postcolonial sensitivities to show how John adapts the symbols of Roman imperial worship to the worship of Christ.[40] Such interpreters have also shown how the vision of Rome's destruction relies upon another imperial trope—the demise of an imperial victim, the enslaved Prostitute.[41] Davina C. Lopez sagely suggests, "while Revelation may entertain resistance as an option in relation to empire, its rhetoric also appears to be thoroughly textured with imperial resonances."[42]

Not all interpreters are troubled by these ambiguities and complications. Writing in the context of apartheid South Africa, Allan A. Boesak has set forth a classic position, as noted in the previous chapters: Roman imperial-

36. Artfully addressed by Emanuel 2020, 116–18.
37. A. Yarbro Collins 1984, 172.
38. Royalty 1998.
39. Carey 1999.
40. Darden 2015.
41. S. Smith 2014.
42. Lopez 2016, 294.

ism established a violent context for Revelation, in turn demanding a violent overthrow. Those who do not know suffering and oppression cannot understand Revelation, Boesak insists.[43] More commonly, Revelation's defenders have appealed to literary considerations. Schüssler Fiorenza acknowledges that violent and misogynistic imagery figures prominently in the book, countering that these images are stock literary devices designed to serve liberating purposes.[44] Along similar lines, interpreters frame Revelation's rhetoric in terms of parody. John takes images, myths, and tropes from Roman imperial discourse and turns them against the empire.[45] According to many interpreters, these literary strategies demonstrate full-throated resistance, turning the empire's discourses against it.

Sarah Emanuel regards these strategies as "a Jewish retooling of Roman humor for Revelation's own gain," but she warns that Revelation's resistance is compromised by its dependence on Roman imperial tropes.[46] The Lamb looks and sounds too much like Caesar.[47] In using and mocking Roman humor, Revelation both resists and "acquiesces" to Roman ways of imagining reality. Like Rome, it "mocks, tortures, and turns into spectacle" its enemies.[48]

Postcolonial interpretation majors on the relationship between parody and ambivalence.[49] In a fundamental sense, debates between ambivalent and liberating interpretations of Revelation are theological. However, the question remains regarding what value Revelation brings to contemporary religious, ethical, and political imagination.[50] We cannot dodge the ethical implications of our assessments, not for long anyway. But a postcolonial sensibility insists that resistance is always and inherently compromised. Resistance inevitably carries the symptoms of its contexts. Parody necessarily relates to its subject as a parasite to its host; it does not roam free of its context. Postcolonial readers

43. Boesak 1987, 38.

44. Schüssler Fiorenza 1991, 122–24.

45. See deSilva 2009, esp. 37–48, 112–14; Howard-Brook and Gwyther 1999, esp. 223–35; and Emanuel 2020.

46. Emanuel 2020, 130.

47. Emanuel 2020, 169.

48. Emanuel 2020, 199–200 and n. 49.

49. With a view toward Revelation, Stephen D. Moore (2014, 13–37) surveys the intertwined concepts of ambivalence, mimicry, and hybridity in the work of postcolonial critic Homi Bhabha. Other postcolonial readings rely upon Bhabha in similar ways (see Carey 1999; S. Smith 2014; Darden 2015; and Emanuel 2020). Darden (2015, 62–77) offers a most helpful assessment of Homi Bhabha on these points.

50. On the tension between postcolonial and liberationist interpretations, see Sugirtharajah 2002, 103–23.

press the question: should we ever expect to encounter a literary resistance unencumbered by ambivalence?

RESISTANCE AND THE SYMPTOMS OF EMPIRE

This essay began with a question: what do we mean when we categorize Revelation as resistance literature? Beneath this question lies a criticism: interpreters often appeal to resistance as a self-evident or "obvious" category when it is not.

The literary apocalypses of ancient Judaism and Christianity, especially the ones composed before or contemporaneously with Revelation, offer a helpful starting point for pursuing this question. In these texts, we often find sympathy for violent revolt but only rarely calls for the audience to take up arms. We also observe an inward turn, that is, the exhortation to rigorous fidelity in an apostate society. These apocalypses voice keen awareness of imperial oppression, including a sense that the righteous are vulnerable to violence. They typically hope for salvation through either messianic deliverance or in the heavenly realms. These patterns all resonate within Revelation.

We then turned to the language of *hypomonē*, a prominent concept in Revelation. Translators usually render *hypomonē* as endurance, patient endurance, or perseverance. Only a few commentators read *hypomonē* in terms of resistance. I argue that by associating *hypomonē* with *nikē* (conquest or victory), Revelation welcomes more overtly political readings. In Revelation, *hypomonē* means the kind of resistance that contributes to Rome's eventual overthrow, the means of victory for the saints. We find an analog for this use of *hypomonē* in 4 Maccabees, where the martyrs' faithfulness leads to the tyrant's destruction. We cannot construct a detailed picture of Revelation's historical moment, but the book insists that its hearers are subject to persecution and repression. In Revelation, the primary practices of resistance are abstention from all the trappings of imperial idolatry and exploitation along with consistent testimony to Jesus Christ, even to the point of death. I suggest that Revelation calls believers to resistance that is communal but not collective. That is, the saints participate together in these practices of resistance, but Revelation offers no sign that they organize, strategize, or collaborate.

Beyond daily practices, Revelation also voices resistance through its literary strategies. In particular, it acknowledges Roman pretensions to glory while "unveiling" the empire's debasement. In this essay, we focused upon the images of the Beast and the Prostitute. Through these symbols, John dramatizes Roman idolatry, cruelty, and exploitation. Both images also provide a means for

John to dehumanize emperor and empire and to envision their destruction. By juxtaposing the Beast and the Prostitute over against the Lamb and the Bride (i.e., the New Jerusalem), Revelation suggests that true glory accompanies the Lamb. These literary devices reinforce the book's call to abstain from imperial idolatry and exploitation, even at mortal risk.

We conclude by attending to a conflict among interpreters, some of whom treat Revelation as a prime example of counterimperial resistance, while others regard its resistance with ambivalence. The absence or presence of post-colonial sensitivities weighs heavily in these conflicting assessments. In the end, I suggest that while Revelation does indeed offer a program of practical and literary resistance, it cannot avoid bearing the symptoms of empire. Nor should we expect it to.

Agamben, Giorgio. 2011. *The Kingdom and the Glory: For a Theological Geneal-ogy of Economy and Government.* Translated by Lorenzo Chiesa. Stanford: Stanford University Press.

Ahmed, Sara. 2014. *The Cultural Politics of Emotion.* 2nd ed. New York: Routledge.

Alkier, Stefan. 2012. "Witness or Warrior? How the Book of Revelation Can Help Christians Live Their Political Lives." Pages 125–41 in *Revelation and the Politics of Apocalyptic Interpretation.* Edited by Richard B. Hays and Stefan Alkier. Waco: Baylor University Press.

Allen, Garrick V. 2017. *The Book of Revelation and Early Jewish Textual Culture.* SNTSMS 168. New York: Cambridge University Press.

Allison, Dale C., Jr. 2016. *Night Comes: Death, Imagination, and the Last Things.* Grand Rapids: Eerdmans.

Applebaum, Anne. 2020. *Twilight of Democracy: The Seductive Lure of Authoritar-ianism.* New York: Doubleday.

Aune, D. E. 1990. "The Form and Function of the Proclamations to the Seven Churches (Revelation 2–3)." *NTS* 36:182–204.

———. 1998. *Revelation.* 3 vols. WBC 52A–C. Dallas: Word.

Bakhtin, Mikhail. 1984. *Problems of Dostoevsky's Poetics.* Edited and translated by Caryl Emerson. Theory and History of Literature 8. Minneapolis: University of Minnesota Press.

Barnhill, Gregory M. 2017. "Seeing Christ through Hearing the Apocalypse: An Ex-ploration of John's Use of *Ekphrasis* in Revelation 1 and 19." *JSNT* 39:235–57.

Barr, David L. 1998. *Tales of the End: A Narrative Commentary on the Book of Revelation.* Storytellers Bible 1. Santa Rosa, CA: Polebridge.

———. 2009. "Women in Myth and History: Deconstructing John's Characteriza-tions." Pages 55–68 in *A Feminist Companion to the Apocalypse of John.* Ed-ited by Amy-Jill Levine with Maria Mayo Robbins. New York: T&T Clark.

Battle, Michael. 2017. *Heaven on Earth: God's Call to Community in the Book of Revelation.* Louisville: Westminster John Knox.

Bauckham, Richard. 1993a. *The Climax of Prophecy: Studies on the Book of Revelation*. Edinburgh: T&T Clark.

———. 1993b. *The Theology of the Book of Revelation*. New Testament Theology. New York: Cambridge University Press.

———. 1998. *The Fate of the Dead: Studies on the Jewish and Christian Apocalypses*. NovTSup 93. Leiden: Brill.

Beale, G. K. 1999. *The Book of Revelation*. NIGTC. Grand Rapids: Eerdmans.

Ben-Ghiat, Ruth. 2020. *Strongmen: Mussolini to the Present*. New York: Norton.

Berlant, Lauren, and Michael Warner. 1995. "What Does Queer Theory Teach Us about X?" *PMLA* 110:343–49.

Blount, Brian K. 2005. *Can I Get a Witness? Reading Revelation through African American Culture*. Louisville: Westminster John Knox.

———. 2009. *Revelation*. NTL. Westminster John Knox.

Boesak, Allan A. 1987. *Comfort and Protest: The Apocalypse of John from a South African Perspective*. Philadelphia: Westminster.

———. 2015. *Kairos, Crisis, and Global Apartheid: The Challenge to Prophetic Resistance*. New York: Palgrave Macmillan.

Bonhoeffer, Dietrich. 1971. *Letters and Papers from Prison*. Exp. ed. New York: Macmillan.

Bowens, Lisa Marie. 2019. "God and Time: Exploring Black Notions of Prophetic and Apocalyptic Eschatology." Pages 213–24 in *T&T Clark Handbook of African American Theology*. Edited by Antonia Michelle Daymond, Frederick L. Ware, and Eric Lewis Williams. New York: T&T Clark.

Bowden, Anna M. V. 2021. *Revelation and the Marble Economy of Roman Ephesus: A People's History Approach*. Lanham, MD: Lexington Books/Fortress Academic.

Boxall, Ian. 2006. *The Revelation of Saint John*. BNTC. Peabody: Hendrickson.

Boyarin, Daniel. 2012. *The Jewish Gospels: The Story of the Jewish Christ*. New York: New Press.

Bray, Karen, and Stephen D. Moore. 2020. "Introduction: Mappings and Crossings." Pages 1–17 in *Religion, Emotion, Sensation: Affect Theories and Theologies*. Edited by Karen Bray and Stephen D. Moore. New York: Fordham University Press.

Brenner, Athalya. 1997. *The Intercourse of Knowledge: On Gendering Desire and "Sexuality" in the Hebrew Bible*. BibInt 26. Leiden: Brill.

Briggs, John. 1987. "Reflectaphors: The (Implicate) Universe as a Work of Art." Pages 414–35 in *Quantum Implications: Essays in Honor of David Bohm*. Edited by B. J. Hiley and J. David Peat. New York: Routledge & Kegan Paul.

Brown, Wendy. 2018. "Neoliberal Frankenstein: Authoritarian Freedom in Twenty-First Century 'Democracies.'" Pages 7–44 in *Authoritarianism: Three Inqui-*

ries in Critical Theory, by Wendy Brown, Peter E. Gordon, and Max Pensky. Chicago: University of Chicago Press.

Bühner, Ruben A. 2021. *Messianic High Christology: New Testament Variants of Second Temple Judaism.* Waco: Baylor University Press.

Bultmann, Rudolf. 1958. *Jesus Christ and Mythology.* New York: Scribners.

Byron, Gay L., and Vanessa Lovelace. 2016. "Introduction: Methods and the Making of Womanist Biblical Hermeneutics." Pages 1–18 in *Womanist Interpretations of the Bible: Expanding the Discourse.* Edited by Gay L. Byron and Vanessa Lovelace. SemeiaSt 85. Atlanta: SBL Press.

Caird, G. B. 1993. *The Revelation of Saint John.* BNTC. San Francisco: HarperSanFrancisco, 1966. Repr., Peabody: Hendrickson.

Carey, Greg. 1998. "Apocalyptic Ethos." Pages 731–61 in vol. 2 of *SBL Seminar Papers 1998.* SBLSP 37:2. Atlanta: Scholars Press.

———. 1999. *Elusive Apocalypse: Reading Authority in the Revelation to John.* StABH 15. Macon: Mercer University Press.

———. 2005. *Ultimate Things: An Introduction to Jewish and Christian Apocalyptic Literature.* St. Louis: Chalice.

———. 2006. "Revelation and Empire: Symptoms and Resistance." Pages 169–80 in *The Reality of Apocalypse: Rhetoric and Politics in the Book of Revelation.* Edited by David L. Barr. SymS 39. Atlanta: Society of Biblical Literature.

———. 2008. "Moving an Audience: One Aspect of Pathos in the Book of Revelation." Pages 163–78 in *Words Well Spoken: George Kennedy's Rhetoric of the New Testament.* Edited by C. Clifton Black and Duane F. Watson. Waco: Baylor University Press.

———. 2009. "A Man's Choice: Wealth Imagery and the Two Cities in the Book of Revelation." Pages 147–58 in *A Feminist Companion to the Apocalypse of John.* Edited by Amy-Jill Levine and Maria Mayo Robbins. New York: Continuum.

———. 2016. *Apocalyptic Literature in the New Testament.* Core Biblical Studies. Nashville: Abingdon.

———. 2022. *Faithful and True: A Study Guide to the Book of Revelation.* Cleveland: Pilgrim.

———. 2023. *Death, the End of History, and Beyond: Eschatology in the Bible.* Interpretation. Louisville: Westminster John Knox.

Charles, R. H. 1920. *A Critical and Exegetical Commentary on the Revelation of St. John.* 2 vols. ICC. Edinburgh: T&T Clark.

Christerson, Brad, and Richard Flory. 2017. *The Rise of Network Christianity: How Independent Leaders Are Changing the Religious Landscape.* New York: Oxford University Press.

Collins, Adela Yarbro. 1976. *The Combat Myth in the Book of Revelation.* HDR 9. Missoula, MT: Scholars Press.

———. 1980. "Revelation 18: Taunt Song or Dirge?" Pages 185–204 in *L'Apocalypse johannique et l'Apocalyptique dans le Nouveau Testament*. Edited by Jan Lambrecht. Leuven: Leuven University Press.

———. 1984. *Crisis and Catharsis: The Power of the Apocalypse*. Philadelphia: Westminster.

———. 1987. "Women's History and the Book of Revelation." Pages 80–91 in *SBL Seminar Papers 1987*. Edited by Kent Howard Richards. SBLSP 26. Atlanta: Scholars Press.

———. 1993. "Feminine Symbolism in the Book of Revelation." *BibInt* 1:20–33.

———. 1999. "The Apocalyptic Ekphrasis." Pages 449–64 in *1900th Anniversary of Saint John's Apocalypse: Proceedings of an International and Interdisciplinary Symposium*. Athens: Holy Monastery of St. John the Theologian in Patmos.

———. 2021. "Time and History: The Use of the Past and the Present in the Book of Revelation." Pages 187–214 in *Dreams, Visions, Imaginations: Jewish, Christian and Gnostic Views of the World to Come*. Edited by Jens Schröter, Tobias Nicklas, and Armand Puig i Tàrrech. BZNW 247. Berlin: de Gruyter.

Collins, Adela Yarbro, and John J. Collins. 2008. *King and Messiah as Son of God: Divine, Human, and Angelic Messianic Figures in Biblical and Related Literature*. Grand Rapids: Eerdmans.

Collins, John J. 1979. "Introduction: Towards the Morphology of a Genre." *Semeia* 14:9–20.

———. 2007. "Pre-Christian Jewish Messianism: An Overview." Pages 1–20 in *The Messiah in Early Judaism and Christianity*. Edited by Magnus Zetterholm. Minneapolis: Fortress.

———. 2016. *The Apocalyptic Imagination: An Introduction to Jewish Apocalyptic Literature*. 3rd ed. Grand Rapids: Eerdmans.

Concannon, Cavan W. 2021. *Profaning Paul*. Class 200. Chicago: University of Chicago Press, 2021.

Crossan, John Dominic. 2015. *How to Read the Bible and Still Be a Christian: Struggling with Divine Violence from Genesis through Revelation*. San Francisco: HarperOne.

Darden, Lynn St. Clair. 2015. *Scripturalizing Revelation: An African American Postcolonial Reading of Empire*. SemeiaSt 80. Atlanta: SBL Press.

Davies, Jamie. 2019. "4 Ezra and Revelation 13:1–18: Blasphemous Beasts." Pages 116–22 in *Reading Revelation in Context: John's Apocalypse and Second Temple Judaism*. Edited by Ben C. Blackwell, John K. Goodrich, and Jason Maston. Grand Rapids: Zondervan Academic.

———. 2023. *Reading Revelation: A Literary and Theological Commentary*. Macon: Smyth & Helwys.

Davies, W. D. 1962. "Ethics in the New Testament." *IDB* 2:167–70.

Decock, Paul B. 2012. "Images of War and Creation, of Violence and Non-Violence in the Revelation of John." Pages 185–200 in *Coping with Violence in the New Testament*. Edited by Pieter G. R. de Villiers and Jan Willem van Henten. STR 16. Leiden: Brill.

deSilva, David A. 2009. *Seeing Things John's Way: The Rhetoric of the Book of Revelation*. Louisville: Westminster John Knox.

Dorrien, Gary. 2021. *American Democratic Socialism: History, Politics, Religion, and Theory*. New Haven: Yale University Press.

Downs, David J. 2013. "Economics, Taxes, and Tithes." Pages 156–68 in *The World of the New Testament: Cultural, Social, and Historical Contexts*. Edited by Joel B. Green and Lee Martin McDonald. Grand Rapids: Baker Academic.

Du Mez, Kristin Kobes. 2021. *Jesus and John Wayne: How White Evangelicals Corrupted a Faith and Fractured a Nation*. New York: Liveright.

Duff, Paul B. 2001. *Who Rides the Beast? Prophetic Rivalry and the Rhetoric of Crisis in the Churches of the Apocalypse*. New York: Oxford University Press.

Edelman, Lee. 1994. *Homographesis: Essays in Gay Literature and Cultural Theory*. New York: Routledge.

Edsall, Thomas. 2016. "Purity, Disgust and Donald Trump." *New York Times*, January 6, 2016. https://www.nytimes.com/2016/01/06/opinion/campaign-stops/purity-disgust-and-donald-trump.html.

Elliott, Neil. 2008. *The Arrogance of Nations: Reading Romans in the Shadow of Empire*. Paul in Critical Contexts. Minneapolis: Fortress.

Emanuel, Sarah. 2020. *Humor, Resistance, and Jewish Cultural Persistence in the Book of Revelation: Roasting Rome*. New York: Cambridge University Press.

Enos, Richard Leo, and Karen Rossi Schnakenberg. 1994. "Cicero Latinizes Hellenic *Ethos*." Pages 191–209 in *New Essays in Rhetorical and Critical Theory*. Edited by James S. Baumlin and Tita French Baumlin. Dallas: Southern Methodist University Press.

Family Research Institute. "Getting the Facts: Same-Sex Marriage." February 3, 2009. http://www.familyresearchinst.org/category/pamphlets/.

Felton, Gale Carton. 2005. *This Holy Mystery: A United Methodist Understanding of Holy Communion*. Nashville: Discipleship Resources.

Frankfurter, David. 2001. "Jews or Not? Reconstructing the 'Other' in Rev 2:9 and 3:9." *HTR* 94:403–25.

Frantz, Erica. 2018. *Authoritarianism: What Everyone Needs to Know*. New York: Oxford University Press.

Fredriksen, Paula. 2018. *When Christians Were Jews: The First Generation*. New Haven: Yale University Press.

Freedom House. 2023. "Freedom in the World, 2023: Marking 50 Years in the Struggle for Democracy." https://freedomhouse.org/sites/default/files/2023 -03/FIW_World_2023_DigtalPDF.pdf.

Friesen, Steven J. 2001. *Imperial Cults and the Apocalypse of John: Reading Revelation in the Ruins.* New York: Oxford University Press.

———. 2004. "Poverty in Pauline Studies: Beyond the So-called New Consensus." *JSNT* 26: 323–61.

Frilingos, Chris. 2003. "Sexing the Lamb." Pages 297–317 in *New Testament Masculinities.* Edited by Stephen D. Moore and Janice Capel Anderson. SemeiaSt 45. Atlanta: Society of Biblical Literature.

Gaddafi, Muammar. 1998. *Escape to Hell and Other Stories.* Toronto: Hushion House.

Gagné, André. 2024. *American Evangelicals for Trump: Dominion, Spiritual Warfare, and the End Times.* Translated by Linda Shanahan. New York: Routledge.

García Ureña, Lourdes. 2021. "The Book of Revelation and Visual Culture." Pages 487–504 in *Dreams, Visions, Imaginations: Jewish, Christian and Gnostic Views of the World to Come.* Edited by Jens Schröter, Tobias Nicklas, and Armand Puig i Tàrrech. BZNW 247. Berlin: de Gruyter.

Glancy, Jennifer A., and Stephen D. Moore. 2011. "How Typical a Roman Prostitute Is Revelation's 'Great Whore'?" *JBL* 130:551–69.

Gordon, Peter E. 2018. "The Authoritarian Personality Revisited: Reading Adorno in the Age of Trump." Pages 45–84 in *Authoritarianism: The Inquiries in Critical Theory,* by Wendy Brown, Peter E. Gordon, and Max Pensky. Chicago: University of Chicago Press.

Gorman, Michael J. 2011. *Reading Revelation Responsibly: Uncivil Worship and Witness: Following the Lamb into the New Creation.* Eugene: Cascade.

Gorski, Philip S., and Samuel L. Perry. 2022. *The Flag and the Cross: White Christian Nationalism and the Threat to American Democracy.* New York: Oxford University Press.

Graybill, Rhiannon. 2023. "Jezebel and Sexual Violence." Pages 52–53 in *Revelation,* by Lynn R. Huber with Gail R. O'Day. Wisdom Commentary 58. Collegeville: Liturgical.

Grimsrud, Ted. 2022. *To Follow the Lamb: A Peaceable Reading of the Book of Revelation.* Eugene, OR: Cascade.

Gushee, David P. 2023. *Defending Democracy from Its Christian Enemies.* Grand Rapids: Eerdmans.

Haidt, Jonathan. 2006. *The Happiness Hypothesis: Finding Modern Truth in Ancient Wisdom.* New York: Basic.

———. 2012. *The Righteous Mind: Why Good People Are Divided by Politics and Religion.* New York: Random House.

Hansen, Ryan Leif. 2014. *Silence and Praise: Rhetorical Cosmology and Political Theology in the Book of Revelation*. Emerging Scholars. Minneapolis: Fortress.

Harland, Philip A. 2003. *Associations, Synagogues, and Congregations: Claiming a Place in Ancient Mediterranean Society*. Minneapolis: Fortress.

Harlow, Barbara. 1987. *Resistance Literature*. New York: Methuen.

Harris, Dana M. 2019. "4 Ezra and Revelation 5:1–14: Creaturely Images of the Messiah." Pages 59–65 in *Reading Revelation in Context: John's Apocalypse and Second Temple Judaism*. Edited by Ben C. Blackwell, John K. Goodrich, and Jason Maston. Grand Rapids: Zondervan Academic.

Hays, Richard B. 2012. "Faithful Witness, Alpha and Omega: The Identity of Jesus in the Apocalypse of John." Pages 69–83 in *Revelation and the Politics of Apocalyptic Interpretation*. Edited by Richard B. Hays and Stefan Alkier. Waco: Baylor University Press, 2012.

Hays, Richard B., and Stefan Alkier. 2012. Introduction to *Revelation and the Politics of Apocalyptic Interpretation*. Edited by Richard B. Hays and Stefan Alkier. Waco: Baylor University Press.

Henning, Meghan. 2014. *Educating Early Christians through the Rhetoric of Hell: "Weeping and Gnashing of Teeth" as Paideia in Matthew and the Early Church*. WUNT 2/382. Tübingen: Mohr Siebeck.

Henning, Meghan, and Nils Neumann, eds. 2024a. *Vivid Rhetoric and Visual Persuasion: Ekphrasis in Early Christian Literature*. Grand Rapids: Eerdmans.

———. 2024b. "Before the Eyes: A History of Vivid Rhetoric and Ekphrasis in the New Testament." Pages 1–16 in *Vivid Rhetoric and Visual Persuasion: Ekphrasis in Early Christian Literature*. Edited by Meghan Henning and Nils Neumann. Grand Rapids: Eerdmans.

Henten, Jan Willem van. 2000. "Nero Redivivus Demolished: The Coherence of the Nero Traditions in the Sibylline Oracles." *JSP* 21:3–17.

Hick, John. 1966. *Evil and the God of Love*. London: Macmillan.

Hill, Charles E. 2001. *Regnum Caelorum: Patterns of Millennial Thought in Early Christianity*. 2nd ed. Grand Rapids: Eerdmans.

Hodson, Gordon, and Kimberly Costello. 2007. "Interpersonal Disgust, Ideological Orientations, and Dehumanization as Predictors of Intergroup Attitudes." *Psychological Science* 18.8:691–98.

Hoffmann, Matthias Reinhard. 2005. *The Destroyer and the Lamb: The Relationship between Angelomorphic and Lamb Christology in the Book of Revelation*. WUNT 2/203. Tübingen: Mohr Siebeck.

Horsley, Richard A. 2007. *Scribes, Visionaries, and the Politics of Second Temple Judea*. Louisville: Westminster John Knox.

Houck, Davis W., and David E. Dixon, eds. 2006. *Rhetoric, Religion, and the Civil Rights Movement, 1954–1965*. Waco: Baylor University Press.

Howard-Brook, Wes, and Anthony Gwyther. 1999. *Unveiling Empire: Reading Revelation Then and Now*. Maryknoll: Orbis.

Huber, Lynn H. 2007. *Like a Bride Adorned: Reading Metaphor in John's Apocalypse*. ESEC. New York: T&T Clark.

———. 2013. *Thinking and Seeing with Women in Revelation*. LNTS 465. London: Bloomsbury T&T Clark.

Huber, Lynn H., with Gail R. O'Day. 2023. *Revelation*. Wisdom Commentary 58. Collegeville: Liturgical.

Humphrey, Edith McEwan. 1995. *The Ladies and the Cities: Transformation and Apocalyptic Identity in Joseph and Aseneth, 4 Ezra, the Apocalypse and the Shepherd of Hermas*. JSPSup 17. Sheffield: Sheffield Academic.

Hurtado, Larry W. 2005. *How on Earth Did Jesus Become a God? Historical Questions about Earliest Devotion to Jesus*. Grand Rapids: Eerdmans.

Hylen, Susan. 2003. "The Power and Problem of Revelation 18: The Rhetorical Function of Gender." Pages 205–19 in *Pregnant Passion: Gender, Sex, and Violence in the Bible*. Edited by Cheryl A. Kirk-Duggan. SemeiaSt 44. Atlanta: Society of Biblical Literature.

———. 2011. "Metaphor Matters: Violence and Ethics in Revelation." *CBQ* 73:777–96.

———. 2020. "Feminist Interpretation of Revelation." Pages 467–82 in *The Oxford Handbook of the Book of Revelation*. Edited by Craig R. Koester. New York: Oxford University Press.

Jacob, Sharon. 2015. *Reading Mary alongside Indian Surrogate Mothers: Violent Love, Oppressive Liberation, and Infancy Narratives*. The Bible and Cultural Studies. New York: Palgrave Macmillan.

Jacob, Sharon, and Jennifer T. Kaalund. 2016. "Flowing from Breast to Breast: An Examination of Dis/placed Motherhood in African American and Indian Wet Nurses." Pages 209–38 in *Womanist Interpretations of the Bible: Expanding the Discourse*. Edited by Gay L. Byron and Vanessa Lovelace. SemeiaSt 85. Atlanta: SBL Press.

Jeffcoat Schedlter, Justin P. 2023. *Royal Ideologies in the Book of Revelation*. New York: Cambridge University Press.

Jenkins, Philip. 2023. "The Literary Drama of Church History." *Christian Century* 140.11, November 2023. https://www.christiancentury.org/column/voices/literal-drama-church-history.

Johns, Loren L. 2003. *The Lamb Christology of the Apocalypse of John: An Investigation into Its Origins and Rhetorical Force*. WUNT 2/167. Tübingen: Mohr Siebeck.

———. 2005. "Conceiving Violence: The Apocalypse of John and the Left Behind Series." *Direction* 34:194–214.

———. 2020. "Jesus in the Book of Revelation." Pages 223–39 in *The Oxford Handbook of the Book of Revelation*. Edited by Craig R. Koester. New York: Oxford University Press.

Johnson, Jessica. 2018. *Biblical Porn: Affect, Labor, and Pastor Mark Driscoll's Evangelical Empire*. Durham: Duke University Press.

Johnson, Luke Timothy. 2018. *Miracles: God's Presence and Power in Creation*. Interpretation. Louisville: Westminster John Knox.

Jones, Robert P. 2020. *White Too Long: The Legacy of White Supremacy in American Christianity*. New York: Simon & Schuster.

———. 2023. *The Hidden Roots of White Supremacy and the Path to a Shared American Future*. New York: Simon & Schuster.

Jung, Carl Gustav. 1954. *Answer to Job*. Translated by R. F. C. Hull. London: Routledge & Kegan Paul.

Kastely, James L. 2004. *Pathos: Rhetoric and Emotion*. Pages 221–37 in *A Companion to Rhetoric and Rhetorical Criticism*. Edited by Walter Jost and Wendy Olmstead. Blackwell Companions to Literature and Culture 22. Malden: Blackwell.

Keller, Catherine. 1996. *Apocalypse Now and Then: A Feminist Guide to the End of the World*. Minneapolis: Fortress.

———. 2005. *God and Power: Counter-Apocalyptic Journeys*. Minneapolis: Fortress.

———. 2021. *Facing Apocalypse: Climate, Democracy, and Other Last Chances*. Maryknoll: Orbis.

Kennedy, George A. 1998. *Comparative Rhetoric: An Historical and Cross-Cultural Introduction*. New York: Oxford University Press.

———. 2003. *Progymnasmata: Greek Textbooks of Prose Composition and Rhetoric*. WGRW 10. Atlanta: Society of Biblical Literature.

Kidwell, Jeremy, and Sean Doherty, eds. 2015. *Theology and Economics: A Christian Vision of the Common Good*. New York: Palgrave Macmillan.

Kiel, Micah D. 2017. *Apocalyptic Ecology: Revelation, the Earth, and the Future*. Collegeville: Liturgical.

Kim, Jean K. 1999. "'Uncovering Her Wickedness': An Inter(con)textual Reading of Revelation 17 from a Postcolonial Feminist Perspective." *JSNT* 73:61–81.

King, Martin Luther, Jr. 1986. "Letter from Birmingham City Jail." Pages 289–312 in *A Testament of Hope: The Essential Writings and Speeches of Martin Luther King, Jr.* Edited by James Melvin Washington. San Francisco: Harper & Row.

Kinzig, Wolfram. 2021. *Christian Persecution in Antiquity*. Waco: Baylor University Press.

Klassen, William. 1966. "Vengeance in the Apocalypse of John." *CBQ* 28:300–311.

Klauck, Hans-Josef. 2001. "Do They Never Come Back? *Nero Redivivus* and the Apocalypse of John." *CBQ* 63:683–98.

Koester, Craig R. 2014. *Revelation: A New Translation with Introduction and Commentary*. AY 38. New Haven: Yale University Press.

Koosed, Jennifer L., and Stephen D. Moore. 2014. "Introduction: From Affect to Exegesis." *BibInt* 22:381–87.

Kotrosits, Maia. 2016. "How Things Feel: Biblical Studies, Affect Theory, and the (Im)personal." *Brill Research Perspectives in Biblical Studies* 1:1–53.

Kraybill, J. Nelson. 1996. *Imperial Cult and Commerce in John's Apocalypse*. JSNTSup 132. Sheffield: Sheffield Academic.

———. 2010. *Apocalypse and Allegiance: Worship, Politics, and Devotion in the Book of Revelation*. Grand Rapids: Brazos.

Lakoff, George. 2004. *Don't Think of an Elephant! Know Your Values and Frame the Debate*. White River Junction, VT: Chelsea Green.

Lakoff, George, and Mark Johnson. 2003. *Metaphors We Live By*. 2nd ed. Chicago: University of Chicago Press.

Lateiner, Donald. 2017. "Evoking Disgust in the Latin Novels of Petronius and Apuleius." Pages 203–33 in *The Ancient Emotion of Disgust*. Edited by Donald Lateiner and Dimos Spatharas. Emotions of the Past. New York: Oxford University Press.

Lateiner, Donald, and Dimos Spatharas. 2017. "Introduction: Theories of Disgust, Ancient and Modern." Pages 1–40 in *The Ancient Emotion of Disgust*. Edited by Donald Lateiner and Dimos Spatharas. New York: Oxford University Press.

Lateiner, Donald, and Dimos Spatharas, eds. 2017. *The Ancient Emotion of Disgust*. New York: Oxford University Press.

Lawrence, D. H. 1980 (1931). *Apocalypse and the Writings on Revelation*. New York: Penguin.

Laws, Sophie. 1988. *In the Light of the Lamb: Imagery, Parody, and Theology in the Apocalypse of John*. Wilmington: Glazier.

LeVine, Marianne. 2023. "Trump Calls Political Enemies 'Vermin,' Echoing Dictators Hitler, Mussolini." *Washington Post*, November 13, 2023. https://www.washingtonpost.com/politics/2023/11/12/trump-rally-vermin-political-opponents/.

Levine, Amy-Jill, with Maria Mayo, eds. 2009. *A Feminist Companion to the Apocalypse of John*. Feminist Companion to the New Testament and Early Christian Writings 13. New York: T&T Clark.

Lindsey, Hal, with C. C. Carlson. 1970. *The Late Great Planet Earth*. Grand Rapids: Zondervan.

Linton, Gregory. 1991. "Reading the Apocalypse as an Apocalypse." Pages 161–86 in *SBL Seminar Papers 1991*. Edited by Eugene H. Lovering Jr. SBLSP 30. Atlanta: Scholars Press.

Lonas, Lexi. 2023. "1 in 4 High School Students Identifies as LGBTQ." *The Hill*, April 27, 2023. https://thehill.com/homenews/education/3975959-one-in -four-high-school-students-identify-as-lgbtq//.

Long, D. Stephen. 2000. *Divine Economy: Theology and the Market*. London: Routledge.

Longenecker, Bruce W. 2010. *Remember the Poor: Paul, Poverty, and the Greco-Roman World*. Grand Rapids: Eerdmans.

———. 2016. "Peace, Security, and Propaganda: Advertisement and Reality in the Early Roman Empire." Pages 15–46 in *An Introduction to Empire in the New Testament*. Edited by Adam Winn. RBS 84. Atlanta: SBL Press.

Lopez, Davina C. 2008. *Apostle to the Conquered: Reimagining Paul's Mission*. Paul in Critical Contexts. Minneapolis: Fortress.

———. 2016. "Victory and Visibility: Revelation's Imperial Textures and Monumental Logics." Pages 273–95 in *An Introduction to Empire in the New Testament*. Edited by Adam Winn. RBS 84. Atlanta: SBL.

Luiza, Marco Tullio, Torun Lindholm, Caitlin B. Hawley, Marie Gustafsson Sendén, Ingrid Ekström, Mats J. Olsson, and Jonas K. Olofsson. 2018. "Body Odour Disgust Sensitivity Predicts Authoritarian Attitudes." *Royal Society Open Science* 5.2: 171091. https://doi.org/10.1098/rsos.171091.

Luther, Susanne. 2024. "Topographies of Conduct? Ethical Implications of the Ekphrastic Description of Jerusalem in Revelation 21." Pages 273–302 in *Vivid Rhetoric and Visual Persuasion: Ekphrasis in Early Christian Literature*. Edited by Meghan Henning and Nils Neumann. Grand Rapids: Eerdmans.

Mangina, Joseph L. 2010. *Revelation*. BTCB. Grand Rapids: Brazos.

Marchal, Joseph A. 2012. "Queer Approaches: Improper Relations with Paul's Letters." Pages 209–27 in *Studying Paul's Letters: Contemporary Perspectives and Methods*. Edited by Joseph A. Marchal. Minneapolis: Fortress.

———. 2019. "The Disgusting Apostle and a Queer Affect between Epistles and Audiences." Pages 113–40 in *Reading with Feeling: Affect Theory and the Bible*. SemeiaSt 95. Edited by Fiona C. Black and Jennifer L. Koosed. Atlanta: SBL Press.

———, ed. 2021. *After the Corinthian Women Prophets: Reimagining Rhetoric and Power*. SemeiaSt 97. Atlanta: SBL.

Marsh, Charles. 1997. *God's Long Summer: Stories of Faith and Civil Rights*. Princeton: Princeton University Press.

———. 2001. *The Last Days: A Son's Story of Sin and Segregation at the Dawn of a New South*. New York: Basic.

———. 2014. *Strange Glory: A Life of Dietrich Bonhoeffer*. New York: Knopf.

Marshall, John W. 2001. *Parables of War: Reading John's Jewish Apocalypse*. Waterloo: Wilfrid Laurier University Press.

———. 2005. "Collateral Damage: Jesus and Jezebel in the Jewish War." Pages 35–50 in *Violence in the New Testament*. Edited by Shelly Matthews and E. Leigh Gibson. New York: T&T Clark.

———. 2009. "Gender and Empire: Sexualized Violence in John's Anti-Imperial Apocalypse." Pages 17–32 in *A Feminist Companion to the Apocalypse of John*. Edited by Amy-Jill Levine with Maria Mayo Robbins. New York: T&T Clark.

Martin, Clarice J. 2005. "Polishing the Unclouded Mirror: A Womanist Reading of *Revelation* 18:13." Pages 82–109 in *From Every People and Nation: The Book of Revelation in Intercultural Perspective*. Edited by David Rhoads. Minneapolis: Fortress.

Mathews, Mark D. 2013. *Riches, Poverty, and the Faithful: Perspectives on Wealth in the Second Temple Period and the Apocalypse of John*. SNTSMS 154. New York: Cambridge University Press.

McDonough, Sean M. 2008. "Revelation: The Climax of Cosmology." Pages 178–88 in *Cosmology and New Testament Theology*. Edited by Jonathan T. Pennington and Sean M. McDonough. LNTS 355. New York: T&T Clark.

McGrath, James F. 2009. *The Only True God: Early Christian Monotheism in Its Jewish Context*. Urbana: University of Illinois Press.

McKnight, Scot, with Cody Matchett. 2023. *Revelation for the Rest of Us: A Prophetic Call to Follow Jesus as a Dissident Disciple*. Grand Rapids: Zondervan.

McLaurin, Charles. 1982. "Voice of Calm." *Sojourners*, December 11, 1982: 12–13.

Meeks, M. Douglas. 1989. *God the Economist: The Doctrine of God and Political Economy*. Minneapolis: Fortress.

Meier, Harry O. 2002. *Apocalypse Recalled: The Book of Revelation after Christendom*. Minneapolis: Fortress.

———. 2020. "Post-Colonial Interpretation of the Book of Revelation." Pages 499–516 in *The Oxford Handbook of the Book of Revelation*. Edited by Craig R. Koester. New York: Oxford University Press.

Mendel, Arthur P. 1992. *Vision and Violence*. Ann Arbor: University of Michigan Press.

Mercieca, Jennifer. 2020. *Demagogue for President: The Rhetorical Genius of Donald Trump*. College Station: Texas A&M University Press.

Metzger, Bryan. 2023. "Speaker Mike Johnson Frets That High Schoolers Increasingly Identify as LGBTQ in Fundraising Email: 'We Have Much to Repent For.'" *Business Insider*, December 5, 2023. https://www.businessinsider.com

/mike-johnson-frets-high-schoolers-increasingly-lgbtq-in-campaign
-email-2023-12.

Middleton, J. Richard. 2014. *A New Heaven and a New Earth: Reclaiming Biblical Eschatology.* Grand Rapids: Baker Academic.

Middleton, Paul. 2018. *The Violence of the Lamb: Martyrs as Agents of Divine Judgment in the Book of Revelation.* LNTS 586. New York: T&T Clark.

Miller, Patrick R., Andrew R. Flores, Donald P. Haider-Markel, Daniel C. Lewis, Barry L. Tadlock, and Jami K. Taylor. 2016. "Transgender Politics as Body Politics: Effects of Disgust Sensitivity and Authoritarianism on Transgender Rights Attitudes." *Politics, Groups, and Identities* 5.1:4–24.

Miller, William Ian. 1997. *The Anatomy of Disgust.* Cambridge: Harvard University Press.

Moloney, Francis J. 2020. *The Apocalypse of John: A Commentary.* Grand Rapids: Baker Academic.

Moltmann, Jürgen. 1967. *Theology of Hope: On the Ground and the Implications of a Christian Eschatology.* New York: Harper & Row.

———. 2004. *In the End—The Beginning: The Life of Hope.* Minneapolis: Fortress.

Moore, Stephen D. 1995. "The Beatific Vision as a Posing Exhibition: Revelation's Hypermasculine Deity." *JSNT* 60:27–55.

———. 2006. *Empire and Apocalypse: Postcolonialism and the New Testament.* Bible in the Modern World 12. Sheffield: Sheffield Phoenix.

———. 2014. *Untold Tales from the Book of Revelation: Sex and Gender, Empire and Ecology.* RBS 79. Atlanta: SBL Press.

Moore, Stephen D., and Jennifer A. Glancy. 2014. "The Empress and the Brothel Slave." Pages 103–24 in *Untold Tales from the Book of Revelation: Sex and Gender, Empire and Ecology,* by Stephen D. Moore. RBS 79. Atlanta: SBL Press.

Morales, Helen. "Ooze and Orifices: Aspects of Disgust in Classical Times," review of *The Ancient Emotion of Disgust,* ed. Donald Lateiner and Dimos Spatharas. *Times Literary Supplement,* July 21, 2017. https://www.the-tls.co.uk/articles/disgust/.

Moss, Candida. 2013. *The Myth of Persecution: How Early Christians Invented a Story of Martyrdom.* New York: HarperOne.

Mounk, Yascha. 2018. *The People versus Democracy: Why Our Freedom Is in Danger and How to Save It.* Cambridge: Harvard University Press.

Moxnes, Halvor. 2003. *Putting Jesus in His Place: A Radical Vision of Household and Kingdom.* Louisville: Westminster John Knox.

Moyise, Steve. 2001. *The Old Testament in the New: An Introduction.* Continuum Biblical Studies Series. New York: Continuum.

———. 2012a. *The Later New Testament Writings and Scripture: The Old Testa-*

ment in Acts, Hebrews, the Catholic Epistles, and Revelation. Grand Rapids: Baker Academic.

———. 2012b. "Models for Intertextual Interpretation of Revelation." Pages 31–45 in Revelation and the Politics of Apocalyptic Interpretation. Edited by Richard B. Hays and Stefan Alkier. Waco: Baylor University Press.

———. 2020. "The Old Testament in the Book of Revelation." Pages 85–100 in The Oxford Handbook of the Book of Revelation. Edited by Craig R. Koester. New York: Oxford University Press.

Mullen, E. Theodore, Jr. 2007. "Divine Assembly." NIDB 2:145–46.

Murphy, Frederick J. 1998. Fallen Is Babylon: The Revelation to John. Harrisburg: Trinity Press International.

Murphy, Nancy. 2011. "Immortality versus Resurrection in the Christian Tradition." Annals of the New York Academy of Sciences 1234:76–82.

Nasrallah, Laura. 2003. "An Ecstasy of Folly": Prophecy and Authority in Early Christianity. Cambridge: Harvard University Press.

Nickelsburg, George W. E. 1977. "Apocalyptic and Myth in 1 Enoch 6–11." JBL 96:383–405.

Nickelsburg, George W. E., and James C. VanderKam. 2004. 1 Enoch: A New Translation. Minneapolis: Fortress.

Nicklas, Tobias. 2012. "The Eschatological Battle According to the Book of Revelation: Perspectives on Revelation 19:11–21." Pages 227–44 in Coping with Violence in the New Testament. Edited by Pieter G. R. de Villiers and Jan Willem van Henten. STR 16. Leiden: Brill.

Nietzsche, Friedrich. 1965 (1887). The Birth of Tragedy and the Genealogy of Morals. Translated by Francis Golffing. Garden City: Anchor.

Novenson, Matthew V. 2015. Christ among the Messiahs: Christ Language in Paul and Messiah Language in Ancient Judaism. New York: Oxford University Press.

Nussbaum, Martha C. 2004. Hiding from Humanity: Disgust, Shame, and the Law. Princeton: Princeton University Press.

Oakes, Peter. 2020. Empire, Economics, and the New Testament. Grand Rapids: Eerdmans.

O'Brien, Julia M. 2008. Challenging Prophetic Metaphor: Theology and Ideology in the Prophets. Louisville: Westminster John Knox.

O'Leary, Stephen D. 1994. Arguing the Apocalypse: A Theory of Millennial Rhetoric. New York: Oxford University Press.

Olbricht, Thomas H. 2001. "Pathos as Proof in Greco-Roman Rhetoric." Pages 7–22 in Paul and Pathos. Edited by Thomas L. Olbricht and Jerry L. Sumney. SymS 16. Atlanta: Society of Biblical Literature.

Orbán, Viktor. 2018. "Orbán Viktor's Ceremonial Speech on the 170th Anniversary of the Hungarian Revolution of 1848." March 18, 2018. https://www.miniszt erelnok.hu/orban-viktors-ceremonial-speech-on-the-170th-anniversary-of -the-hungarian-revolution-of-1848/.

Osiek, Carolyn. 1983. *Rich and Poor in the Shepherd of Hermas: An Exegetical-Social Investigation*. CBQMS 15. Washington, DC: Catholic Biblical Association of America.

Oslington, Paul, ed. 2014. *The Oxford Handbook of Christianity and Economics*. New York: Oxford University Press.

Paul, Ian. 2001. "The Book of Revelation: Image, Symbol and Metaphor." Pages 131–47 in *Studies in the Book of Revelation*. Edited by Steve Moyise. New York: Continuum.

Pernot, Lauren. 2005. *Rhetoric in Antiquity*. Translated by W. E. Higgins. Washington, DC: Catholic University of America Press.

Phelan, John E., Jr. 2004. "Revelation, Empire, and the Violence of God." *ExAud* 20:65–84.

Pippin, Tina. 1992. *Death and Desire: The Rhetoric of Gender in the Apocalypse of John*. Louisville: Westminster John Knox.

Pippin, Tina, and J. Michael Clark. 2006. "Revelation/Apocalypse." Pages 753–68 in *The Queer Bible Commentary*. Edited by Deryn Guest, Robert E. Goss, Mona West, and Thomas Bohache. London: SCM.

Portier-Young, Anathea E. 2010. "Languages of Identity and Obligation: Daniel as Bilingual Book," *VT* 60:98–115.

———. 2011. *Apocalypse against Empire: Theologies of Resistance in Early Judaism*. Grand Rapids: Eerdmans.

Rainbow, Jesse. 2007. "Male μαστοί in Revelation 1:13." *JSNT* 30:249–53.

Reddish, Mitchell G. 2001. *Revelation*. SHBC. Macon: Smyth & Helwys.

Reed, Annette Yoshiko. 2022. *Jewish-Christianity and the History of Judaism*. Minneapolis: Fortress.

Reid, Barbara E. 2023. "Editor's Introduction to Wisdom Commentary: 'She Is the Breath of the Power of God' (Wis 7:25)." Pages xxiii–xlii in *Revelation*, by Lynn R. Huber with Gail R. O'Day. Wisdom Commentary 58. Collegeville: Liturgical.

Reid, Barbara E., and Shelly Matthews. 2021. *Luke 1–9*. Wisdom Commentary 43A. Collegeville: Liturgical.

Richard, Pablo. 2015. *Apocalypse: A People's Commentary on the Book of Revelation*. Maryknoll, NY: Orbis.

Robbins, Vernon K. 2016. "Rhetography: A New Way of Seeing the Familiar Text." Pages 367–92 in *Foundations for Sociorhetorical Interpretation*. Edited by Vernon K. Robbins, Robert H. von Thaden Jr., and Bart B. Bruehler. Rhetoric of Religious Antiquity 4. Atlanta: SBL Press.

Rosenmeyer, Patricia A. 2001. *Ancient Epistolary Fictions: The Letter in Greek Literature*. New York: Cambridge University Press.

Rossing, Barbara R. 1999. *The Choice between Two Cities: Whore, Bride, and Empire in the Apocalypse*. Harrisburg: Trinity Press International.

———. 2004. *The Rapture Exposed: The Message of Hope in the Book of Revelation*. Boulder: Westview.

———. 2005. "For the Healing of the World: Reading Revelation Ecologically." Pages 165–82 in *From Every People and Nation: The Book of Revelation in Intercultural Perspective*. Edited by David Rhoads. Minneapolis: Fortress.

Royalty, Robert M. 1998. *The Streets of Heaven: The Ideology of Wealth in the Apocalypse of John*. Macon: Mercer University Press.

———. 2004. "Don't Touch *This* Book! Revelation 22:18–19 and the Rhetorical of Reading (in) the Apocalypse of John." *BibInt* 12:282–99.

Ruiz, Jean Pierre. 1994. "Hearing and Seeing but Not Saying: A Look at Revelation 10:4 and 2 Corinthians 12:4." Pages 182–202 in *SBL Seminar Papers 1994*. Edited by E. H. Lovering Jr. SBLSP 33. Atlanta: Scholars Press.

Schaefer, Donovan O. 2015. *Religious Affects: Animality, Emotion, Power*. Durham: Duke University Press.

———. 2019. "The Codex of Feeling: Affect Theory and Ancient Texts." *Ancient Jew Review*, January 16, 2019. https://www.ancientjewreview.com/read/2019/1/11/the-codex-of-feeling-affect-theory-and-ancient-texts.

Schearing, Linda S., and Valarie H. Ziegler. 2014. *Enticed by Eden: How Western Culture Uses, Confuses, (and Sometimes Abuses) Adam and Eve*. Waco: Baylor University Press.

Scheidel, Walter, and Steven J. Friesen. 2009. "The Size of the Economy and the Distribution of Income in the Roman Empire." *JRS* 99:61–91.

Schippers, A. M. 2019. "Dionysius and Quintilian: Imitation and Emulation in Greek and Latin Literary Criticism." PhD diss., Leiden University.

Schüssler Fiorenza, Elisabeth. 1988. "The Ethics of Biblical Interpretation: Decentering Biblical Scholarship." *JBL* 107:3–17.

———. 1991. *Revelation: Vision of a Just World*. Proclamation Commentaries. Minneapolis: Fortress.

———. 1998. *The Book of Revelation: Justice and Judgment*. 2nd ed. Minneapolis: Fortress.

Schwarzkopf, Stefan, ed. 2019. *The Routledge Handbook of Economic Theology*. London: Routledge.

Scott, James C. 1985. *Weapons of the Weak: Everyday Forms of Peasant Resistance*. New Haven: Yale University Press.

———. 1990. *Domination and the Arts of Resistance*. New Haven: Yale University Press.

Seidel, Andrew L. 2022. "Events, People, and Networks Leading Up to January 6." Pages 14–24 in *Christian Nationalism and the January 6 Insurrection.* https://ffrf.org/uploads/legal/Christian_Nationalism_and_the_Jan6_Insurrection-2-9-22.pdf.

Shook, Natalie J., Cameron G. Ford, and Shelby T. Boggs. 2017. "Dangerous Worldview: A Mediator of the Relation between Disgust Sensitivity and Social Conservatism." *Personality and Individual Differences* 119:252–61.

Siker, Jeffrey S. 2011. "Yom Kippuring Passover: Recombinant Sacrifice in Early Christianity." Pages 65–82 in *Ritual and Metaphor: Sacrifice in the Bible.* Edited by Christian A. Eberhart. RBS 68. Atlanta: Society of Biblical Literature.

Skaggs, Rebecca, and Thomas Doyle. 2007. "Violence in the Apocalypse of John." *CBR* 5:220–34.

Slater, Thomas B. 2019. *Revelation as Civil Disobedience.* Nashville: Abingdon.

Smith, Brandon D. 2022. *The Trinity in the Book of Revelation: Seeing Father, Son, and Holy Spirit in the Apocalypse.* Studies in Christian Doctrine and Scripture. Downers Grove, IL: InterVarsity.

Smith, David A. 2020. *The Epistles for All Christians: Epistolary Literature, Circulation, and the Gospels for All Christians.* BibInt 186. Leiden: Brill.

Smith, Shanell T. 2014. *The Woman Babylon and the Marks of Empire: Reading Revelation with a Postcolonial Womanist Hermeneutics of Ambiveilence.* Minneapolis: Fortress.

Spencer, Richard A. 2001. "Violence and Vengeance in Revelation." *RevExp* 98:59–75.

Spurr, David. 1993. *The Rhetoric of Empire: Colonial Discourse in Journalism, Travel Writing, and Imperial Administration.* Chapel Hill: Duke University Press.

Stanton, Elizabeth Cady, et al. 1988 (1898). *The Woman's Bible. Part II: Comments on the Old and New Testaments from Joshua to Revelation.* New York: European Publishing Company. Repr., Salem: Ayer.

Stenström, Hanna. "'They Have Not Defiled Themselves with Women . . .': Christian Identity According to the Book of Revelation." Pages 33–54 in *A Feminist Companion to the Apocalypse of John.* Edited by Amy-Jill Levine with Maria Mayo Robbins. New York: T&T Clark.

Stewart, Alexander E. 2017. "*Ekphrasis*, Fear, and Motivation in the Apocalypse of John." *BBR* 27:227–40.

Stuckenbruck, Loren T. 1995. *Angel Veneration and Christology: A Study in Early Judaism and the Christology of the Apocalypse of John.* WUNT 70. Tübingen: Mohr Siebeck.

———. 2007. "Messianic Ideas in the Apocalyptic and Related Literature of Early Judaism." Pages 90–113 in *The Messiah in the Old and New Testaments.* Edited by Stanley E. Porter. Grand Rapids: Eerdmans.

Sugirtharajah, R. S. 2002. *Postcolonial Criticism and Biblical Interpretation*. New York: Oxford University Press.

Sumney, Jerry L. 2009. "Post-Mortem Existence and Resurrection of the Body in Paul." *HBT* 31:12–26.

Swartley, Willard M. 2006. *Covenant of Peace: The Missing Peace in New Testament Theology and Ethics*. Grand Rapids: Eerdmans.

Tanner, Kathryn. 2005. *Economy of Grace*. Minneapolis: Fortress.

Terrizzi, J. A., Jr., N. J. Shook, and W. L. Ventis. 2010. "Disgust: A Predictor of Social Conservatism and Prejudicial Attitudes toward Homosexuals." *Personality and Individual Differences* 49.6:587–92.

Thompson, Leonard L. 1990. *The Book of Revelation: Apocalypse and Empire*. New York: Oxford University Press.

Thompson, Marianne Meye. 2012. "Reading What Is Written in the Book of Life: Theological Interpretation of the Book of Revelation Today." Pages 155–71 in *Revelation and the Politics of Apocalyptic Interpretation*. Edited by Richard B. Hays and Stefan Alkier. Waco: Baylor University Press.

Tonstad, Sigve K. 2019. *Revelation*. Paideia Commentaries on the New Testament. Grand Rapids: Baker Academic.

Trites, Allison A. 1973. "Μάρτυς and Martyrdom in the Apocalypse: A Semantic Study." *NovT* 15:72–80.

Vickers, Brian. 1988. *In Defence of Rhetoric*. Oxford: Clarendon.

Villiers, Pieter G. R. de. 2012. "Unmasking and Challenging Evil." Pages 201–22 in *Coping with Violence in the New Testament*. Edited by Pieter G. R. de Villiers and Jan Willem van Henten. STR 16. Leiden: Brill.

Volf, Miroslav. 1993. *Exclusion and Embrace: A Theological Exploration of Identity, Otherness, and Reconciliation*. Nashville: Abingdon.

Wall, Robert W. 1991. *Revelation*. New International Bible Commentary. Peabody: Hendrickson.

Wall Street Journal. 2008. "Rahm Emanuel on the Opportunities of Crisis." YouTube, November 19, 2008. https://www.youtube.com/watch?v=_mzcbXi1Tkk.

Warren, Meredith J. C. forthcoming. "Rape Jokes, Sexual Violence, and Empire in Revelation and *This Is The End*." In *The Bible and the Postsecular World: Essays in Honour of Philip Davies*. Edited by Thomas Bolin and James Crossley. London: Routledge.

Weinfeld, Moshe. 1973. "'Rider of the Clouds' and 'Gatherer of the Clouds,'" *JANES* 5:421–26.

Wengst, Klaus. 1897. *Pax Romana and the Peace of Jesus Christ*. Translated by John Bowden. Minneapolis: Fortress.

Whitaker, Robyn J. 2015. *Ekphrasis, Vision, and Persuasion in the Book of Revelation*. WUNT 2/410. Tübingen: Mohr Siebeck.

———. 2023. *Revelation for Normal People: A Guide to the Strangest and Most Dangerous Book in the Bible*. The Bible for Normal People. Harleysville: The Bible for Normal People.

———. 2024. "Vivid Vignettes: Lakes of Fire, Grotesque Feasts, and the Idea of Hell in Revelation 19:17–21." Pages 254–72 in *Vivid Rhetoric and Visual Persuasion: Ekphrasis in Early Christian Literature*. Edited by Meghan Henning and Nils Neumann. Grand Rapids: Eerdmans.

Whitehead, Andrew L., and Samuel L. Perry. 2020. *Taking America Back for God: Christian Nationalism in the United States*. New York: Oxford University Press.

Wilson, Stephen G. 1995. *Related Strangers: Jews and Christians 70–170 C.E.* Minneapolis: Fortress.

Winn, Adam. 2016a. "A Brief Word of Introduction and Acknowledgment." Pages ix–xi in *An Introduction to Empire in the New Testament*. Edited by Adam Winn. RBS 84. Atlanta: SBL Press.

———. 2016b. "Striking Back at the Empire: Empire Theory and Responses to Empire in the New Testament." Pages 1–14 in *An Introduction to Empire in the New Testament*. Edited by Adam Winn. RBS 84. Atlanta: SBL Press.

Wire, Antoinette Clark. 1990. *The Corinthian Women Prophets: A Reconstruction through Paul's Rhetoric*. Minneapolis: Fortress.

Wisse, Jakob. 1989. *Ethos and Pathos from Aristotle to Cicero*. Amsterdam: Hakkert.

Works, Carla Swafford. 2014. *The Church in the Wilderness: Paul's Use of Exodus Traditions in 1 Corinthians*. WUNT 2/379. Mohr Siebeck: Tübingen.

Yeatts, John R. 2003. *Revelation*. Believers Church Bible Commentary. Scottdale: Herald.

Yrigoyen, Charles, Jr. 1996. *John Wesley: Holiness of Heart and Life*. Nashville: Abingdon.

Zhuang, Ganlin. 2023. "Rethinking Ethos: A Comparative Analysis of Persuasive Character Building in Classical Antiquity through the Lenses of Aristotle, Cicero, and Quintilian." *SHS Web of Conferences* 178:02016. https://doi.org /10.1051/shsconf/202317802016.

Ziegler, Philip G. 2018. *Militant Grace: The Apocalyptic Turn and the Future of Christian Theology*. Grand Rapids: Baker Academic.

———. 2024. "God's Adversary and Ours: A Brief Theology of the Devil." Paper presented as the 2024 Annie Kinkead Warfield Lectures, Princeton Theological Seminary. Princeton, NJ. March 18–21.

Index of Authors

Agamben, Giorgio, 125n41
Ahmed, Sara, 33n28
Alkier, Stefan, 67n8, 152
Allen, Garrick V., 6n10, 31
Allison, Dale C., Jr., 83n37
Applebaum, Anne, 26n3
Aune, David E., 12n28, 17n41, 49n8, 55nn30–31, 74n17, 114n16

Bakhtin, Mikhail, 21nn57–58
Barnhill, Gregory M., 91n14
Barr, David L., 132n23, 132n26, 147
Battle, Michael, 67
Bauckham, Richard, 50–51, 58n43, 59n45, 77, 79n27, 80n29, 81n31, 113n9, 116n23, 158n12, 165n29
Beale, G. K., xv n4, 31n14, 49n11, 67n6, 114n16
Ben-Ghiat, Ruth, 97n29
Berlant, Lauren, 129n13
Blount, Brian K., 65nn67–68, 143, 144n19, 161, 165n29
Boesak, Allan A., 41–42, 64, 143, 152, 167–68
Boggs, Shelby T., 34n34
Bonhoeffer, Dietrich, xiv
Bowden, Anna M. V., 10n20, 58n41, 121, 122

Bowens, Lisa Marie, 86
Boxall, Ian, 81n31, 81n33, 149n34, 161
Boyarin, Daniel, 53n25, 55, 56n34
Bray, Karen, 89n7
Brenner, Athalya, 136
Briggs, John, 13n29
Brown, Wendy, 26
Bühner, Ruben A., 53, 55n31
Bultmann, Rudolf, 69
Byron, Gay L., 128

Caird, G. B., 74n19, 81n31
Carey, Greg, 3n2, 5n5, 9n16, 13n29, 14n34, 20n51, 21n55, 26n2, 27n8, 31n22, 32nn25–26, 49n12, 56n37, 57n38, 59n46, 63n60, 66n1, 73n16, 79n27, 82n35, 85n40, 87n1, 94n24, 99n30, 107n51, 107n52, 117n26, 118n28, 135n36, 137n46, 147n29, 151n49, 155n6, 159n13, 159n15, 166n31, 167n39, 168n49
Carlson, C. C., 68n9
Charles, R. H., 137, 138n49
Christerson, Brad, 64n63
Clark, J. Michael, 138
Collins, Adela Yarbro, xiv n2, 44, 52n21, 53n25, 56n34–35, 70n11, 91n14, 93n23, 100, 127, 132n24,